LONDON'S
PRIDE

LONDON'S PRIDE

The Glorious History
of The Capital's Gardens

Introduction by
Sir Roy Strong

Edited by
Mireille Galinou
of The Museum of London

Anaya Publishers Ltd
London

First published in Great Britain in 1990
by Anaya Publishers Ltd,
49 Neal Street, London WC2H 9PJ

ISBN 1–85470–032–4 (hardback)
ISBN 1–85470–031–6 (paperback)

Designed by Adrian Morris

British Library Cataloguing in Publication Data
A CIP catalogue record for this book
is available from the British Library

Phototypeset by Keyspools Ltd, Golborne, Lancs.

Printed and bound in Great Britain by
Clays Ltd, Bungay, Suffolk

Preceding pages: *In the
eighteenth century the Mall
in St James's Park was the
place to see and be seen. It
attracted all classes of society
and institutionalized
Londoners' enduring
relationship with their parks.
Note that the walled garden of
No. 10 Downing Street is
visible in the left background
(see p. 202 for a view inside
the garden)*

Contents

Introduction

In the decade between two major exhibitions – *The Garden* at the Victoria and Albert Museum in 1979, and *London's Pride* at the Museum of London in 1990 – the subject of garden history has taken off. What might be described as a growth industry reveals itself in the new impetus towards replanting historic gardens, the listing of important gardens by the Historic Buildings Council and the discovery of long forgotten gardens, as well as in a wealth of new research. The trickle of academic attention from such pioneers as John Harvey, Miles Hadfield and Kenneth Woodbridge became a flood.

The ten years have been marked by major publications covering every period of gardening history in this country (detailed in the Bibliography at the end of this book) – John Harvey and Teresa McLean on the Middle Ages; my own work on the Renaissance garden; David Jacques and Arend van der Horst, and a volume of the *Journal of Garden History* on the baroque age; David Stuart and David Jacques on Georgian gardens; Brent Elliott on the Victorian and David Ottewill on the Edwardian periods. We can add to this countless articles besides major studies of individuals, including Peter Willis on Charles Bridgeman and John Dixon Hunt on William Kent.

One area that has, however, remained little explored is the history of town gardens. In this the exhibition *London's Pride* represents the turning point. This beautiful book and the exhibition it accompanies together move across a wide canvas far beyond the pleasure garden to take in the development of parks and open spaces, nursery and market gardens, all of which were crucial in the development of the metropolis. It also puts into perspective a topic very much at the heart of today's debate on the regeneration of the inner city. What is the future role of public spaces and parks and private gardens? The discussion is relevant not only to London but also to many of Britain's other major cities.

Although the Garden History Society was founded in 1965, garden history is a young subject, rich in unexplored avenues of research. Documentary evidence is still emerging, but aerial photography and garden archaeology have opened up new vistas – providing a corrective to the tendency of the subject to be a branch of the history of ideas or of English literature, obsessed with the country house garden to the exclusion of other types.

A celebration of London's gardens is a timely demonstration of this wider perspective. The imaginative displays of the *London's Pride* Exhibition bring the gardening past of the capital to life, giving visitors a new understanding of its horticultural reality and fresh insights into the green areas of London today. This book with its feast of paintings, prints, photographs and other objects shown in the exhibition, is both a complement to this

The Hackney garden in which the Butters family posed for their photograph in 1875 suggests both comfortable affluence and an awareness of 'state of the art' urban gardening practices

(alas) ephemeral event at the London Museum and a valuable study in its own right. The issues raised and evidence produced by the writers of the interesting chapters that follow continue the dynamic *furor hortensis* in garden history of the last decade.

To be of significance an exhibition and its accompanying publications should be not only a contribution to knowledge past but, in addition, a catalyst and a polemic for the present and future. May *London's Pride* achieve just that.

SIR ROY STRONG
January 1990

EDITOR'S
FOREWORD

London's environment is exceptionally green. How many capital cities can boast such a proliferation of private gardens? In Rome, Paris or Vienna, housing blocks dominate the urban environment, and the inhabitants' need for open space must be fulfilled by communal courtyards and a few municipal parks and piazzas. Already in the nineteenth century London was prominent as a green capital. Regent's Park alone covered an area of 149 hectares, while Paris in 1855 had only 88 hectares of gardens. Napoleon III noted the lack of 'promenades' and squares in Paris, and after visiting London, he embarked on a programme of improving Parisian open spaces.

The need for parks and gardens was built into the fabric of the city at a very early date. As far back as 1580 Queen Elizabeth I was making a proclamation aiming to slow down new building which would attract yet more inhabitants, and advocating that each family should have its own house.

The voracious expansion of the city into the countryside, leaving rural enclaves to placate a yearning for the lost greenery, has been a fascinating process and provided the basis of the Museum of London's 1990 exhibition which shared its title with, and acted as the motive force for, this book. Our contributors offer a broad analysis of the nature of this open space: the gardens of great houses, small back gardens, medium-sized gardens, the market gardens, the parks, the squares, all the way down to the windowbox. Many of London's open spaces are accessible to the public; private ones are enjoyed by their gardening owners as well as vicariously by passers-by in buses and trains.

The vast subject of garden history in the context of London, the capital city and seat of the Court, offers an almost overwhelming array of material. What ground should this book set out to cover? Where should we draw the line? Although the geographical limitation provided a set of manageable boundaries within which to work, we considered narrowing the scope further by focusing on private gardens and excluding public parks and gardens, despite their being better documented.

This option, as it turned out, was naïve in the extreme. It very rapidly became clear that public and private sectors were so intimately bound up together that to separate the two would provide an inadequate picture. In addition, determining what constitutes public and private in this context would involve a minefield of difficulties since so many of today's public parks and gardens were once private.

It is in fact precisely the interaction between public and private open space which offers a key to understanding London's exceptionally green environment. Already in 1418 an Ordnance was issued for the protection of Moorfields: citizens were required to remove the gardens and hedges they had erected in an attempt to secure from the common fields a little space for themselves. Later, when Moorfields was turned into London's first pleasure park, its layout of walks and squares of

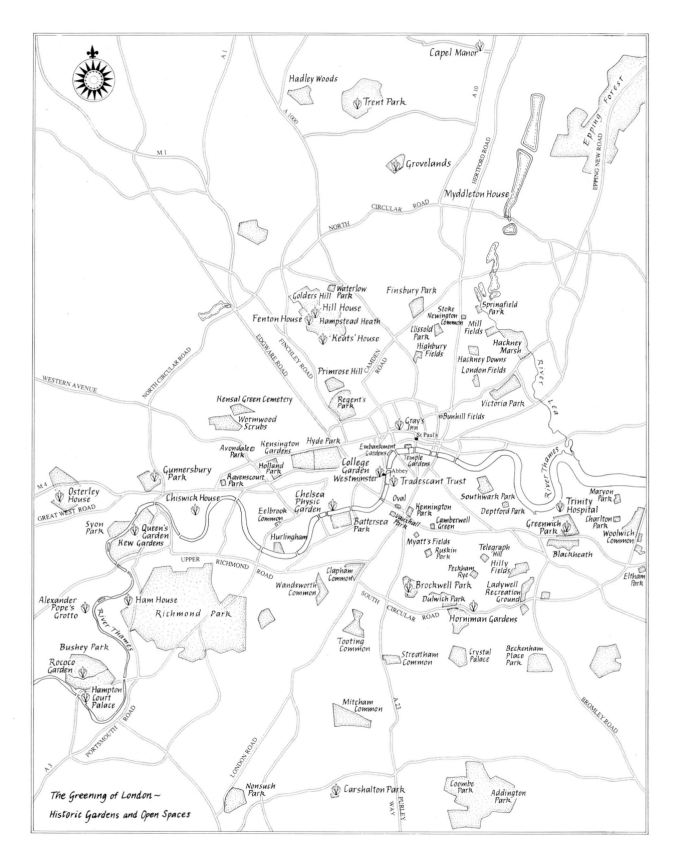

The Greening of London ~
Historic Gardens and Open Spaces

9

grass surrounded by trees gave the character of an enclosed private garden.

The passage from private to public often followed a consistent pattern; first there was enclosure of the countryside, then the land was gradually opened up to the citizens, and as it became increasingly used, it was integrated into the social scene – finally being landscaped or relandscaped. Almost immediately public open space acted as a magnet for private gardens. Historians who would instinctively argue that private gardens developed more rapidly in areas devoid of public amenities would have to recognize that, in London at least, the opposite was true. This is observable not only at Moorfields but more spectacularly at St James's Park which became surrounded on all sides by private gardens.

The historical evolution of London's green spaces is covered in many of these essays, from 'Open Space in Tudor and Early Stuart London' to 'Victorian Parks' and the twentieth-century 'Garden Suburb, Green Belt and Windowbox'. However, just how far back in time should we go to trace the history of the private garden?

Roman gardens in London must have existed but they remain virtually undocumented. When the Governor's Palace near Cannon Street was excavated, archaeologists were able to suggest it was built round a large open court containing pools and probably fountains. In addition, a site in Warwick Square, near St Paul's Cathedral, yielded a few gardening clues; a hand-dug garden bed was found showing a row of deep spade cuts and root holes from cultivated plants. But substantial archaeological evidence has so far only been discovered outside London. By the Middle Ages London indulged, as indeed did other European cities, in gardening for pleasure, alongside gardening for necessity. 'The Medieval Garden' brings to life those gardens created by Londoners for their own enjoyment.

This initial scarcity of evidence contrasts with later essays, perhaps most notably with 'A Tour of London's Gardens with John Rocque'. A detailed comparison of Rocque's map with later and with modern-day maps gives extraordinary insights into the layouts of the grand gardens of the eighteenth century and their subsequent fate. On the other hand 'Gardening and the Middle Classes' presents for the first time recent research on the small urban garden in the eighteenth century.

The more functional aspects of London gardens are also covered. 'Market Gardens' brings together a range of sources on early commercial food gardening, while 'Medicinal and Kitchen Gardening' deals with a number of aspects of the domestic use of gardens up to the eighteenth century.

What emerges throughout the book are preoccupations that transcend period – the garden for relaxation, display and production were themes already evident in the Middle Ages. The nineteenth and twentieth-century introduction of sports grounds and playing fields is anticipated by the bowling greens and archery ranges of the seventeenth. The plant rental business of James Cochran during the Regency led on to the late Victorian floral extravaganzas created by firms such as Wills and Segar; and many of these ongoing themes are brought out in the essay 'Citizens, Gardens and Meanings'.

Parks and gardens in the urban context are inevitably a rich area of study. We have aimed at a lively balance and hope that this all too brief survey will provoke others to take up the challenge offered by those issues we have not been able to pursue.

Mireille Galinou
January 1990

These archetypal back-to-back gardens are so common in London that this scene could be almost anywhere in the inner city

Gardens and Their Meanings

In *The City Gardener*, Thomas Fairchild speaks both of the eighteenth century and for London's perennial gardening enthusiasts, many of whose preoccupations seem to have remained remarkably constant since the earliest records. The proliferation in London not only of gardens, but of squares and parks, and the survival of many ancient tracts of common, forest and heath is at least remarkable, if not unique. How are these open spaces used by Londoners and visitors? What purpose do they serve and does their meaning change with time?

Opposite: *A* Punch *cartoon of 1909 exposed both the pride suburban dwellers had in their small gardens and their 'Pooterish' pretensions to grandeur*

'The garden should fit its master . . . as clothes do'

CITIZENS,
GARDENS AND MEANINGS

'I find that most persons whose business requires them to be constantly in town will have something of a garden at any rate. One may guess the general love my fellow citizens have of gardening in furnishing their rooms and chambers with basons of flowers and bough pots, rather than not have something of a garden before them.'

Thomas Fairchild   *The City Gardener*

City dwellers have had to experience the erosion of access to open countryside from the time of the Emperor Augustus to the present day. Vestiges of common land such as Wimbledon, Barnes and Wanstead Commons still offer Londoners an urban playground; in some respects Epping Forest and Hampstead Heath stand for much the same as did the Roman Campagna two thousand years ago. What has changed dramatically is the total

A London Transport poster of 1915 whose imagery offers escape to the free – although by then already sometimes overcrowded – delights of Epping Forest

Opposite: *In the mid-sixteenth century, the royal gardens at Whitehall had a number of individual beds, bounded by painted railings, in which were 'planted' carved heraldic beasts relevant to the Tudors*

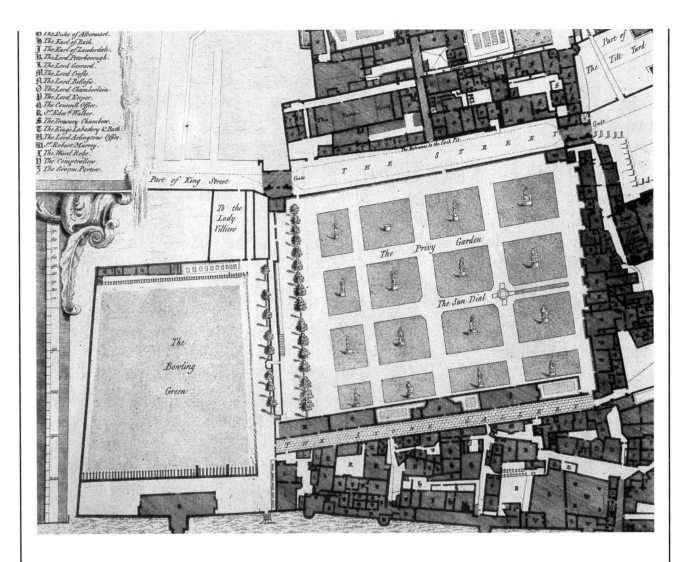

According to this plan of Whitehall Palace, taken from a survey of 1680, the Privy Garden has acquired a formal 'Continental' layout, and its heraldic statuary has disappeared

area of such land available to city dwellers – as well as the loss of most common rights of grazing and gathering.

Until the nineteenth century, Londoners were sustained – sometimes literally – by the woods, parks and common land around the city to which they had various rights of access and of use. Successive enclosures, purchases and gifts of land for services rendered increasingly restricted the citizens' freedom of movement and exercise of rights, but it was not until the massive expansion of the late eighteenth and the nineteenth centuries that the urban park and private garden-space acquired their acute significance as substitutes for an unattainable countryside.

A privileged few have always been able to keep a foot in both camps, enjoying the benefits of a rural retreat and the stimulus of the city at will. Fulham Palace was once the country estate to which early Bishops of London retired when life at their urban palace became too demanding. Virgil, in the first century BC, needed to return to Rome periodically from his country estate, in order to maintain his position as 'man of the world', visit libraries, engage in debate and so on. In fifteenth-century Italy, Cosimo de' Medici travelled daily in summer between his Florentine commercial base and one or other of his villas in the hills around the city.

Cutting a good figure in the city or at court was largely dependent upon the maintenance of an efficiently run rural or suburban 'servicing unit'. Whereas in Europe the town house was normally considered to be the main residence, the great London houses were sometimes little more than luxuriously appointed *pieds-à-terre* used when the court was in residence at Whitehall, or, later, during the London season.

Such country estates over the centuries provided the urban household with its very means of existence in the form of grain, meat and dairy produce, wine and beer, fruit and vegetables, vitally important honey, and so forth. Often, as was the case with the Bishop of Ely's suburban estate at Holborn, there was a surplus for sale.

In turn, the mercantile, diplomatic and social activities centred on the town house were the source of the wealth or status which made the owning of a country property a viable proposition. A particularly good example of this relationship existed in the Theobalds estate developed by Lord Burghley and his son Robert Cecil in the second half of the sixteenth century. A few miles north of London, the manor supplied the Cecils' town house in the Strand, and the gardens at both houses were overseen by the herbalist John Gerard. But Theobalds was important to the Cecil family's well-being in more than the strictly physical sense. The layout of the vast formal gardens was dense with emblematic and classical allusions to the glory of the Tudor dynasty and Elizabeth in particular. Thus, when Lord Burghley and later his son diverted Elizabeth with mazes, heraldic knot-gardens, classical references in statuary, boat trips and elaborate allegorical entertainments, they were also ensuring their continuing prestige as men of the court, the city and the world.

Gardens of the mind

Large and intellectually elaborate gardens were to be found in and around the city, as well as in the surrounding countryside. In his *Survey of London* first published in 1598, the historian John Stow complained that land was being enclosed 'not so much for use or profit as for show and pleasure, bewraying the vanity of mens' minds'. The 'vanity of mens' minds', with respect to gardens at least, was undoubtedly being fed by accounts of the great Renaissance gardens on the Continent, particularly in Italy and France. The possession of a modern Italianate garden meant admiration and envy from those less fortunate and fashionable.

Of especial practical as well as intellectual interest to Italian garden designers from the late fourteenth century onwards were the detailed accounts of the gardens of the Younger Pliny, rediscovered in his Letters written during the late first and early second centuries AD. His descriptions of multi-levelled gardens with lawns, topiary, shaded arcades and secret arbours, fountains and watercourses were of overwhelming influence. A garden laid out along received Plinian lines not only had the advantages of classical antecedence and archaeological accuracy. It could also be seen as a reflection of the intellectual interests of its owner and its historical meaning was thus overlaid with academic and philosophical ones. The popularity of the archaeologically erudite garden was long lasting. Returning from a trip to Italy with Inigo Jones in 1615, the Earl of Arundel brought a collection of antique statues with which to people the gardens of Arundel House in the Strand. The gardens of the villas which were built along the Thames in the eighteenth century were rich with remains and references of often staggering complexity.

It is clear that in Italy, and later elsewhere, such gardens were frequently designed as settings for philosophical discussion, intellectual exercise being complemented by entertainment and physical activity just as in the Athenian gymnasia. Plato's recipe for healthy civic and intellectual life centred on the balancing of apparently conflicting human needs. Thus the Greek gymnasia were devoted to the training of the body, through competitive sport, and the mind, through competitive debate in the classes held by the philosophers in the gymnasium grounds. Plato himself held classes in his own private garden and the notion of the 'philosopher's

garden' is one which recurs frequently. Such resonances were not lost north of the Alps, and Sir Thomas More entertained friends and visiting scholars in his Chelsea gardens in much the same spirit as Cosimo de' Medici had done at his villas at Carregi and Fiesole a century before. The gardens at Lambeth and Fulham Palaces were frequently used in a similar spirit. Such gardens were quite distinct in meaning from monastic gardens, although both were clearly used to stimulate intellectual activity and aid reflection and meditation. The secular 'thinker's garden' was open to the world and its influences, whereas the conventual garden served a community whose *raison d'être* was usually the exclusion of the outside world.

In many ways the garden as an escape into solitude is related to the similar functions of a private study or other personal space. It is very much part, too, of the debate which focused on the relative merits of the active versus the contemplative life. Should we be people 'of the world', or 'of the spirit'? Are the two necessarily irreconcilable? The garden offered one possible way of maintaining a foot in both camps, particularly for city dwellers. The argument ran roughly as follows: to appreciate fully the delights of the garden/*locus amoenus* (delightful place) one had to experience them in relation to urban activity. Conversely, one needed frequent regenerative trips to the garden in order to function most advantageously in urban life.

Gardens as retreats

The 'original' garden is familiar to most people through its expression in Christian and other mythologies. In various guises the Garden of Eden or Paradise garden reappeared in countless literary and real gardens of the Middle Ages and Renaissance. Such gardens arguably reached their highest point of refinement in the

Fifteenth-century artists frequently depicted the Virgin in enclosed gardens which imposed elaborate symbolism on representations of contemporary secular gardens. Everything from the fountain to the plant species has Biblical resonances

hortus conclusus or enclosed garden of the Virgin, whose iconography was drawn as much from the highly erotic Song of Solomon as from Genesis. This reconciliation of the sacred with the profane set the pattern for symbolic gardens of love and defended virtue, where every element of the garden was endowed with a symbolism which enriched and elucidated its cumulative meaning. Thus, the fountain in the garden could represent, among other things, the four rivers flowing from the Garden of Eden, the four gospels, or youth, while the lily might stand for purity, the rosebud for virginity and so on. Most of what we can reconstruct of European gardens of the Middle Ages is necessarily gathered from manuscript illustrations and paintings, and it is clear that there is an interesting overlap between imagined and real gardens.

The 'contemplative' gardens of the many monastic and conventual establishments which existed in London before the Dissolution offer a variety of types of enclosed garden. Individual gardens attached to each cell at the Charterhouse, for example, were quite distinct from those productive garden areas which served the community as a whole. Each monk cultivated this personal patch according to his own taste, and in an exceptionally rigorous order such as the Carthusians', this contrast of the garden as recreation to the solitude and silence of the cell must have provided a vital outlet. Infirmary gardens, with their herbs and medicinal plants, were both essential to the efforts of the monks in healing the sick and therapeutic in a less specific way, since they could be used as recreation areas while maintaining a necessary segregation from the rest of the community. In most cases, cloister gardens – arguably the most 'pure' of enclosed gardens – were designed for exercise and discussion. Their generally symmetrical layout, with a central fountain or basin, was both redolent of the 'paradise' garden and a link with the earliest monasteries established by Benedict at Subiaco in the sixth century. There, small communities took over abandoned Roman villas, with their enclosed peristyle gardens surrounded by rows of

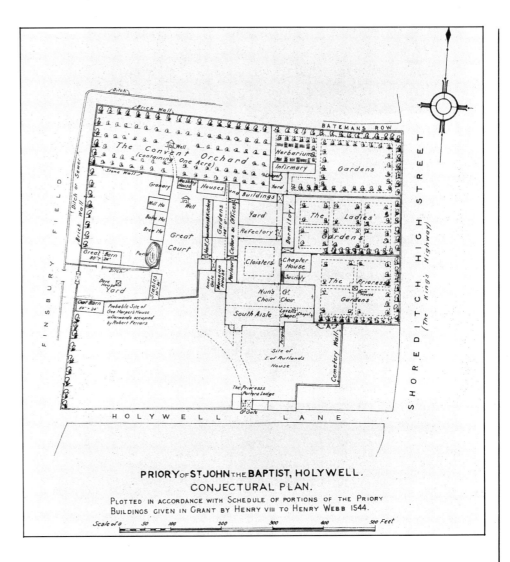

The various open spaces within the confines of St John's Priory, Holywell, suggest that their gardens offered both produce and secluded leisure to the Benedictine nuns who lived there

PRIORY OF ST JOHN THE BAPTIST, HOLYWELL.
CONJECTURAL PLAN.
PLOTTED IN ACCORDANCE WITH SCHEDULE OF PORTIONS OF THE PRIORY BUILDINGS GIVEN IN GRANT BY HENRY VIII TO HENRY WEBB 1544.

columns. Gardens at large and politically significant foundations such as Westminster and Bermondsey could sometimes become surprisingly worldly, offering as they did the opportunity for discreet diplomacy in comparatively safe surroundings. In this respect, they were perhaps closer to the gardens at the clerical palaces of Lambeth and Fulham than to those of the Charterhouse.

Such blurring of the distinction between 'contemplative' and 'active' gardens is particularly evident in the case of the gardens attached to the Inns of Court. The gardens at the Temple, of course, were inherited by the lawyers from the religious foundation after the Knights Templar were officially disbanded early in the fourteenth century. Thus, while for some time they retained their monastic layout and possibly planting, their invasion by lawyers, students and citizens brought them into that private/public realm also occupied by the gardens of the Livery Companies and those of the Cambridge and Oxford colleges (Fellows' gardens excepted). The Temple gardens continue to suggest that slight sense of privileged invasion into another protected and vaguely exclusive world which must have constituted much of their meaning to Londoners over the past six hundred years. Like the Bishop of Ely's garden, which is mentioned in *Richard III*, the Temple gardens have acquired a quite particular meaning through Shakespeare's use of them. Just as he could presumably rely on the fame of the Bishop's strawberry garden, so his use of the Temple garden as a setting for the initial exchange which escalated into the Wars of the Roses suggests that Shakespeare was able to exploit Londoners' familiarity with the gardens and their planting, and with the elaborate symbolism which had by then accrued to the rose.

The complex nature of the gardens of the Inns of Court is perhaps best exemplified by the Grays Inn garden around the turn of the seventeenth century. In 1586 the lawyer-philosopher Francis Bacon became a Bencher. Although this was more than a decade before the publication of his famous essay 'On Gardens' – a theoretical reflection which was probably based on the reality of the Cecil garden at Theobalds – it is reasonable to suppose that Bacon's involvement in the ordering of the Grays Inn garden represents an early practical exploration of his intellectual interest. There is little absolutely unquestionable evidence of Bacon's garden today, but in its time it clearly attracted considerable notice. Lewis Mumford suggests in *The City in History* that Grays Inn, as it was laid out at the beginning of the seventeenth century, marks the transition from the introspective and essentially non-public enclosed garden of the Middle Ages to the relatively public one which was conceived as integral to later city planning. If this is so, then one may assume that the meaning of the Grays Inn garden was similarly transitional: what had once been a retreat from the world was becoming a retreat for the world.

As planned spaces within the built environment, the gardens of the seventeenth- and eighteenth-century squares are supreme and uniquely English examples. On one hand, they were, and are, obviously public; on the other they flaunt the privacy of social and financial privilege. In many instances only people with homes around the squares hold keys – and the holding of a key to such a garden can render that garden overgrown with meaning. The eighteenth century laid the foundations for London's position as the European capital with the highest proportion of individual dwellings with their own outdoor spaces. On the whole such spaces, usually at the rear, were necessarily fairly small and their layout was conceived in architectural unity with the house. Thus, ground-planted trees and shrubs – as opposed to those grown in pots – were generally confined to the communal square garden. Many small

town gardens were paved or gravelled and there is little to indicate that suggestions of the countryside were considered appropriate.

The eighteenth-century Londoners' wholehearted indulgence of the *rus in urbe* fantasy was manifested by the huge popularity of the pleasure gardens. Although themselves strictly suburban rather than rural, the gardens at Vauxhall and Ranelagh, particularly, offered the opportunity to indulge in the kind of romanticized ruralism that was so well expressed in the decorative acts and in paintings of the period – among them those executed for the Vauxhall supper boxes. The pleasure gardens meant many different things to different people, of course. To their owners they represented profit; to the musicians who provided entertainment they meant employment; to citizens and visitors of many social backgrounds they could mean anything from innocent enjoyment of the trees, birds and fountains to a freedom which to the vociferous disgust of the more inhibited slid happily into licence.

Gardens of knowledge

Botanical curiosity has provided another essentially different escape into fantasy. The gardens at Kew have since the eighteenth century fed the imagination, not with romanticized visions of rural delight, but with the unfamiliar and the exotic. Kew's reputation as a botanical wonderland excited popular interest long before the Gardens' official opening to the general public in the 1840s.

Acquisition of plant specimens in conjunction with exploration and colonization, as in the Chelsea Physic Garden and at Kew, reflects a particularly interesting form of control over the natural world. Colonized peoples could be subjugated by force and the subjugation of animals and plants in new territories was equally horrifyingly straightforward. One can, however, gain ascendancy through knowledge. In addition to an entirely laudable desire to know everything possible about the world in which we live, there developed the acquisition of plant specimens as a form of symbolic possession of newly discovered lands. Very often, it was clear

that indigenous populations benefited from a symbiotic relationship with the plant life around them. This gave them, by implication, a threatening superiority over their conquerors which could be negated by the gathering of plant specimens which under experiment would yield their secrets and thus reduce the native inhabitants' advantage.

Private specimen collections perhaps have rather different meanings. The eighteenth-century surgeon Sir Hans Sloane appears to have collected plants in much the same spirit as he collected almost everything from illuminated manuscripts to fossils – with the fervour of the encyclopaedist. For Bishop Compton, an enforced temporary retirement to Fulham Palace during the reign of James II offered the

Above: Enclosed parks and gardens were inaccessible to most eighteenth-century Londoners. The privileged held keys – examples here include ones to Hyde Park and Kew Gardens – and servants were not admitted 'without masters'

opportunity to indulge in a deep and long-held interest in collecting for the love of the plants themselves. To Lord Burghley, plants from the Americas held great intrinsic interest – but they could also be displayed as flattering effects of England's power under Elizabeth's rule. The exotic trees which survive in parks and larger suburban gardens expressed elements of imperial and colonial control in the nineteenth century, to say nothing of the crowded conservatories of suburban villas, where fashion was clearly fed by foreign policy.

In various guises, the garden as expressive of control is a dominant motif in its history. It partly explains, too, the current resurgence of

'The dangers of the enclosed garden.' A satirical 1930s look at the ability of the English to retreat to their plots and delude themselves that 'everything in the garden is lovely'

interest in gardens and the attendant gardening boom. Many of us feel that we live in an increasingly confusing and unknowable world which no longer offers the anchors of permanent residence, extended family and stable community. Gardens, particularly for city dwellers, offer spaces which are reassuringly comprehensible and controllable oases in a desert of rapid 'progress' and apparently arbitrary destruction and dislocation. They are areas over which we, as autonomous individuals, rather than as frequently impotent members of society, have control. In our gardens, we can all be anarchists – at least until a neighbour complains about our encroaching Russian vine.

Gardens for ourselves

Given comparably sized plots, town and country people tend to use them somewhat differently and thus to impose different meanings upon them. Village dwellers can, after all, at least see the countryside around them, even if freedom of access to fields and woods is less common than one would wish, and proportionally greater space is often devoted to productive planting than in the 'escapist' town garden. Londoners are increasingly compensating for the visual and spiritual absence of countryside by bringing elements of it into their

gardens. The proliferation of so-called cottage gardens and 'wild' areas is not simply a manifestation of the greening of the city: it also, surely, expresses an historical loss and a manufactured nostalgia which is magnified by the current pressure of urban values.

Londoners have made their gardens into playgrounds for fantasy. The fantasies expressed need not, of course, be strongly related to rural yearnings. Observant travellers on suburban railways will know that our gardens can offer anything from a shedded paradise of tropical birds to a re-created Sissinghurst-in-miniature or a Dutch landscape complete with windmills, canals and clog-wearing inhabitants. Gardens such as these, often deemed 'tasteless' by self-appointed arbiters of such things, are supreme and valuable expressions of individuality and private delight which offer a wonderfully robust challenge to urban conformity, and are thus intense with meaning on many levels. On a larger scale, but essentially related to these 'fantasy' gardens was the roof garden above Derry and Tom's store in Kensington. There, one could wander through the Elizabethan country garden of the designers' vision or imagine oneself in the water gardens of the Alhambra in Granada. Related, too, were the temporary fantasies of the gardens created for

Their beautifully kept garden in East London must have meant a great deal to the McSweeney family, most of whom worked in the London Docks during the depressed 1930s

the many exhibitions at Earls Court, Olympia and the White City around the turn of the century, and at the Festival of Britain site: their somewhat reduced progeny appear annually at the Ideal Homes exhibition. And all for a few shillings under a grey London sky.

Among the most inventive of garden fantasists, of course, are young children. To them their gardens are safe and familiar territories for digging, pouring, slopping and paddling, for keeping pets, climbing and making noise. Their meanings can be extended and changed by pitching tents, making dens, planting seeds, playing football, imagining landscapes and ruinous riding of mountain bikes. Other people's gardens can be strange worlds of mystery and difference: a garden spied upon from a bedroom window has an entirely different meaning from the same garden entered, particularly if the entry is by delicious trespass. At least in children's literature, the delightful daring of such an enterprise is frequently offset by a terrifying or misanthropic owner: paradise soured yet again.

As an element of a garden's individual meaning, fantasy is probably as old as pleasure gardening itself. However, on a more mundane and essentially horticultural level, gardens are, or can be, intensely personal. Plants are given,

inherited, exchanged, brought back from holidays, rescued and not infrequently 'liberated' on visits to other gardens. All this gives meaning to the most modest planting – and it is meaning which is enhanced by the desire the gardener understandably feels to explain it all. A productive garden acquires meaning beyond that represented by actual produce taken from it, particularly within an urban context. The Bishop of Ely could win approval by providing the Duke of Gloucester with strawberries, and urban allotment-holders, similarly, are doing more than giving away marrows when they offer vegetables to colleagues at work. Both gifts carry with them many meanings that the donors have given to the garden and to themselves as gardeners, or as garden-owners.

Those elements of friendship, exchange, sharing and reciprocation which are characteristic of the best kind of gardening have their darker side in the cut-throat competitiveness that gardeners are occasionally prey to. Harmless delight in 'besting' other gardeners can develop into open warfare, and the close proximity to one another that characterizes city gardens makes them somewhat more liable to such disturbance. This kind of energy is often harmlessly channelled into competition gardening, and the old London County Council was

For the Victorians, a well-stocked conservatory offered both an extension to the house and hints of the exoticism of the furthest parts of the British Empire

among the first urban authorities actively to encourage organized gardening competitions and shows.

It is in back gardens and on allotments that Londoners most usually express and indulge their individuality. Front gardens, in any case, are generally smaller and for some reason seem more controlled in appearance by neighbourhood consensus. In this respect, an interesting feature distinguishes urban gardens in London from those in northern cities. In Leeds and Newcastle, for example, houses in clearly quite affluent nineteenth-century terraces have almost all their garden space in front of the house, re-

sulting in subtle shifts in significance. Thus, the arrangement of exterior space in these northern houses more directly corresponds in meaning to the arrangement of interior space: front parlour extends into front garden as an area of potential relaxation and self-expression while the back yard extends and encloses the activities of the back kitchen which are common to almost everyone. There can be little doubt that front and rear outdoor spaces had rather different meanings in London and Leeds, but how this difference developed from a similarity in the use of private urban spaces before the nineteenth century is rather less clear.

Meaning, of course, changes with ownership and use. Let us imagine, for example, the possible shifts in meaning which might be imposed upon Mr Pooter's 'nice little back garden which runs down to the railway' at 'The Laurels', Brickfield Terrace, Holloway. As recorded in *The Diary of a Nobody*, Mr Pooter's practical gardening did not extend much beyond the purchase of a second-hand gardening manual and the sowing of a few radishes, half-hardy annuals and mustard and cress 'in a nice sunny border'. But the possession of a garden around which to 'take a turn' was clearly vital to his sense of self-importance. It was also, as gardens continue to be, the battleground on which tensions with the neighbours were played out: a brick thrown among the geraniums, a parcel of greasy bones dumped on the path. . . . The overhanging branch, collapsing fence or encroaching creeper all seem to engender in us a degree of emotional unreasonableness which we would never consider exhibiting in other spheres of social interaction, or, for that matter, in our front gardens, so strong is our defence of the garden as an extension of our private and personal being.

To successive generations of children, the proximity of 'The Laurels' to the railway line must have been a source of delight and entertainment. During wartime it might have acquired significance as a productive area with vegetables, and perhaps a few hens at the bottom. With an immigrant family living in the house during the 1950s the layout and use of the garden might have expressed a nostalgia for a warmer and more colourful outdoor environment. To later bed-sit dwellers, the garden may have meant little more than a communal liability and a dumping ground for unwanted furniture. Recent 'gentrification' of such areas has brought the garden's meaning full circle. The need to look out on, and entertain friends in, an instantly mature garden purchased from a garden centre or provided by a designer is as much a statement of social and material aspiration as 'taking a turn or two' in the garden with visitors was to Mr Pooter. The most that one is likely to learn of the owners and creators of such gardens in the late twentieth century is that they had an accurate and acute sense of current style. But many London gardens continue to express an individuality and personal meaning which is seldom evident in city gardens abroad, and which renders them delightful oases in the urban environment.

The tensions of a day on the production line, behind a shop counter or in the office can be almost miraculously alleviated by an hour of planting, pottering or simply sitting in a garden. Four or five hundred years ago, a day spent in the noise and stench of mercantile Cheapside no doubt generated similar stress which was reduced by going to the countryside beyond the city walls or sitting in a courtyard herb garden. There has been surprisingly little change in the uses and meanings which, over the centuries, Londoners have given to their gardens. It is true that as the number of private garden spaces increased so their individual extent decreased considerably, but the gardens themselves, along with London's parks and open spaces, represent an historical continuity of meanings which is arguably less detectable in most other spheres of city life. There are gardens at the Inns of Court which represent much the same things to Londoners as they always have done. Although the Cecils' Theobalds garden has disappeared, we can still detect the vestiges of a different but similarly complex iconography in Lord Burlington's villa at Chiswick or at Hampton Court Palace. We still colonize the world with knowledge from Kew and the Chelsea Physic Garden. The remaining gardens at Westminster Abbey, Fulham and particularly Lambeth at least suggest the worldly privacy of the great ecclesiastical gardens. A few Livery Company gardens survive as reminders of the type of small enclosed gardens which existed in the wealthier City merchants' establishments. Gardens in the squares, with their often exclusive access, accentuate privilege just as in the past.

And it is not just to physical survivals and similarities that we can look for evidence of continuity. We continue to use our gardens for entertaining and impressing, for quiet retreat or lively discussion, as horticultural encyclopedias and expressions of botanical erudition, as knowable areas of control and self-expression through both their planting and their architecture. Above all, perhaps, it is to the fact that they *are* gardens in London's vast conurbation that they owe their particular and enduring attraction, continuity and their many meanings.

The Middle Ages

Our first glimpse of the leisure aspect of London gardens created specifically for pleasure occurs with the medieval period. Sadly it remains a fragmented vision as there are no contemporary illustrations of the capital's gardens. However this chapter brings to life gardens known through written descriptions, by matching them with details from European illustrations which highlight similar features.

Opposite: *This illustration concludes the* Roman de la Rose *and depicts the moment when the Lover is finally reunited with the Rose. The story was a central theme in the courtly world of the Middle Ages and focuses entirely on the garden which is seen to be rich in allegorical meaning*

'Gardens of the citizens . . . spacious and fair'
THE MEDIEVAL GARDEN

Up until the eleventh century, only the monasteries possessed any systematic knowledge of plants, and each order handed down information on the properties of individual plants and cultivation details for the practical benefit of its members. Other evidence of the existence of horticultural standards during these times is fragmentary: in about AD 800 the Emperor Charlemagne issued a list of plants which he considered suitable for growing in the cities of his Frankish empire, not only revealing the Emperor's megalomania, but also implying a degree of horticultural sophistication, at least in concept. In general, however, and particularly in England, the unsettled nature of the period, marked by migrations into these islands from north-west Europe, did not prove conducive to encouraging the pleasures of gardening. The soil was used to aid survival, not to supply entertainment, and there is little evidence for advanced gardening texts in the Dark Ages.

When the Normans invaded England in 1066 they were also reaching south to the Mediterranean. There they came into contact with Arabic and classical gardening traditions. These traditions filtered through to England, and it is from this time that we can date the development of the pleasure garden in England. In the early twelfth century, Henry I appears to have paid especial attention to the creation and

This late fifteenth-century town garden illustrates the familiar grid-pattern of beds. It included a cistern, probably of lead, at one end, and would have supplied local businesses with produce

Opposite: *Gathering fruit from an orchard surrounded by a wattle fence, late fifteenth century. The disturbance caused by the pig on the right would have been a familiar sight in medieval London's streets*

30

development of gardens at his residences, one of which was at Havering in Essex, where the post of gardener was hereditary. The name Havering-atte-Bower no doubt bears witness to one of the garden's most attractive features.

Royal gardens and those of the nobility were responsible for the main developments in garden aesthetics, whereas monasteries continued to concentrate on the development of plants in the medical and culinary sciences. It was at the Hospital of St Mary Rouncival of Charing Cross, for example, that the Rouncival pea was developed in the later Middle Ages. This does not imply, however, that religious houses were ignorant of the beauties of the garden. Flowers were required to decorate altars and chapels on Holy Days and Feast Days, and infirmary gardens were places of convalescence where contemplation of nature might aid the patient's recovery.

The thirteenth and fourteenth centuries

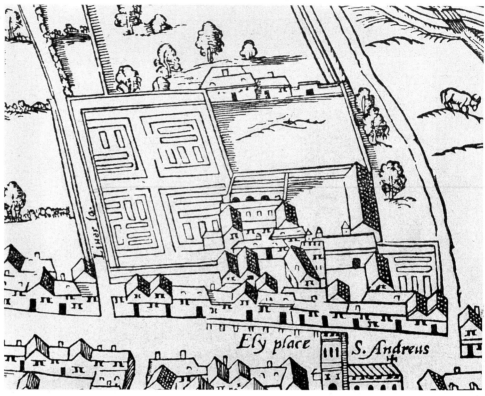

A sixteenth-century view of the Bishop of Ely's garden of Holborn, one of the largest and most productive in medieval London

witnessed the zenith of medieval gardening. Developments were spearheaded by Henry III and his son Edward I, most notably at the Tower and Westminster Palace, where Edward was presumably inspired to make extensive changes during the 1270s by the Arabic gardens he had encountered while on crusade. By comparison, the fifteenth century was static, the kings and nobility of England more concerned with dynastic upheavals than with horticulture.

London is of paramount importance when discussing medieval gardens. The city was the seat of royal power. The main royal residences were situated there, and several others were near by in the surrounding countryside. The nobility and the most prominent of the lay clergy had residences in the city and the chief English houses of religious orders were located there. All of these had gardens attached, which were in some cases very extensive, so that there was in London a concentration of high-quality gardens, of expertise and of the service industries and supplies which fuelled the work of the gardeners. As early as the 1170s, William Fitz-stephen commented on 'the gardens of the citizens that dwell in the suburbs, planted with trees, spacious and fair, adjoining one another. On the north are pasture lands and a pleasant space of flat meadow, intersected by running waters, which turn revolving mill wheels with merry din.'

Much later, the area is still shown to be rich in gardens on the map of London of the 1560s attributed to Ralph Agas. This map offers a bird's-eye view of what many medieval gardens looked like, as several of those depicted are documented during the medieval period. One such, in Holborn, is the extensive garden of the Bishop of Ely of Ely Place, already mentioned as the site of a scene in Shakespeare's *Richard III*. In 1373, Adam Vynour, the Bishop's gardener, compiled an account for the previous year's work in the garden and of supplies to it, demonstrating it to be productive and a lucrative source of income for the Bishop. A large expanse of gardens may be seen on the Agas map between London Wall, Broad Street, Throgmorton Street and Lothbury.

There are no contemporary illustrations or plans of any of London's medieval gardens. Indeed, there are very few gardens of any type illustrated in English manuscripts. Most details of gardens are found in foreign illustrations of the fourteenth century and later, and most show pleasure gardens, not as the central subject, but as a decorative setting or incidental detail of some larger scene. The absence of English garden illustrations should not be taken to imply that the English were unappreciative of the art of horticulture. On the contrary, garden accounts documenting work carried out at royal, noble, livery-company and ecclesiastical gardens demonstrate a high level of care and attention to aesthetics. If we combine details from several of these accounts with features included in pictorial evidence, then we can gain some impression of the appearance of medieval London gardens, or at least those belonging to the upper echelons of society.

The larger residences and ecclesiastical establishments would often have more than one garden; there might be a great garden, private garden, kitchen garden and, in the case of monasteries, an infirmary garden. At the Tower, there was a garden within the fortress and another outside the walls. Other gardens might be constructed for specific purposes such as entertainment or, as in the case of the gardens of the king's falconry at Charing Cross Mews, they might have formed part of one of the annexes of the main residence.

Needless to say, the size of gardens varied depending on their use and the number of people likely to use them or, in the more densely inhabited areas of the City, on the amount of space available, although some gardens like that of the Austin Friars sprawled, often to the annoyance of neighbours. Actual dimensions are difficult to determine. In the case of Ely Place, we are told in Adam Vynour's account of 1373 that 121 perches of hedge were erected around the great garden (1 perch = $5\frac{1}{2}$ yards). This was obviously a very large garden, even if we assume that the hedge was constructed around the edge of the garden and not about its interior, giving a perimeter of at least 665 yards. The hedge was made using four cartloads of thorns which, together with brambles and shrubs such as willow and hawthorn, were deemed appropriate protection for the garden's perimeter.

Inside the garden

In the town many gardens were surrounded by walls which were intended primarily to keep others out but which also might enhance the garden's beauty when decked with plants. In 1365 a wall at Westminster Abbey was topped by a reed thatch. Edward I's reorganization of the Tower garden included the construction of earthen walls and in 1313 the Austin Friars built an earthen wall around their garden to replace a hedge. Wattle fences were also employed, as were paling fences providing rather less substantial barriers. A further defence, lining the outer side of the wall, was the ditch, used at larger houses such as the Black Prince's Palace at Kennington, also a favourite residence of Richard II. In 1275, Edward I lined the moat of the Tower with willow trees. The later medieval mind saw no incongruity in beautifying military structures in this way and elsewhere flowers were grown on castle battlements. Castles were designed to be lived in as well as fought for, and the pleasures of life were not always subjugated by military requirements.

Much attention was paid to lawns. Albertus Magnus, writing about 1260, regarded a tightly laid and closely cropped lawn as vital to the appearance of the garden and gave advice on its manufacture and maintenance. He recommends that the turves should be beaten down with wooden mallets and this may possibly have been the technique used when turves were laid at Westminster Palace in 1298, although in 1259 a roller had been used to level a lawn there.

Albertus's lawns formed a square with flowers and herbs planted around its edge and trees to provide shade from the sun. Flowers, herbs and shrubs were also grown in beds rectangular in shape and laid out in a grid pattern with walkways between. It is also thought that knot gardens existed before the end of the fifteenth century. Beds might be raised and framed by a low wall or by a low wooden rail or fence as was the case at Westminster Abbey. Albertus also recommended that raised benches of turf should be positioned at the edge of the lawn next to the herb and flower border. Turf benches recur frequently in illustrations either

as seats or planted with flowers, and not all are situated as Albertus suggests. They were evidently a distinctive and regular feature of medieval gardens and certainly existed in London. Those at Westminster Palace, for example, were repaired with new turf during the 1380s.

The types of plants grown in London's gardens are too numerous to name here. It is thought that Friar Henry Daniel had about 250 species growing in his garden in Stepney during the fourteenth century, but Daniel was a botanist and interested in plants from a scientific point of view, so many of the plants grown by him would not have been common in other London gardens. Even so, a considerable list would have to be compiled. We can assume those flowers mentioned by Albertus – violet, columbine, lily, rose and iris – to have been regular. Certainly the lily and rose are mentioned in London accounts on several occasions and seem to have been particularly in demand. Herbs mentioned by Albertus were rue, sage and basil, to which might be added such others as borage, fennel, thyme, hyssop, parsley and mint. In addition to their value in the kitchen,

Above: *Some gardens offered a peaceful retreat. This late fourteenth-century manuscript illumination is almost the only English view of a royal garden: the King and Queen play chess, sitting on turf benches (known to have featured at Westminster Palace) in a fenced garden*

Right: *In this early fifteenth-century* Garden of Paradise, *plants include a cherry tree, borage, rose campion, cowslip, daisy, purple flag iris, hollyhock, madonna lily, lily of the valley, scarlet lychnis, peony, periwinkle, sweet rocket, rose, sage, snowdrop, strawberry, violet and yellow wallflower*

herbs were used decoratively and to delight the sense of smell. Their aesthetic properties were obviously in mind when a new herb garden, which included benches and a pool, was constructed at Westminster Abbey in 1305–6. Here they would also have been important for use in the Abbey infirmary. Given the trade of the members of the Grocers' Company, it is no sur-

34

prise that the herb garden features prominently in their fifteenth-century garden accounts. Albertus's trees were also chosen for their scent as much as the shade they cast. Trees and bushes purchased during the 1270s for the gardens of Westminster Palace and the Tower included pear, rose, quince, peach, gooseberry, cherry, willow and yew, and Westminster Abbey was noted for its damson trees. Trees might also be decoratively trimmed, although there is no evidence of true topiary in English gardens before the sixteenth century.

Frequent mention is made of the vine, which was extremely popular and widespread as an ornament, particularly when trained over a trellis or arbour, a technique repeatedly depicted in contemporary illustrations and paintings. In 1362 new timber and poles were acquired to repair the tunnel arbours at Kennington Palace, and in 1395 the chronicler Froissart shaded himself from the sun in the vine-covered alleys at Eltham Palace; a new garden was made there around this time for Richard II. In the fifteenth century, the vines in the Grocers' Company garden were sufficiently successful to allow members of the company to take home bunches of grapes in season.

Walkways around gardens varied in form and construction. Paths at Westminster Abbey were strewn with sand in 1359. There were paved walks around the garden of Westminster Palace in 1307, while at the royal palace at Sheen, a cloister was paved and a garden made within it in 1366–7. More elaborate raised walkways were built at Eltham in 1388–9 and at the Grocers' Company during the fifteenth century, where steps led down into the garden.

Other man-made structures were designed to provide shelter and aid appreciation of the garden. The tower next to the Grocers' Company garden may have served this purpose. There were 'chambers', probably summer-houses, at both Westminster Abbey and Westminster Palace. In 1440–1, a gazebo was built at Charing Cross Mews, which housed the king's falconry but was used as much as a pleasure garden in the fifteenth century. A pavilion was built by Richard II on an island in the Thames next to Sheen Palace, and we may suppose this to have been set in a garden, and used for royal entertainments both public and private. Gardens were planned to be viewed from the main residential buildings. The royal palace at Greenwich, where the garden in the fifteenth century included a hedge and arbour, was furnished with an overlooking gallery.

Water was an important component in medieval gardens, perhaps the most spectacular example being the island garden at Sheen, where the River Thames was enlisted to augment the pleasures of a visit to the garden. Otherwise, the provision of water was on a much slighter scale, consisting of wells, cisterns and fountains. At Westminster Palace there was a conduit with taps and at Charing Cross Mews there was a lead bath with a central image of a falcon, to which water was conveyed by aqueduct and poured into the bath through four brass leopard-head spouts. There were also, of course, ponds. One of these at Westminster Abbey was situated in the Infirmarer's herb garden, newly built in 1305–6. The Earl of Lincoln's large garden in Holborn had a fish-pond containing pike which were fed on small fish, small frogs and eels, the provision of which, for the year 1295–6 took 8s 0½d from the Earl's annual budget. Other animals contributed to the garden entertainment. Caged songbirds added the beauty of sound to the sights and smells of the garden, peacocks and pheasants roamed across lawns. The doves which provided the Charing Cross falcons with food may also, before their fate, have provided pleasure to visitors. The mention of deer in the Earl of Lincoln's Holborn accounts implies a parkland extension to the garden. The open spaces of thirteenth-century Holborn certainly permitted this, and coneygarths or rabbit warrens were also part of the area's park landscape.

The uses of the garden

Our tour around the medieval pleasure garden in London must not end without a glimpse of people taking their leisure in it. As in any other age, medieval Londoners used their gardens not only as places to which they might retreat in peace to refresh their thoughts but also as settings for social gatherings, where music would be played and food and drink consumed. The garden attached to London Bridge House in Southwark included an arbour, ponds and a fountain, and was the scene of a regular celebration after the audit of the Bridgemaster's accounts. At Eltham in 1388–9, a walled garden was built so that Richard II and his queen could take their meals in the open air. Games and sports such as chess, bowling and archery were also held in gardens. During the fifteenth century there were, rather anomalously, archery butts in the Infirmary garden at Westminster Abbey. People were also employed as integral parts of the garden for the entertainment of

owners and their guests. Boys were paid to sit fishing from ponds and presumably garden workers were employed in a similar manner on occasions.

Garden produce provided a source of income for royal and noble households, although the sale of grapes and other fruit and verjuice (expressed fruit juice) was not a major part of the revenues of royal residences. It is likely, nevertheless, that some gardens were more geared towards production than others. In about 1270, Westminster Abbey expected its garden to grow beans, apples, cherries, plums, pears, nuts, medlars and herbs. In 1321–2 seeds purchased by Lambeth Palace included leeks, parsley, skirret, cress, cabbage, cucumber, hyssop, spinach, borage and lettuce. Several gardens also contained vineyards, such as the Earl of Lincoln's garden, that of the Bishop of Ely and another in Smithfield belonging to the Canons of Holy Trinity which flourished before 1137. Due to

Some larger suburban gardens extended into parkland and were stocked with animals such as rabbits, deer, peacocks and pheasants, either for purely decorative purposes or for hunting

the generally warmer climate, southern England was, before the fifteenth century, a wine-producing region, a characteristic it has regained in recent times, although England was not self-sufficient in wine, which was the country's major import. Much of this produce would have been consumed within the households themselves, where it was necessary to hold large and lavish banquets as befitted the owner's status, and with the concentration of

royal and noble residences in London, socializing required considerable resources.

Otherwise produce was sold. Sales from the Earl of Lincoln's garden in 1295–6 included pears, apples, nuts, herbs, beans, verjuice, roses, hemp, onions, garlic, vines and leeks as well as some of the Earl's deer. A major sales outlet for the produce of earls', barons' and bishops' gardens was a market held in St Paul's Churchyard, which evidently thrived. Such was the commotion it caused that it had to be moved in 1345 from the Churchyard to avoid disturbing the devotions of those in the Cathedral. A flourishing market like this also suggests that Londoners ate more fruit and vegetables than might be implied by other dietary evidence, though much of the produce was for general household needs. This market, and perhaps other outlets, was a likely source of materials needed for gardens. The provision of seeds, turves, trees and so on for a reorganization on the scale of that undertaken by Edward I at the Tower and

Far left: *The raised walkways in such gardens as those of Eltham Palace and the Grocers' Company may have been comparable with this detail from Jan Van Eyck's* The Madonna with Chancellor Rolin

Left: *The recreational use of larger gardens included sporting activities. Rather unexpectedly, the Infirmary garden at Westminster Abbey possessed an archery butt*

Above: *A walled garden containing a tunnel arbour rising to a tower at one end. The approach to the garden from the adjacent building was by way of a viewing gallery and stairway, perhaps similar to those documented at the royal palace at Greenwich*

Left: *A late medieval walled garden with tunnel arbour, trellis, trees and chequered pattern of beds. Kennington Palace on the south bank is known to have had tunnel arbours*

Westminster indicates that there was an extensive nursery trade.

We must not imagine that large-scale production resulted in the kind of regimentation in garden design which characterizes modern market gardens and factory farms. Medieval gardens did not feed a mass market and the requirements of production did not conflict with attention to aesthetics. Orchards, for example, were as much places of retreat as of food production.

Pests

So far, a picture has been painted of gardens under constant maintenance, flowering colourfully, sweetly scented and bountiful in their production. It should of course be appreciated that there were gardens suffering from neglect, from the ravages of pests or from incompetent gardeners. Adverse weather conditions might damage the best laid plans, as would shortage of money. Archaeological evidence shows that at the very end of the Middle Ages, the garden of

The privacy and security of gardens, where beehives were often kept, was difficult to maintain. There are several reports of stealing and vandalism in medieval London gardens. These scenes come from the fourteenth-century Luttrell Psalter

the Greyfriars' monastery near Newgate was overgrown and probably flooded, one possible reason being a withdrawal of public support for the friars in the decades leading up to the Dissolution, forcing them to cut down on their activities. Vermin caused problems, as implied by Albertus Magnus when he suggested planting rue in order to get rid of them. Medieval gardens presumably had their share of aphids and birds which pecked away at fruit and seeds. Some men made a living out of mole-catching.

Among the greatest of pests were people. This was especially true of those living in the most densely populated areas of London. The Copperplate Map (c. 1557) shows some large gardens in the centre of the City but there were many others so small that they were hidden from the view of the draughtsman. We gain little from manuscripts on what such gardens looked like, the illustrators preferring to depict perhaps often idealized images for the benefit of wealthy patrons, but we can infer the difficulties of maintaining these little gardens when living cheek by jowl with other citizens. Stealing from gardens was common and they sometimes became the route of short cuts. In 1363, Margery de Honeylane, who lived near Bishopsgate, complained that the wall separating her garden from that of her neighbour had fallen into disrepair, with the effect that 'strange men and animals enter her garden and trample down the grass and other things growing there, and carry off the fruit, and see the private business of the plaintiff and her servants'.

Greater encroachments than this were suffered. In 1356, in the parish of St Dunstan in the East, John de Martin's neighbour, John Bengeo, allowed water from his gutter to fall into the former's garden, and his earthen wall between the two properties was ruinous. Furthermore, Bengeo had dug a 12 × 8-foot cellar beneath Martin's garden without including any supports, so that the earth in the garden had subsided into it.

Animal life

A larger diversity of mammals than is presently the case in town centres would have contribu-

ted to the destruction. Skeletal remains discovered at Greyfriars included a dog, cat, rabbit, house mouse, field mouse, yellow-necked mouse, field vole, bank vole, water vole, common shrew, water shrew, weasel and hedgehog. It is not difficult for any gardener to imagine his medieval predecessor seeking to prevent a neighbourhood cat from digging up flowerbeds while performing its natural functions. Dogs were especially blamed for rampaging through gardens, crushing plants, and pigs rooted through backyards, sometimes causing harm to more than just plants. There are records of children sustaining serious injuries, sometimes death, as a result of encounters with street-wandering pigs.

Medieval society was predominantly rural; only one in ten of medieval England's population lived in towns and the prevailing attitudes to life were those of the country. Even London, by far the largest town in England and the only English town that could compete in size and status with the great cities of the Continent, was inhabited to a large extent by people whose hearts and minds were rooted in the land rather than in the more urban pursuits of commerce and industry. The holding of the hustings courts had to be suspended during harvest time. Migration between town and country was constant. For those citizens who were more established in the town, there were constant reminders of the country in the animals which roamed the streets, and all the filth and smells they left behind.

It is thus difficult to apply to medieval society a sharp distinction between town and country. The notion of the garden as an idealized, condensed reconstruction of nature was applicable only to those medieval Londoners who could afford to treat their gardens as luxury items. From the existence of pigsties and the keeping of hens in backyards, we can imagine many gardens in the centre of town having the character of farm smallholdings. This is perhaps a truer reflection of most medieval Londoners' perceptions of their gardens than the impression created by the foregoing descriptions of the pleasure gardens of the well-to-do.

The Tudor and Stuart Period

The Tudor and Stuart period is a key period in the development of London as a green city. It saw the creation of the royal parks and their opening to the public, the first pleasure gardens, the London square, as well as the birth of the commercial seed and nursery trades and of market gardening. Moorfields became London's first 'leisure park', and in the seventeenth century we have the first painted views of London gardens. The new public open spaces created in this period acted as magnets for private gardens. This evidence should balance the view that truly British gardening only emerged in the eighteenth century.

Opposite: *Although the earliest illustrations of the Chelsea Physic Garden date from the eighteenth century, it was in fact founded in 1673 by the Society of Apothecaries for the purpose of growing medicinal plants. The aloe plant shown on the right-hand side is probably based on the botanical drawing by Jacob van Huysum shown on page 66*

'Whither wilt thou build?'

GARDENS AND OPEN SPACE IN TUDOR AND EARLY STUART LONDON

The sixteenth century witnessed a sharp acceleration in the pace of change in London's physical appearance. In 1500, a century and a half after the Black Death, the population of London had still not recovered to its pre-plague level, and the capital was smaller and greener than it was ever to be again. The inhabitants, probably not more than 50,000 or 60,000 in number, were concentrated in the City itself and in the two satellites of Southwark and Westminster, the latter linked to the City by the Strand, but still a distinct entity. There were gardens and open spaces within the built-up area, and even the centre was not far distant from the country outside. But by the early seventeenth century it is estimated that London's population had reached over 200,000, with a corresponding impact on the size and density of the metropolis.

Most of this expansion of the capital's population took place in the second half of the sixteenth century and the first half of the seventeenth. The tide of immigration greatly increased the demand for housing and the value of land, and there were considerable incentives to infill, to encroach, and to appropriate space, despite all official attempts to prevent this. Gardens, together with private and public open space, were very often the casualty of this process; in London as a whole they could only survive where the pressure on land was weaker – as in the new outer suburbs – or where a positive value was set on their preservation, as in the case of grand households and Livery Company halls. At the same time, Londoners' access to open countryside was reduced, as the boundaries of the built-up area expanded and the suburban fringe spread more widely.

Some of the physical changes that this rapid expansion of population brought about are depicted for us both in the map-views of the mid-century – the Copperplate Map of c. 1557, Braun and Hogenberg's version of the same published in 1572 and the 'Agas' woodcut map – and by the pen of John Stow, historian and eulogizer of the city of his birth in his *Survey of London* first published in 1598. These Tudor map-views can be compared with those of the seventeenth century, to show how the metropolis had grown; Stow was himself an historian of change, noting, often lamenting, the alterations to the City and its surroundings during the course of his long life. These sources, together with a wide range of other evidence, enable us to examine the impact of the demographic and economic changes of sixteenth-century London on the environment and amenities enjoyed by its inhabitants.

The impact of growth

The medieval city was a compact entity, compared with its successors, but the long period of stable or falling population levels since the fourteenth-century plagues meant that gaps had appeared in the urban fabric; unwanted houses had been abandoned and derelict house-sites

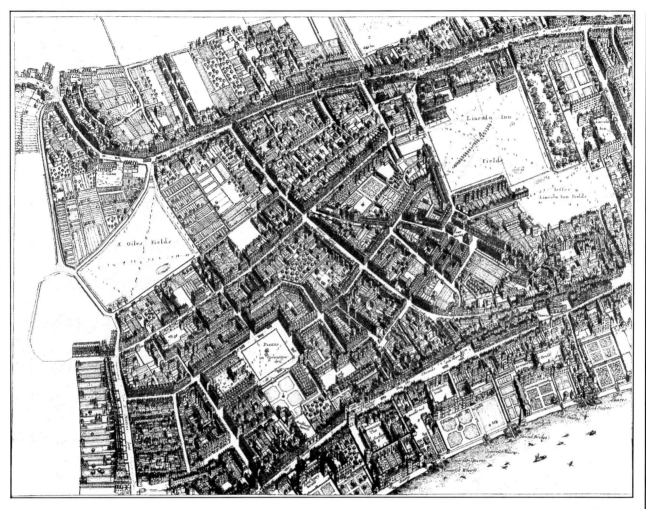

By 1658, the western suburbs were spreading, characterized by handsome houses for gentlemen, with private gardens. The former 'convent garden' has been laid out as a piazza and streets of houses

had become yards, gardens or part of the common street, even in the centre of the City. There had always been more space in the suburbs, and some gardens within the City boundaries were large enough for commercial cultivation and market gardening. With increased population pressure in the sixteenth century this spaciousness began to disappear, as more people were fitted into the existing housing and as gardens and yards were built over to provide new accommodation.

An opportunity for infilling gaps in the built-up area was provided when the Dissolution of the monasteries in the 1530s released many properties on to the commercial land market for the first time in centuries. It is important not to overstate the importance of this development either on the population of London – the greater part of the monastic estates in London was made up of tenanted housing anyway, and most of the initial transfers of monastic land had taken place by 1550, before the great expansion of population – or on the amount of open space in the capital, since most of the religious precincts were enclosed and private and offered no direct amenity to the other inhabitants of London. Some of these houses and precincts were acquired by nobles and courtiers, who took over the establishments to provide themselves with the kind of town house that was becoming fashionable; those along the Strand and towards Westminster were particularly desirable. In most cases, however, some land was released for building, and in a few the whole precinct was converted to

Opposite: Mid sixteenth-century London was still relatively compact, linked to Westminster by the Strand, lined with houses and gardens of nobles and leading churchmen

This charming reconstruction of an Elizabethan central garden at 47–8 Fenchurch Street is based on the early seventeenth-century plan shown on page 55

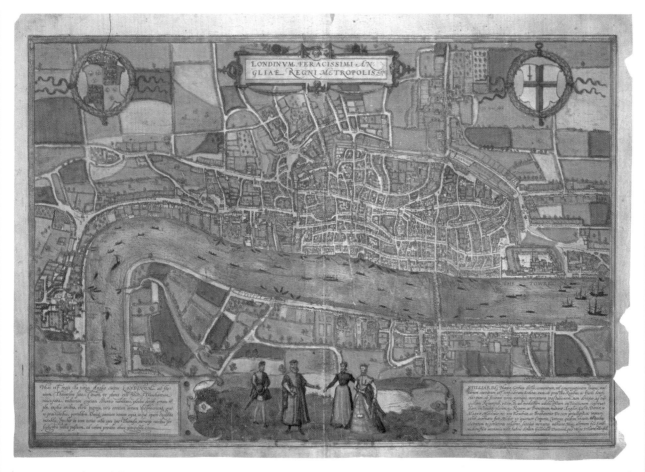

commercial and housing uses. At Austin Friars in the City, Sir William Paulet enjoyed the house, cloister and gardens, while the conventual church was partly used for storage and partly by the Dutch congregation; the precincts of Whitefriars, St Martin le Grand, and Holy Trinity Priory became densely packed with poor housing, so that no trace survived of their former spaciousness.

Both wealth and poverty made demands on space. By the early seventeenth century, Cheapside, probably the most commercially desirable area of the City, was so densely built up with merchants' houses, shops and warehouses, that there were few gardens and not every house had even a yard; some used the leads or flat roofs of adjacent properties or warehouses as their only outdoor space. In the old suburbs on the fringe of the medieval city, where the need was to crowd in as many dwellings for the poor as possible, the long gardens of houses in the Minories and Houndsditch were gradually built over and broken up into separate tenements,

forming alleys of houses along what had once been a garden path. Many of the courts and closes that characterized the seventeenth-century city, and contained some of its worst housing, were probably developed in this way. What had once been garden – or at least open space – behind a street-front house, was colonized by numbers of small dwellings, without any private open space, sharing only the semi-public area of the court.

In addition to infilling of this kind, early modern growth extended the built-up area well beyond its medieval limits. In 1598 Stow described the highway outside Aldgate, where there were formerly 'some few tenements, thinly scattered here and there, with many void places between them up to the bars' (the boundary of the City); by the time he wrote the area was now 'fully replenished with buildings … to White chappell and beyond'. Towards the west, 'many fair houses … for the most part being very new' stretched almost to St Giles in the Fields; there were 'divers fair tenements

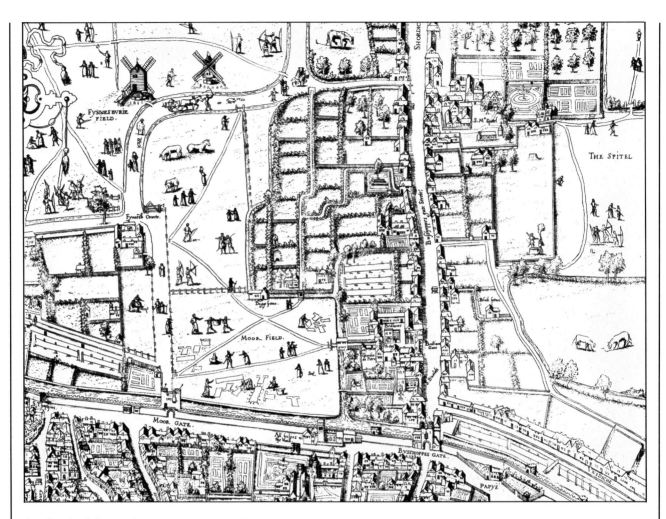

Moorfields, shown here c. 1550, provided open space for many essential activities, while the northern suburb in general contained many private gardens and enclosures

latelie built' at Charing Cross, and continuous building in Southwark along the Thames and towards Newington and Bermondsey. Thomas Freeman, in *London's Progress* (1614), depicted the urban sprawl linking areas hitherto quite distinct:

> Why how now, Babel, whither
>   wilt thou build?
> The old Holborn, Charing
>   Cross, the Strand,
> Are going to St Giles' in the
>   Fields,
> Saint Katherine she takes
>   Wapping by the hand,
> And Hogsdon will to Highgate
>   ere't be long.

Overall, this new sixteenth-century suburban growth was of mixed character; towards Westminster especially, it included good-quality housing for gentry and government officials, as well as the great houses of people like Protector Somerset and Lord Burghley. Much of it, however, was poor housing, cottages and shed dwellings, not always as densely packed as the older suburbs were becoming but still with very limited facilities and amenities. The phenomenon of uncontrolled growth and the spectre of poverty alarmed the Crown and Privy Council, but their attempts to prevent London's expansion were largely unavailing. In

1590 they had to admit that the latest proclamation against new building had 'taken so slendre effect as sithence ... the building of houses and tenements about the Citie hath ben continued and greatlie increased'. Gradually the government came to see its role as limiting growth and controlling its character, rather than banning it altogether. By the second quarter of the seventeenth century, the Crown was licensing development, provided it was of suitable quality, as in the case of Covent Garden.

Surveys of a number of properties in the east and west ends in the middle of the seventeenth century provide a useful index of the varied character of the new suburbs. On the Bishop of London's estate of more than 700 dwellings in Shadwell, the houses were small and two-storey, and only about 40 per cent of them had gardens; a group of 100 houses in High Holborn were on average much larger and taller, and over 70 per cent had gardens; in Piccadilly, still very much the fringe of the built-up area, houses were of medium size, high value and almost all had gardens. Hollar's map of the Covent Garden area in *c.* 1655 shows not only the extension of building since the mid-sixteenth century but also that many of the better houses had clearly been built with reasonably generous gardens.

The spread of the City also had an impact on areas not yet built over but coming under pressure from the needs of the city dwellers. Outside the suburban fringe of houses and gardens there was competition for the use of land, which was valuable for food production, industrial uses, and recreation. The open land at Moorfields to the north of the City, as the Copperplate Map shows, was used in the mid-sixteenth century for grazing, archery, recreation, the City's doghouse and drying washing; the space along the City ditch was occupied by tenterframes for stretching and drying finished cloth. Digging for clay and brickearth and dumping of rubbish were also frequent in the suburbs.

The impact of the City's demand for food on the surrounding areas – resulting in enclosure and more intensive cultivation – conflicted with the citizens' desire for access to open space. In 1515 the people of London broke down the enclosures and hedges and ditches of the villagers of Islington and Shoreditch, which prevented their access to the fields for pleasure and archery. But in the long run attempts to prevent the enclosure of the lands round the City proved unavailing, and open fields and common pasture lands disappeared: in the second half of the sixteenth century the parish of St Martin in the Fields waged a series of lawsuits contesting the illegal enclosure of several hundred acres of their common fields. Stow described how Hog Lane (now Petticoat Lane or Middlesex Street) had once given direct access to the open fields, but by the end of the sixteenth century was lined with cottages, and the fields beyond 'turned into garden-plots, tenter yards, bowling alleys, and such like, from Houndsditch in the West as far as White Chappell, and further towards the east'.

The survival of open space

Open land, inside and outside the City, could not survive these pressures unless ownership, including common ownership, was asserted and a positive value was placed on it. Although very frequently economic considerations prevailed, and green space made way for housing and commercial uses, there were a number of cases in which the amenity value of preserving the space as space was upheld. Even so, it was necessary to define the space, sometimes changing its character, to secure its future.

Moorfields, the nearest large open space to the city centre, belonged to the City, and was used in the sixteenth century for a variety of activities. But it too was in danger of encroachment and abuse: in 1593 the City ordered that it be inspected and 'that the same be kept clean and no be annoyed ... with anye donge, fylthe, or rubbyshe at anye tyme hereafter'. In 1605–7 major works were undertaken to level and drain the ground, lay out walks, and plant it with elm trees. This was done to provide 'a garden ... and a pleasurable place of sweet ayres for Cittizens to walk in', though apparently the drying of clothes there was still allowed. The

central part of Moorfields remains open space now, as Finsbury Circus, though surrounded by nineteenth-century buildings.

To the west of the City, near Lincoln's Inn, three large fields, formerly the property of the Knights Hospitallers and the Hospital of St Giles at Holborn, came under pressure from would-be developers in the early seventeenth century. An application to build there was turned down in 1613, and in 1617 the members of the Inns of Court and nearby gentry residents appealed that the fields 'commonly called Lincoln's Inn Fields . . . might for their general commoditie and health be converted into

walkes after the same manner as Morefields are now made to the great pleasure and benefit of the Citty'. Inigo Jones was apparently involved in the plans to lay out 'walks, partitions or other for publique health and pleasure'; this plan came to nothing, but it may have helped to ensure the ultimate preservation of part of the fields. But while their fate was uncertain residents found that the space was being used to dump dung and dirt, and a horsepool had been made there, so that they were 'almost quite deprived of their former liberty of walking, training, drying of cloathes, and recreating themselves in the said fields'. Ironically, it was

probably only the development of the housing round the fields in the second half of the seventeenth century which defined and hence secured the remaining open space.

There was very little in the way of public green space in the City itself; perhaps the nearest to this were the churchyards of the hundred parish churches. Many of these were tiny, however, and most, in the demographic conditions of the early modern period, were crowded with burials. They too were in danger of encroachment by building, as at St Michael Cornhill. Tenements were built along the north side of the church, in place of a 'green churchyard'; the

The original 'fields' west of Lincoln's Inn were mostly built over in the seventeenth century, but part of the open space survived, given physical and social definition by the elegant houses that surrounded it

'green churchyard' at St Mary-le-Bow had also been built over by the end of the sixteenth century, and sheds and houses were built in St Paul's Churchyard. Parishioners tended to appropriate the churchyard space for their own uses: in 1580 the vestry of St Michael Cornhill ordered everyone who kept cocks, hens and pigeons in the churchyard to remove them, and in 1588 said that only those whose houses opened on to the churchyard could dry clothes there. Other parishes complained of locals mixing mortar and storing building materials in churchyards, or setting up stalls to trade there.

The use of the phrase 'green churchyard' suggests that others were not green, and it appears from parish records that many were paved or gravelled. But several had trees: there were ash trees at St Anne Aldersgate, a yew or yews at St Mary-at-Hill. One of the most pleasant of the city churchyards must have been that of St Helen's, Bishopsgate, formerly a combined parish and conventual church, and hence perhaps with an unusually large churchyard. There were several large sycamore trees, at least one large ash tree and one small one, willows, a plum tree, a cherry tree, a gooseberry tree, a vine, a sweetbriar and a rose tree, as well as a great grass plot and a little grass plot, which the sexton was paid for mowing. Planting of this kind suggests more than a utilitarian view of the space, and indeed one of the parishioners was said to have 'made a garden' within the churchyard, near which she was later buried. Some other churchyards may have been similar green oases in the City; St Helen's may be unusual only in that it is well documented.

Private gardens

There were many private gardens in sixteenth-century London, though most of these, large and small, were in the outer suburbs. Before the Reformation, the London monasteries and the town houses of provincial abbots and bishops provided an example of private town gardening which was taken over, literally, by their noble successors. The garden of the dissolved Charterhouse was spectacularly plundered in

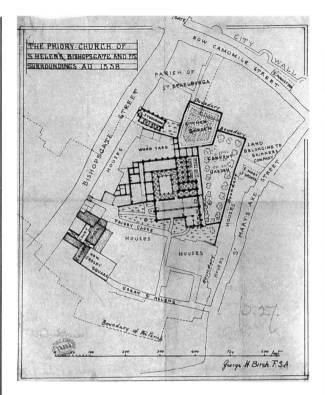

Many of London's monastic precincts and gardens passed straight into private hands at the Dissolution. At St Helen's, Bishopsgate, the church survived as a parish church, but the conventual buildings passed to the Leathersellers' Company

Right: Gardens contained an increasing variety of flowers grown for their beauty alone, including Sweet John, 'a kind of gillofloure ... bearing most fine and pleasant white flowers' (Gerard's Herbal, *1597)*

1538 when the king's gardener and the gardeners of Richard Cromwell took away load after load of bay trees, rosemary grafts and fruit trees; the bailiff in charge of the property counted the holes left in the ground and estimated that in all 91 trees were taken from the orchard. More usually, the establishments were taken over intact: the Earl of Arundel acquired Bath House from the Bishop of Bath and Wells, the Russells obtained the Bishop of Carlisle's house, and the former convent garden of Westminster Abbey, Ely Place, with its famous garden, even-

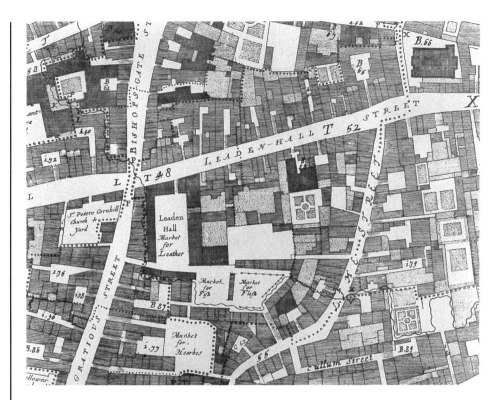

The East India Company's headquarters in Leadenhall Street was formerly a merchant's house. This view, c. 1676, indicates that they maintained the formal garden, presumably for their own pleasure

tually became the home of Sir Christopher Hatton. The Inns of Court, which in some way resembled monasteries in their communal life and economy, remained in uninterrupted possession of their medieval gardens but updated them to conform to new tastes and uses.

Despite the pressure on space, later sixteenth-century London was a natural centre for the art of gardening, since courtiers and nobles competed there in fashionable activities and the display of wealth, and the city's trading links with distant and newly discovered parts of the world facilitated the collection of specimens and rare plants. London was also a focus for scientific and medical enquiry and practice to which gardening made an important contribution. John Gerard, John Parkinson and the Tradescants settled in London to be near sources of patronage, plant supply, and fellow professionals. Gerard lived in Holborn, Parkinson in Long Acre, the Tradescants in Lambeth, all on the outskirts of the capital, where space was not too expensive and they could develop their plant collections, despite the air pollution of which Parkinson was complaining as early as 1629. Professional gardening developed in London at this time: the Gardeners' Company obtained its first charter of incorporation in 1605, and some of the earliest commercial nurseries were established on the fringes of London in the seventeenth century.

An appreciation of gardens and their value was shared by the City 'aristocracy' as well as the gentry and nobility of the West End. The gardens surviving in the City centre belonged to a few important individuals or the City Livery Companies, who chose to keep them as gardens and could afford to forgo the profits of development. This had to be a deliberate choice: the Carpenters' Company in 1568 decided to enlarge their garden by taking in a nearby garden formerly let to a tenant at 15s a year, but the troubled conditions of the mid-seventeenth century caused the Fishmongers' Company to let out their garden in Lime Street, since 'the taxes and charges of keeping the same [were] very great'. Others may have kept gardens in the suburbs, where land was cheaper, while continuing to live in the centre. The garden houses Stow noted in the suburbs outside Bishopsgate and Aldgate belonged to wealthy citizens, and the Goldsmiths' Company had a small garden at their hall near Cheapside and a larger one, with a garden house and bowling-

St Helen's churchyard, off
Bishopsgate, was a green and
pleasant place, planted with
trees and shrubs, in the
sixteenth century, and it
preserved some of this
character into the twentieth

Opposite: *Many of the City
Companies enjoyed the
amenity of a private space: at
Clothworkers' Hall shown on
the right-hand side of this
plan, the parlour overlooked a
secluded formal garden. The
housing block on the left has
been fully reconstructed, as
shown on page 46*

alley, in Red Cross Street outside Cripplegate.

The accounts and descriptions of the City
gardens of the middling and upper classes all
suggest that their main purpose was pleasure
and recreation, though garden planting always
included an element of utility. The Fishmongers
were left their garden in 1501 'to and for the
recreation and disport of themselves'. Gardens
were for looking into, and for walking, eating
and exercising in. Often they were arranged so
that they were overlooked by the parlour or
private sitting-room of the house to which they

were attached; Parkinson called the enjoyment
of sight and scent in this way 'one of the greatest
pleasures a garden can yeeld his master.'

The City gardens we know of were laid out
with walks and beds, sometimes in the form of
knots, with perhaps a fountain or sundial. Many
private and Livery Company gardens contained
bowling-alleys, often more than one. The Carpenters' Company had an arbour, and several
had garden houses or banqueting houses. The
garden of Sir Robert Lee's house in Leadenhall
Street, later to become East India House, had

benches, paved walks with carved posts and rails, and a banqueting house paved with green and yellow tiles.

The plants grown there included medicinal plants, pot-herbs, flowers, and fruit trees. The Drapers' Company's gardener grew flowers and herbs for company dinners, fruit for the Wardens, and planted the side borders for his own profit, though he was not allowed to grow 'teasels, garlick, onyons, and such like things not sightly'. The Carpenters' Company kept detailed accounts of their expenditure on the garden, often listing the seeds and plants bought. In 1568, when they were enlarging their garden, they bought parsley seed, hyssop seed, bugloss, spinach, marigolds, endive, succory, langue-de-boeuf, clary, beets, thyme, lettuce, sorrel, stock-gillyflowers, monkshoods, rosemary, cotton lavender, lavender and camomile. More permanent planting in other years included box and honeysuckle, and there was a walnut tree in the garden. The Drapers bought fruit trees (pears, plums, cherries), filberts and a hundred damask roses when they relaid their garden in 1570.

Seeds and sets were not a great expense, though bought every year; the greatest charge of keeping a garden was labour, including carriage of earth, dung and rubbish. The Drapers retained a gardener permanently; the Carpenters paid their beadle's wife 7s a year for weeding the garden, but brought in outside gardeners, at 2s a day plus drink, for special work. They were particularly anxious that their garden should look good for their ceremonial occasions, and regularly paid gardeners to mow the grass and trim the hedges before their annual Election Day. A number of companies also replanned and restocked their gardens in the later sixteenth century. In 1598–9 the Grocers undertook a major refurbishment of their garden, employing workmen gardeners and labourers to dig and plant, bricklayers to make borders in the garden, and 'Alleymakers' to lay a new bowling-alley. As well as herbs and plants, bay trees and box hedging, they bought in 106 loads of dung, 42 loads of gravel, and 'founders earth and soap ashes' for the alleys.

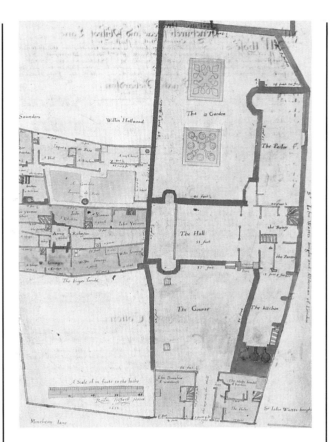

The expenses of the garden that year, not counting the building work, came to £44 2s 5d.

The more modest gardens of lesser citizens and suburban dwellers may have been more utilitarian in character. Even the grand gardens had mundane uses: the Carpenters' Company garden contained a privy or earth closet, and the Drapers' Company had to struggle to prevent the drying of washing in theirs. These were clearly features of smaller gardens, which may also have been used productively, to grow flowers, herbs and fruit for sale. The City's apothecaries in particular cultivated gardens for their supply of medicinal herbs. But it is not clear how widely gardening purely for pleasure spread across the social spectrum, or whether people of modest means could afford to devote space and time to it. It seems likely that drying laundry, keeping poultry and perhaps growing a few herbs and vegetables for the house were the main functions of small private gardens, and that the development of gardens for pleasure for the majority of the community was a feature of a later age.

'Meats to maintain life and medicines to recover health'
MEDICINAL AND KITCHEN GARDENING

John Gerard, writing in 1597 from his house in Holborn in the suburbs of London, encapsulated the philosophy that prevailed from medieval times until well into the seventeenth century: 'The delight [of gardening] is great, but the use is greater, and joined often with necessity... both for meats to maintain life, and for medicines to recover health.'

Gerard emphasized that gardens to most people were a 'necessary provision' to their homes, not as 'ornaments onely'. Although aesthetic considerations in the garden were important, the utilitarian benefits derived from growing herbs, vegetables, fruit and flowers for medicinal and culinary usage were paramount.

This practical approach to gardening had

John Gerard (1545–1612), herbalist, and in 1607 Master of the Barber Surgeon's Company and author of The Herball, or Generall Historie of Plantes, *published in 1597*

Opposite: *'It is impossible to have fine and good gardens, especially kitchen gardens, without being able ... to secure them from their mortal enemy, which is draught,' said de la Quintinie in* The Compleat Gardn'er *(1693), translated by John Evelyn*

long been fostered by the monastic orders; the Renaissance brought it to fruition. Medicinal herbalism as practised by classical scholars and physicians was now reinterpreted by a spate of new writers, stimulated by the introduction of printing. Books on husbandry and gardening, many translated into English from French, Latin and Dutch texts, were characterized by a freshness and pragmatism because they were written by authors who were themselves practising gardeners. New works such as John Gerard's immense *Herball, or Generall Historie of Plantes*, and Thomas Hill's *The Gardener's Labyrinth* none the less invoked classical authority to authenticate their arguments and the efficacy of their herbal remedies. 'It is right necessary (saith Varro) to place Gardens near to the City, as wel for the benefit of Pot-hearbs and roots, as all manner of sweet smelling flowers, that the City greatly needeth,' wrote Hill. A century later John Evelyn, a passionate gardener of independent means, did much to encourage a more scientific interest in the cultivation of herbs,

flowers, fruit and vegetables in the garden with his translation into English of de la Quintinie's monumental work *The Compleat Gard'ner* and of Renutus Rapinus's *Of Gardens*, and in his own prolific writings.

The popularity of gardening and the use to which garden produce might be put is evinced not only by the proliferation of works on the subject, but also by the number of editions which were printed. These books must have found a significant proportion of their market among London's growing population, particularly the increasingly prosperous middle classes. Of course, they would only have been bought and read by a relatively small number of people; most would continue to rely upon oral tradition in growing and using plants. But in spite of all the writing on gardening and husbandry, little hard evidence remains as to the extent to which this advice and information was followed up by the readership and put into practice in smaller London gardens.

The extent and location of many gardens and

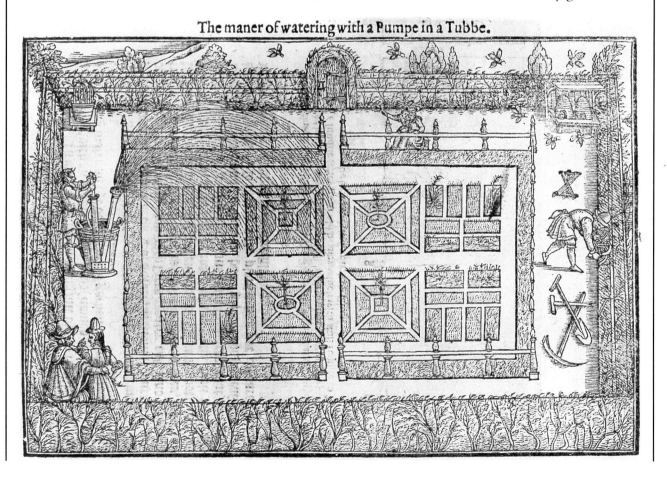

The maner of watering with a Pumpe in a Tubbe.

allotments are shown on contemporary maps, and documentary records – such as those of the Drapers' and other Livery Companies – tell something of who owned and cultivated the plots. According to Sir Hugh Platt, the author with a house and garden in Bethnal Green who in the late sixteenth century was a fund of wisdom on almost any aspect of domestic and

horticultural pursuits, every butcher in the London area possessed a garden in which to bury the 'bloud, offal and entrails of beasts' in order to avoid offence. (If tempered with lime, this mixture was subsequently discovered to be a good fertilizer, especially for vines.) Other aspects of gardening practice must be inferred from a number of different sources. A great deal is known, for example, about the plants cultivated in a number of London gardens – among them those of John Gerard in Fetter Lane and John Parkinson in Long Acre are especially significant.

Necessary provision

One factor that is apparent is that the garden was considered to be a very necessary adjunct both to the kitchen and, for those who possessed them, the still-room.

The kitchen garden, as Parkinson expressed it, was to provide for the 'Master's profit and pleasure, and the meynies content and nourishment...'. One area in a private individual's garden had to serve all purposes: herbs, vegetables and flowers for the pot and for salads; herbs and flowers grown especially for their medicinal and/or aromatic properties.

Plants known to have been commonly

Opposite: *Thomas Dowland of Great Spring Street, Shadwell, combined astrological calculations with botany, to dispense herbal remedies. Plants and herbs are stored in the* materia medica *cabinet with labelled drawers, and in leather bags and pots*

Left: *The earliest painted view of a London garden shows the grounds of Old Corney House, Chiswick, in the 1670s. With its fruit trees and rectangular beds, it conjures up a functional rather than a decorative garden*

grown in London gardens include radishes, peas, parsnips, cress, spinach, tarragon, endive, balm, lettuce, lavender, rosemary, onion, leeks, garlic, mint, nep, sage, sorrel, comfrey, asparagus, coleworts, beets, dock, rocket, bugloss, chicory, clary, chervil, mustard, fennel, marjoram, parsley, basil, angelica, thyme, rue, hyssop, gillyflowers, roses, lilies, marigolds, camomile, columbine and beans. Gerard stated that beans are sown in fields and gardens everywhere about London. 'The blacke beane is found in a few mens gardens who be delighted in varieties and study of herbes. I have great plenty in my garden.'

Not all plants used, fortunately, needed careful husbandry. Many plants grew wild in the fields, lanes and alleys about London, and no doubt these wayside herbs were often gathered to supplement people's diets, or for inclusion in medicinal cures. Rocket, said Gerard, 'grows in most gardens of itself. I found it as ye go from Lambeth bridge to the village of Lambeth...

For intensive cultivation as well as aesthetic appeal, fruit, flowers and vegetables were often grown together and trained up juniper or willow poles, to provide a shaded arbour

Overleaf: Many 'still-room' receipt books contain recipes for fragrant compounds and decoctions. Aromatic water, scented oils and perfumes, were produced through the distillation of flowers, herbs and fruit

over hard by the Thames side . . . a good sallet herb . . . [and] it is also good for the stomach, but causes head-ache if eaten alone.' Then as now, keen gardeners often obtained plants from friends and contacts abroad or from the wild, and these were gradually introduced to other gardens. The Tradescants' introduction of new plant species into their famous garden at Lambeth was especially remarkable, as the explorer Peter Mundy records in 1634 when he saw 'divers outlandish herbes and flowers, whereof some that I had not seene elsewhere but in India, being supplyed by Noblemen, Gentlemen, Sea Commaunders etts'. Such introductions were not always a blessing, as Gerard discovered with French mercury: 'I brought a plant or two into my garden, since which time I cannot rid my garden from it.'

The taste for eating raw, fresh vegetables as a salad developed during the sixteenth and seventeenth centuries so that by 1699 Evelyn could write *Acetaria. A Discourse of Sallets* – a treatise dealing exclusively with salad vegetables. Londoners for most of the year would have had to

rely on dried, preserved and candied garden produce, both to supplement and enrich their diet and for medicinal usage. Cucumbers could be preserved throughout the year by storing them in a barrel with a gallon of 'faire water and a pottle of verjuice' (expressed from crab-apples etc), bay, salt and a handful of green fennel or dill. Roses, gillyflowers and marigolds could be preserved by dipping in a syrup of sugar and rosewater and dried in the sun on paper over a pewter dish. Flowers were commonly incorporated into salads or crystallized for table decoration. Fruit, Sir Hugh Platt argued, could be preserved in vegetable-based 'pitch', and dagberries (a variety of black cherry) having first been dipped should be suspended by their stalks and would last a whole year.

One method advocated for conserving soft fruits, especially strawberries, plums and damsons, was to boil them in white wine and sugar 'til they be stiff'. Strawberries, incidentally, were grown to perfection by Master Vincent Sion who dealt on Bankside near the Old Paris Garden stairs; and who from seven roots, in a year and a half planted half an acre from the increase. Even in the sea-coal-polluted atmosphere of London, plum and fig trees thrived and produced abundant fruit, particularly in the confined alleys near the Barbican and Aldersgate Street. Mr John Miller of Old Street was renowned for his garden plums during the sixteenth century.

Herbs used in cooking were essential not only to add flavour, but also to help disguise the ill-savour of putrefying food. There are recipes for flavouring butter with spices and flowers, and even tobacco could be flavoured by using oil of cinnamon, lavender, cloves and aniseed, thereby perfuming the room and leaving a pleasant taste in the mouth of the smoker.

Domestic uses

Where space allowed, the kitchen garden should, argued Parkinson, be on the far side of the house, away from the best rooms, for 'cabbages and onions are scarce well pleasing to perfume the lodging . . .'. House interiors in the malodorous City needed to be kept fresh from rather more than the smell of onions, and the use of aromatic herbs and flowers was very necessary. Earthenware fuming pots were used to burn aromatic herbs, which helped to perfume the chamber. Thomas Tusser writing in 1573 listed twenty-one herbs commonly grown and used for strewing over the floor, including hyssop, woodruff and meadowsweet. Gerard referred to

> woodruff . . . being made into garllands or bundles and hanged up in the house in the heat of the day, both very well attemper the aire, coole and make fresh the place, to the delight and comfort of such that are therein.

In the early seventeenth century Sir Hugh Platt advised his readers to bring the garden indoors. Sweet marjoram, basil, carnations and rosemary could be planted in pots and suspended from a pulley from the chamber window. Lead or wooden window boxes should be filled with herbs and flowers, and during the summer months the chimney 'may be trimmed with a fine bank of moss and planted with columbine'.

Sweet bags filled with flowers and herbs including rose petals, marjoram and basil were made to lie among linen. Gloves were also scented with violets, orange, lemon and other herbs. 'Dragons' (probably *Arum maculatum*) were grown in every London garden for the starch which they furnished and the roots were useful in making soap. Sir Hugh Platt recommended a method to 'keepe flyes from oile peeces': paintings and hangings could be protected in some measure, he argued, by pricking a cucumber full of barleycorns 'as no man can discerne what strange plant the same should bee' and suspending it in summer months from the ceiling to draw all the flies to it. Decorative tin-glazed earthenware pots were used for potpourris, and would have contained flowers and herbs which were available from the maker's garden.

In the Epistle to his *Delight for Ladies...* (1602), Sir Hugh summarized some of the uses to which garden produce could be put:

> I teach both fruites and flowers
> to preserve . . .
> Th'Artichoke, and th'Apple of
> such strength,
> The Quince, Pomgranate, with
> the Barberie . . .
> Are heere maintained and kept
> most naturally;
> For Ladies closets and their
> stillatories.

The practice of distilling herbs, vegetables and flowers was not uncommon, even on a domestic basis, and the diversity of applications to which the end product might be put was considerable. The still was an extremely useful household item for those fortunate enough to possess one. Jonathan Goddard, a London physician wrote in 1670 that 'worthy ladies and gentlewomen of quality, do employ themselves in making confections, and medicines both internal and external...'. Presumably these

women acquired the majority of their herbs, vegetables and flowers from their own gardens. Among the inventoried items sold to Sir John Trevor in 1588 at Westminster were a 'stilletory to set in brick, four bottles. A flask and a searse [sieve].' In 1653 Samuel Lewis is recorded as having a garden and still house near Bunhill, which he rented out to William Smith for 55s per annum.

Apothecaries needed a garden close by to collect and preserve plant material. Samples were kept in leather bags and wooden boxes suitably labelled for use in the preparation of drugs

Cosmetics

Almost all sixteenth- and seventeenth-century cosmetics were derived from floral or vegetable sources, and there are hundreds of recipes. Artichokes could be used as a deodorant and for a fair complexion; bean blossoms were distilled in an alembic and splashed on the face with water. A rouge could be made from the jaw bones of a hog or sow 'well burnt', ground and mixed with the 'oyle of a white poppy'. Sweet-scented washing water could be produced with the aid of a still, lavender flowers, cloves, orris powder and fresh water. Aromatic and therapeutic saunas could be achieved with a bit of effort and perseverance by using a covered-over bath,

bored with holes to allow the vapours to pass through, lead piping and a large pot filled with sweet herbs 'of such kind as shall bee most appropriate for your infirmatie' with some reasonable quantity of water, the joins to be sealed with a paste of flour and egg white. Provided, Platt enjoined, the bather pokes her head out of the tub, 'you shall sweat most temperately, and continue the same a long time without fainting . . . '.

Pomanders and tussie-mussies (little bouquets of selected herbs and flowers) could be carried to combat offensive smells, and to ward off the plague. In *The City Gardener* (1722) Thomas Fairchild stated that even those without a garden 'content themselves with a nosegay rather than fail'.

Medicinal plants

The use of herbs, flowers and even vegetables for medicinal purposes was extensive, and they were regarded as being of the utmost use in the treatment of all diseases, whether 'chemical or acquired'. Abraham Cowley's poem entitled *The Garden* encapsulated his view:

> Here health it self doth live,
> Thou salt of life which does to
>   all a relish give
> It's standing pleasure and
>   intrinsick wealth
> The Bodies virtue and the Souls
>   good fortune health.

The flowers of lavender were considered to be devoted to the brain, and garden daisy roots were thought beneficial for the hard of hearing. For insomniacs a handful of aniseeds soaked in rosewater and made up into little bags, bound to each nostril, would result in sleep. Children's convulsions could be soothed by placing freshly dug peony roots on the soles of the feet.

John Gerard, Thomas Hill and Nicholas Culpeper among others, listed the virtues and properties of different herbs, vegetables and flowers and remark upon the physical benefits to be derived from their use. Some plants such as garlic were esteemed virtual panaceas. Others such as black thyme were not to be used. Valerian, a popular herb in the garden, was useful for killing mice and warding off the effects of the plague; and water distilled from onions helped to reduce the swellings caused by a rabid dog.

The London apothecaries needed to have gardens close at hand full of plants, so that they could gather and preserve herbs and simples, for immediate or later use. Gerard referred to the gardens belonging to Mr Gray under London Wall and Mr Morgan near Coleman Street. Mr Morgan was a 'curious conserver of rare simples'. Their gardens were notable due to the Nettle Tree or Lotus Arbor that they both possessed, brought originally from Italy. The tree was used medicinally for easing the bloody flux and preventing hair loss. Gerard also commented on an interesting incident where a couple of London gardeners near the 'Bagge and Bottle' were selling at an exorbitant price to misguided and ignorant apothecaries a plant which they claimed was the Holy Wormwood, but which was actually the common Ameos (*Ammi majus*).

It was essential for apothecaries to develop a profound knowledge of plants and herbs, and for this reason botanical excursions or 'simpling days' were arranged on a regular basis for apprentices. One such expedition was organized for 21 June 1627, and it is recorded that apprentices were to gather at 'Grais Inne in Holborne at 5 o'clock in the morning'. By 1673, however, the Worshipful Company of Apothecaries had obtained land at Chelsea, to which many of the plants from the medical garden at Westminster were transferred. John Evelyn, one of many visitors to the Physic Garden at Chelsea, referred in his diary to 'the collection of innumerable rarities' of medicinal plants.

Gardens great and small

Gardens belonging to affluent Londoners, unhampered by the economic necessity to grow plants primarily for their culinary and/or medicinal benefits, could be, above all, aesthetic places for recreation and contemplation. The practical use to which garden produce could be put, although undeniably important, would not have been the prime consideration. Such gardens were a necessary adjunct to the house, a room out of doors, for the entertainment and pleasure of family and friends. Some London gardens were particularly significant, as Evelyn records of Lady Brooke's garden in Hackney, which he says 'was one of the neatest, and most celebrated in England'.

John Evelyn's own garden at Sayes Court in Deptford, then within the County of Kent, was much admired by his contemporaries. A plan of the garden dated 1653 survives with detailed explanatory notes; and includes a private garden for choice flowers and simples. This plan stands alone as an accurate and detailed record of the planting of a large seventeenth-century garden (page 72).

The majority of London gardens were, however, far more modest in scale: private places, where the gardener could retire from the bustle of the City, a secluded spot, a source of infinite pleasure to the gardener, and moreover a profitable place, 'abounding in good things to please the pallate, as well as for the preservation of health'. When space was limited, cultivation on the whole needed to be intensive. Thomas Hill recommended growing briony, cucumber, gourds, rosemary, jasmine, roses and vines up ashen or willow poles, thereby maximizing the produce and providing at the same time a beautiful and shady arbour.

Although Londoners were able to purchase fruit, herbs, vegetables and flowers from London markets, and prepared drugs from apothecaries, private gardens helped to supplement income, and gave incalculable pleasure to the gardener. De la Quintinie encapsulated this view, when he says that many 'take an extreme pleasure in entertaining their friends with herbs and sallets out of their own gardens, stifly maintaining, that they taste much better than those brought to the Markets and of Common Gard'ners.'

It is perhaps this combination of use and pleasure which marks the garden's importance in the life of Londoners during the sixteenth and seventeenth centuries; and the reason for its survival against almost insuperable odds in the urban environment.

FLOWERS AND PLANTS
IN THE SEVENTEENTH CENTURY

Large gardens in London in the seventeenth century were owned by the most important and wealthiest individuals in the country, or were in the hands of institutions and corporate bodies. Most of the poorer people lived in tenements, and maps show that Londoners who had houses or cottages did not on the whole have gardens on any scale. Few surviving documents record any detail of these domestic plots: it is the grander gardens that have been described. Many of the wealthier citizens lived in London all year round, and most of the country gentry visited every year. Their houses would have a permanent staff,

This late seventeenth-century drawing is probably the source for the aloe found on the plan of the Chelsea Physic Garden shown on page 42. It comes from a volume of similar plant material recording the annual gift of plants from the Physic Garden to the Royal Society

Opposite: *Before it became the site of Beaufort House in the seventeenth century, this garden was one of London's most famous. That of Sir Thomas More, 'it was crowned with almost perpetual verdure; it had flowering shrubs, and the branches of fruit trees. . . . appeared like a tapestry woven by Nature itself.' No doubt some of More's layout is preserved here, but under the ownership of the Beauforts (the Duchess was a serious botanist), much gardening activity went on, as lists of plants for 1691 and 1692 testify*

supplemented when the family was in residence; but while there would be some permanent gardeners, extra gardening staff would seldom be taken on at busy times in the gardening calendar. Plants would generally be purchased from London nurseries, rather than being propagated and grown on on a domestic scale.

The prestigious city houses had formal gardens, but on a smaller scale than those of a country estate. The main – often the only – design feature might be a simple parterre. This was a layout of beds geometrically and symmetrically arranged. There were two types: *parterre de broderie* and *parterre anglais*. In the former, within a bed edged with box, was a single kind of low-growing evergreen shrub, such as lavender cotton, rosemary or germander. The box edge and its contents were clipped regularly so as to keep plants low and the lines of the pattern sharp. By selecting plants with different coloured leaves, *parterre de broderie* resembled a

living tapestry when viewed from a distance. In *parterre anglais*, within a clipped box edging was a mixture of many kinds of non-woody plants allowed to grow unchecked. Plants within a *parterre anglais* were grouped according to season or fashion and may have been changed during the year.

A large town house would have courtyards attached, in which there might be statues, and often these areas would be adorned with plants in containers. These may have been there permanently or brought out in summer or when the family was in residence.

Plants

Plants chosen for a garden in the sixteenth and seventeenth centuries were often functional as well as decorative, being used for food, flavouring, medicine or in toiletry. Roses, for example, were important not just for their beautiful flowers, but because their petals could be used for making rosewater or conserves, or as salad

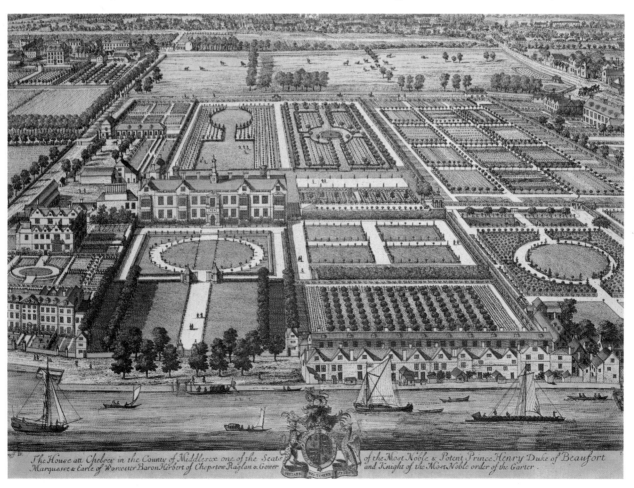

The House att Chelsey in the County of Middlesex one of the Seats of the Most Noble & Potent Prince Henry Duke of Beaufort Marquesse & Earle of Worcester Baron Herbert of Cheprtow Raglan & Gower and Knight of the Most Noble order of the Garter.

ingredients, fresh or pickled, or candied as comfits.

As the seventeenth century progressed, more plants were grown for the sake of their decorative flowers alone, but it was only the wealthy who could afford the extravagance of many of the new species. The majority of gardeners made the most of the subdued beauty of the old favourites, many of which at least had the benefit of scent.

At no time of the year was a garden a mass of colour. The most useful plants had rather dowdy flowers, and those which today are most brilliant had yet to be introduced by plant finders from overseas, or selected and improved by breeders. There were really only two main seasons for gardeners – spring and summer – although the summer blooming would continue into autumn to be supplemented by late-flowering bulbs such as crocus, colchicum, sternbergia and new arrivals such as *Nerine sarniensis* (Guernsey lily) or *Amaryllis belladonna* (naked lady). Very few native plants bloom in winter, and those from other countries – snowdrops, winter aconites, Persian iris and Christmas rose – had arrived too recently to be common. Mezereon, with its sweetly scented flowers, was the most popular winter-flowering shrub, but a newcomer, laurustinus

from the Mediterranean regions, was much coveted.

The climate in the seventeenth century was different from that of today: winters were colder and longer-lasting, and summers were warmer and drier. These favourable summer conditions allowed some plants to perform better than they do today, especially bulbs such as Persian iris, tulips and *Sternbergia lutea*. The keen gardeners of this period seem to have had a particularly adventurous approach, and would try many plants in their gardens which we would not attempt without recourse to glass or heat. Many plants in such experiments died but a surprising number survived. As greenhouses became more common in gardens, these tender plants could be kept alive by giving them winter protection.

Untrained trees allowed to develop naturally were too large for a town garden, although there might be room for the smallest such as Judas tree or laburnum. Some of the larger kinds would be allowed in but these would be regularly clipped to keep them within bounds and to produce a formal shape that could be incorporated into the pattern of the parterre, either permanently planted or in containers. Trimmed in the form of balls, domes, cones, pillars or pyramids might be box, yew, myrtle,

Far left: *This engraving records the appearance of Kensington Palace gardens before they were drastically altered at the beginning of the eighteenth century by Queen Anne, who disliked their Dutch style and the smell of box*

Left: *An extraordinary survival in the churchyard of St Mary's, Bedfont: two yews cut in the shape of peacocks display the date 1704*

Below: *This cast iron gateway is believed to have been designed by Sir Christopher Wren and ornamented his house at Love Lane in the City*

holly, *Rhamnus alaternus* or *Phillyrea angustifolia*. Another form of training was pleaching (interlacing), applied to limes, hornbeam or laburnum to produce screens, alleys or bowers.

Many shrubs would be too large for a town garden. The smallest kinds were used for *parterre de broderie*. Evergreens were looked upon with favour in a country where most of the woody plants are deciduous: those with fragrant foliage – such as lavender, wormwood or hyssop, which would flourish in the prevailing favourable climate – were especially prized. Some of the larger kinds along with trees would be used to make hedges: privet, hornbeam, beech, hawthorn, box, holly, yew, bay, cherry or Portugal laurel. One variation of a hedge was boscage, where the framework of a tree on top of a well developed trunk was clipped.

In an age when transport was slow, those plants which could survive long journeys were particularly useful. Bulbs and corms were therefore desirable; and among the most popular were narcissus, anemone, grape and oriental hyacinths, fritillaries, large bulbous, juno and tuberous iris; and both spring- and autumn-flowering crocuses.

Seeds were then, as now, convenient to carry and probably the easiest way of introducing

new plants into a garden. Annuals which quickly came into flower and provided summer display included common, French and African marigolds, belvedere (*Kockia scoparia*), opium and corn poppies, larkspur and snapdragons. Biennials – among them sweet William, Canterbury bells, foxgloves, honesty and dame's violet – a rather longer-term project, were grown to provide late-spring and early-summer display. Herbaceous plants, which suffer when out of the ground for long periods, would have been divided and transplanted locally from garden to garden just as they are today, but would also have been raised from seed. Because of their often sprawling habit and

century, it was purely for ornament, if it existed at all. Stretches of grass in formal patterns called plattes can be seen at Ham House and Kirby Hall. Grass would not be used in a London garden except as an alternative to other plants in a parterre.

Gardens at this period were intended to impress – by their ingenious and extravagant design, immaculate maintenance or plant content. What, therefore, could be more ostentatious than to grow exotic plants from countries warmer than England? As fruit, oranges had been known in the early sixteenth century, and by the end of that century the first bushes were being grown in Europe. Container-grown

Lavender and santolina edged with box and surrounded by yew hedges in the walled garden at the east end of Ham House. It was known as the Cherry Garden in the seventeenth century, and it has recently been restored to its c. 1671 layout

Opposite: *Orange trees, originating from China, were first grown in Britain in the sixteenth century, but it was not until the following century that orangeries were built on any scale to protect the fruit from the hard British winter. Queen Henrietta Maria had an orangery in Wimbledon which boasted forty-two trees*

untidy appearance after flowering, a particularly careful choice had to be made for admission to the neat pattern of a parterre: soapwort, lily-of-the valley, dusty miller, valerian, Italian starwort and some kinds of geranium were popular candidates in this context.

The lawn – an essential feature of an English garden today – did not become fashionable until the eighteenth century. In earlier times the use of grass had been limited. On country estates it had been used for bowling greens, as swards for archery and as pathways in a wilderness. Whereas today a lawn is used as an amenity and can be walked on, in the seventeenth

plants were placed in the garden in summer and housed before the arrival of cold weather. The orangeries where they were housed might be free-standing buildings, but were sometimes the arcades and loggias characteristic of the architecture of the period, and which might now have been glazed in. These rooms were heated in the coldest weather by charcoal braziers kept stoked day and night. It is surprising that in such ill-lit places with noxious fumes and uneven heat any plants survived. Just to have orange plants was prestigious but there were gardeners sufficiently skilled to produce edible fruit. In the London area there were orangeries at the gardens of the King at St James's, Queen Henrietta Maria at Wimbledon, the Duke of Norfolk at Beddington and Lord Brooke at Hackney. Improved heating was provided by closed stoves within the building. There is a drawing in John Evelyn's *Kalandarium Hortense* of 1676, which shows an external boiler with flues up the back walls.

These buildings now provided protection in winter to tender evergreens, then referred to as greens, and so they became known as greenhouses. Greenhouses now housed a much wider range of plants: citrus of all kinds, cacti, succulents, jasmines, myrtles, canna, banana and Paris daisy. Gardens in London with greenhouses included the Chelsea Physic Garden, the Bishop

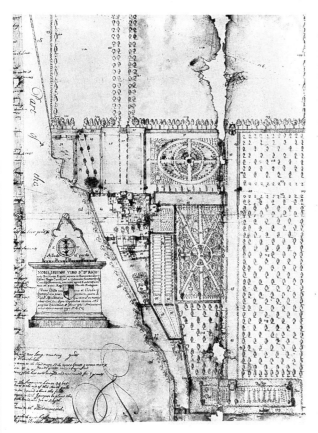

John Evelyn's plan of his own garden at Sayes Court, Deptford, is an exceptionally detailed document which shows the relative position of the decorative and functional elements in a large garden layout

of London's at Fulham Palace, Lord Arlington's at Euston, Sir Thomas Cooke's at Hackney, and Captain Forster's at Lambeth. The largest number of greenhouses was at the Brompton nursery where tender plants from Kensington Palace were housed during the winter. No doubt other wealthy people would hire space at the nursery rather than erect greenhouses of their own.

Nurseries

As most of the wealthy people in England either lived in London or at least visited it regularly it was inevitable that there was the greatest concentration of nurseries around the capital. The largest and most important, already mentioned, was at Brompton Park; it was owned by a series of partners of whom the best known were George London and Henry Wise. Other important nurseries of the seventeenth century were those of George Ricket at Hoxton, Ralph Tuggie at St Margaret's Westminster, Francis Hunt at Putney and James Mouldar of Spitalfields. Most sold a wide range of plants, but there was some specialization: two who grew fruit trees were Leonard Gurle at Whitechapel and John Millen at Old Street. Even more specialized was John Rose, the King's gardener who dealt only in vines. Vegetable and herb seeds were stocked by corn chandlers who might also offer flower seeds. Some nurserymen were also dealing in seeds; the best known was William Lucas at Strand Bridge whose business was to be taken over by Edward Fuller. There was also a Mr Crouch at Bishopsgate, Theophilus Stacy, also at Bishopsgate, and Charles Blackwell at Holborn.

Introducing plants

Nurseries, then as now, depended for their trade on novelty. Where then did they obtain their plants? Nurserymen would have contacts with travellers, merchants, soldiers and sailors who would be commissioned to bring back seeds, bulbs and occasional plants from foreign countries. Some plants would be exchanged or purchased from large country estates where the disposal of surplus plants would be a perk of the gardeners. Most important would be the royal gardens of St James's, Kensington Palace and Hampton Court, which would be recipients of new and rare plants from home and foreign sources as gifts or in exchange from other courts of Europe.

The John Tradescants, father and son, were gardeners to the King, the Earl of Salisbury, the Duke of Buckingham and Sir Edward Wotton. From these gardens and other contacts in this country and overseas, they were able to obtain many new and rare plants. They were to assemble at their garden at Lambeth what was probably the most extensive plant collection in England. In 1610 John Tradescant the elder was sent on a shopping expedition by his master the Earl of Salisbury to bring back fruit trees and other new plants from nurseries in Holland, Flanders and France. In 1618 he was to accompany Sir Dudley Digges to Moscow when he was appointed ambassador to the Imperial court. From this trip John Tradescant was to introduce into England angelica and the Siberian larch. From a visit made to Spain and North Africa in 1621, he brought back *Gladiolus byzantinus* and the African marigold. It was the younger Tradescant who went to North America, making the first of three trips in 1637. He travelled to Virginia and along the eastern seaboard into Canada. His introductions from the New World include the tulip tree, Virginia creeper, bergamot (*Monarda fistulosa*) and a columbine (*Aquilegia canadensis*).

Sir George Wheeler made the grand tour as a young man after coming down from Oxford in 1675. He visited Venice, Greece and Turkey. Having an interest in plants he did some plant collecting and the best known of his introductions is the rose of sharon, *Hypericum calycinum* which in the succeeding two centuries was known as Sir George Wheeler's tutsan.

At Fulham Palace a celebrated garden containing a wealth of plant material was assembled by the Bishop of London, Henry Compton, who had the colonies of North America as part of his see. In 1680 he chose John Banister to be a missionary in Virginia and gave him instructions to send back new plants.

Among Banister's introductions was the first magnolia, *Magnolia virginiana*.

Sir Hans Sloane, a doctor to London society who was to attend Queen Anne, became patron of the Chelsea Physic Garden. His interest in plants began when as a medical student he had to study botany in order to learn about the medicinal uses of herbs. After qualifying he accompanied the Duke of Albemarle to Jamaica in 1687, where he was able to indulge his continuing botanical interests; the introduction to England of *Caesalpinia pulcherrima* is attributed to him.

John Tradescant the Younger published lists

This manuscript plan of the Brompton Park nursery offers a unique glimpse into Britain's first large-scale nursery which covered the site of the present Victoria and Albert Museum during the seventeenth and eighteenth centuries

of plants growing in his garden at Lambeth in 1634 and 1656. Probably these lists were intended as catalogues of plants available for sale. A list of plants in the Botanic Garden at Oxford was produced in 1648 by Jacob Bobart and for the Botanic Garden in Edinburgh by James Sutherland in 1683. At this period the sale of surplus plant material by botanic gardens was an important source of revenue. While both are far from London, they would be important sources of new plant material for nurserymen.

Fashionable plants

The first ornamental plants grown in gardens would be the showier kinds from the countryside: geranium, globeflower, primrose and fritillary. Gardeners were always on the look-out for any which were different: earlier/later bloomers; taller/shorter plants; flowers and foliage that were different in colour or form. Beginning in the sixteenth century but reaching a peak in the following one was a fashion for double flowers. Those from Britain included

Left: *Chelsea Physic Garden has remained a green oasis along the busy Chelsea Embankment. It has been enjoyed by many Londoners since the inception of regular opening hours*

Below: *John Tradescant the Elder was a Londoner, based in Lambeth, who travelled extensively and was responsible for the introduction of many new plants into England.*

Opposite: *Dutch flower paintings found a ready market in seventeenth-century London. The coveted 'Rembrandt' tulips dominate this composition*

the common daisy, various kinds of buttercup, kingcup, celandine, wood anemone, cuckoo flower and primrose. From other countries came wallflower, rose campion, fair maids of France and sweet rocket. Another fashion was for bizarre flowers. Hen-and-chicken was a term applied to any plant whose flowers produced from their centres secondary blooms: these could be found in common daisy, marigold, opium poppy and various buttercups.

Primroses, besides producing double flowers, had other modifications: in hose-in-hose there is one flower within another (Tudor gentlemen wore two pairs of stocking or hose: one came up to the thigh while the other was turned over at the knee); Jack-in-the-greens had a ruff of tiny green leaves behind the flower; pantaloons (also called galligaskins) had inflated calices.

Although there were many flowers grown in

the seventeenth century five reached the height of fashion; three were spring bloomers and two summer. Mention has been made of the importance of bulbous plants in gardens of this period, and pride of place must go to the tulip. It was introduced to Europe from Turkey in 1554 by Ogier Ghislain de Busbecq who was Flemish ambassador at the court of Suleiman the Magnificent. Within a very short space of time tulips had reached most countries of

The Magnolia virginiana *was first grown in Britain at Fulham Palace where it had been sent from Virginia by the missionary John Banister*

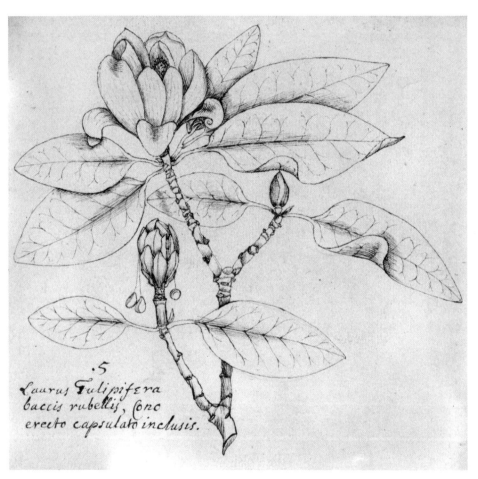

the colour would be overlaid with dots, lines, stripes and flecking of other colours; it was this unpredictable patterning that made these tulips so fascinating and desirable. In Holland between 1634 and 1637, tulipomania swept the country when bulbs exchanged hands for enormous sums of money with the hope that when they flowered there would be fantastic blooms. Fortunes were won and lost and much bankruptcy followed; while other countries in Europe were

Europe, and throughout the seventeenth century, the tulip was the most important spring flower. In England there were already a number of types being grown: earlies, doubles and parrots. Most esteemed though, throughout Europe, were those in which the flowers had broken colours; today these are referred to as Rembrandt. Although the reason was not known in the seventeenth century, it was infection by a virus disease which caused this colour-breaking. Whereas healthy bulbs would produce self-coloured blooms, in infected bulbs

affected, none suffered to the same extent as Holland.

Although three species of anemone were widely grown – *Anemone coronaria, A. hortensis* and *A. pavonina* – it was the many forms with different types and degrees of doubling and the variety and patterning of colours which made them so fashionable.

The auricula was among the earliest of fashionable flowers. Though its attraction has fluctuated, with its flowers embracing many colours of the spectrum, including green, and the dusting of farina on both leaves and flowers, it remains as popular today as it was four hundred years ago. It seems to have arrived in England in 1570 and at least three kinds were being grown in the garden of John Gerard at Holborn in 1596. Throughout the seventeenth century there is no doubt that it was the most fashionable garden plant, and long lists appear in all the garden books which were published in that century. Although it was planted in gardens it was already being cultivated in pots so that protection could be provided to precocious blooms when spring frosts threatened.

The carnation was probably introduced into England by the Normans along with stone which they imported to build their castles. Although its cultivation continued for 500 years it did not become fashionable until a semi-double form arose in the sixteenth century and by the following there were varieties with flowers fully double. More substantial flowers with delicious fragrance and subsequent attractive patterning attracted countless gardeners and, as with the auricula, extensive lists of cultivars appear in books.

There are three species of *Dianthus* native to England which were much grown: Cheddar pink, *D. gratianopolitanus*, Deptford pink, *D. armerius* and maiden pink, *D. plumarius*. At first flowers were single and colours few, but increasingly more doubles appeared and the flower colour range was extended. Although fragrant, their scent never approached that of the carnation, whose larger and more substantial flowers always pushed the pink into second place.

There were other plants widely grown in the seventeenth century but these did not become really fashionable until the following century: polyanthus, narcissus of several kinds, hyacinths, hepatica, Asian ranunculus and hollyhocks.

To escape religious persecution culminating in the Massacre of St Bartholomew in 1572 and the Revocation of the Edict of Nantes in 1685, many Huguenots fled France. They were to settle in many Protestant countries, including Britain, and in London many were to be found in Spitalfields. Among them were professional people from the arts and sciences as well as craftspeople in textiles, glassmaking, printing and precious metals.

Some of the Huguenot immigrants were to have a marked effect on agriculture and horticulture. They introduced the hop and established its cultivation in Kent – until then gentian (*Gentiana lutea*) root had been added to beer as a bitter. The linen industry in Ireland was founded as a result of their introduction of flax. Flax also produces linseed oil, and another oil seed crop which they introduced was rape. Following their arrival the British diet gained many new vegetables and improved varieties – French bean, celery, cauliflower, chicory and globe artichoke among them.

The first flower shows

Many Huguenots with an interest in gardening had brought plants with them, including auricula, carnation, anemone, pink and hepatica. Along with the English gentry, the Huguenots formed florists' societies where interested people could meet to exchange information and plants and to discuss and foster the cultivation of their specialities. (A florist at this time was not a person in trade who made his living by selling cut flowers, but an amateur who specialized in the growing of many different kinds of a single plant.) The first of the florists' societies, that in Norwich, was in existence by 1631 and there was one in London, probably at Spitalfields, by 1676. These societies held floral feasts annually where, after a midday dinner, flowers were exhibited in competition for prizes. Auricula, tulip, anemone and carnation were the first to be shown, but later all the most fashionable of flowers came to be exhibited.

Throughout the eighteenth century floral feasts were held in most towns and cities throughout England, Scotland and Ireland. By 1780, though, they were in decline and by the first decade of the nineteenth century had been mostly abandoned, to be replaced by the flower show we know today, where a much wider range of garden and glasshouse produce is seen in competition.

Feeding the City

The cultivation of vegetables, especially lettuce and other salad plants, had been a highly developed industry in the Low Countries since the fourteenth century. The market gardens outside Amsterdam were well known by the early fifteenth century. This system of food production spread to England, and was particularly encouraged by the arrival of Dutch refugees from 1567 onwards. Ports such as Sandwich, where they first settled, soon benefited, and by the late sixteenth century areas around London were developing market gardens, stimulated by the rapid expansion of London's population. The Fulham parsnip and the Hackney turnip became as famous as the Sandwich carrot.

These relatively intensive growing methods required fertilizer and this was provided by the waste of the city. At the aptly named Dung Quay, huge mountains of dung, both animal and human, awaited the boats to take the refuse of the city to the market gardens. And so the cycle continued.

Opposite: *The cabbage field was a popular means for artists to staple food and had the advantage of being instantly recognizable*

'Oh the incredible profit by digging of Ground!'
LONDON'S MARKET GARDENS IN THE EARLY MODERN PERIOD

The London housewife was affected by the supply and storage requirements of her foodstuffs, their seasonality, the church calendar (especially Lent and fast days) and the manner in which the food was expected to be prepared. She was fortunate in having public markets at Leadenhall, Gracechurch Street, the west end of Cheapside near the church of St Michael-le-querne, and in Newgate Street, where for centuries country people had sold their fruit and vegetables. Gardeners working for important local residents, such as bishops and earls, had sold surplus produce at a regular market near St Paul's since at least the fourteenth century, for in 1343 they were moved to the garden wall of the Blackfriars after complaints from worshippers. 'Foreign' – i.e. non-freemen – fruiterers were restricted to Cheapside between the Standard and the Great Conduit in Gracechurch Street, and by the Greyfriars at Newgate, while freemen and their servants could sell fruit anywhere.

By the sixteenth century trading had been extended to Sundays, such was the demand of London's rapidly expanding population. Made legal in 1588, Sunday trading was permitted before 7 a.m. (8 a.m. in winter), for perishables – milk, herbs, flowers, roots and 'timely fruit' – strawberries, cherries and the like which could be 'cried' in the streets by basketmen. The fifteenth-century poem 'London Lickpenny' gives a vivid impression of the poor wanderer in London tempted by the produce in the capital. A report on the markets in 1588 restricted sellers to three baskets each and the washing of produce in the street was forbidden.

Housewives would then have expected to pay a penny each for large artichokes, a penny per quart green beans, twopence per stone large turnips, twopence per stone yellow carrots (or threepence from January to March) at a period when a labourer's wage was fourpence per day. Market abuses were common, with many vendors in the pillory for sales of underweight goods, or disguising old among fresh produce.

In his *Diary* Henry Machyn recalls sellers being in the pillory for giving short weight: 'The first day of July [1552] there was a man and a woman on the pelere in Chepe-syd; the man sold potts of straberries, the whyche the pott was nott alff fulle, but fyllyed with forne [fern].'

In 1593, a proposal was made 'for restraint of those that let out cellars and sheds under stalls where herbs, roots, fruits, bread, and victuals are noisomely kept till they be stale and unwholesome for man's body, and then, mingled with fresh wares of the same kind, are brought forth into the markets and there sold to the great deceit and hurt of the people'.

John Stow in his famous *Survey of London* in 1598 refers to the many 'garden plottes' in the newly developing areas in the east end outside the City, notably Aldgate and Hackney, and mentions a commercial gardener named Cawsway who held land in Houndsditch until 1553,

By the early eighteenth century, vegetables were coming into daily use. The novel idea of the time was that of growing garden vegetables as field crops

as 'one that served the market with herbs and roots'. Within a few years, Stow reports, Cawsway's land was 'parcelled into gardens wherein are now many fair houses of pleasure built'. Such was the fate of every market garden that lay in the way of London's development. The mid-sixteenth-century Copperplate Map of London shows the many gardens prior to the development to which Stow refers.

Plants for food

What exactly was this produce and what part did it play in the citizen's diet? From medieval plant lists we learn of the range of fruit and vegetables familiar to all levels of society. Some of these were native plants, formerly wild, such as crab-apple, wild cherry, cabbage, leeks and field garlic. Others had a Mediterranean origin and were first introduced by the Romans.

Although the better-off could afford roast meats, for which England was famous, a 'national dish' of all classes until at least the seventeenth century (and much later in remote regions of Britain) was stew or 'pottage', in which the poor cooked root vegetables, cereals and possibly minced meat. (Samuel Pepys's nettle porridge was probably a variant.) 'Pottage', said Andrew Boorde in 1542, 'is not so much used in all Crystendom as it is in England.' Piers Plowman explains (*c.* 1400) how he had to eat vegetables when too poor to buy even white meats:

> I have no salt bacon
> Ne no coleney [egg] by Crist!
> Coloppes [fried egg and bacon]
>   for to maken
> Ac [but] I have percile [parsley]
>   and porettes [leeks]
> And manye cole plauntes...
>   [cabbages].

Radishes, cabbage, parsnips, turnips, carrots,

beet, lettuce and the newly introduced spinach were all known to the sixteenth-century housewife. Contemporary recipes show that the majority of these were regarded as pot-herbs (even lettuce) for cooking in stews and sauces, others, like boiled spinach with sugar and vinegar, were also used in salads. Salads were eaten as an appetizer at the main meal at noon, or at supper, as an accompanying side dish. Flowers, herbs and fruit were included as well as the usual lettuce, radish, onion and cucumber.

Fresh fruit was regarded with suspicion, although it might be safely used in moderation to treat feverish conditions marked by an excess of 'heat' and 'dryness', fruit being considered 'cold' and 'moist' by nature. Fruit was especially to be avoided during the summer months, since popular fancy saw a connection with the diarrhoea and dysentery then common, and the laxative effect of overeating fruit during a glut. In 1618, Busoni, Chaplain to the Venetian Ambassador in London, reported that the English did not put fruit on the table 'but between meals one sees men, women and children, always munching through the streets, like so many goats, and yet more in places of public amusement'. Fruit played a smaller role in the English diet than in the French, but was used as an appetizer at the tables of the better off, or eaten roasted or with sugar, comfits, fennel seed or aniseed at the end of the meal to 'close up' the stomach. Pepys habitually ate cooked fruit in the mid-seventeenth century.

In the sixteenth century Kent was the leading county growing fruit for the London market and William Lambarde extolled the apple, pear, cherry and plum orchards there in his *Perambulation* of 1576. Busoni was more critical and thought our apples were 'really very good and cheap, of various sorts and procurable all the year round. The pears are scarcely eatable and the other fruit most abominable, their taste resembling that of insipid masticated grass. The numerous sorts of cherries and egriots which one sees in Italy may well be desired in this Kingdom, though certainly not enjoyed, for generally in the markets they sell one single sort

In the eighteenth century Chelsea remained a village and supplied Westminster and London markets. The market gardens were obliterated at the beginning of the nineteenth century when the low ground was raised by soil brought from the site of St Katharine's Dock, then under construction

of very bad morella. Yet the English are extremely greedy of them, especially the women, buying them at the beginning of the season in bunches at the cost of an eye.'

It was during the seventeenth century that fruit growing was greatly improved on a commercial scale, so as to produce more variety and larger and sweeter crops. Although our native apples, pears and cherries benefited, strawberries and gooseberries remained small and unim-

proved. While the rich like Sir John Evelyn of Godstone, Surrey, might cultivate exotic fruit such as oranges, peaches, apricots, grapes, melons and figs under glass, such produce did not reach the general market. Although Londoners might appear well supplied, the growing season for native fruit was short and prices were generally high. Around 1600, for example, a London housewife would have expected to pay about eightpence a pound for English cherries, three-pence per quart for gooseberries and imported lemons at sixpence each, when a labourer's wage was sixpence a day.

The sixteenth century marked the beginning of a new interest in gardening and in fruit and vegetables. New and better strains of the standard English vegetables – cabbages, carrots, peas, beans and onions – were introduced in the early and mid-seventeenth century from the Low Countries, where their cultivation was

Buy my wheat
Payres Fyn
Fha rype straberies
Buy a hair lyne
Fyn potatos fyn
Fresh Cheese & Creame
Buy a longe brush
Hats or caps to dres
Any Cornes to pick
Good morrow.
Buy al my smelts
Whyt redish whyt
Buy a case for a hat
Buy any pompeons
Whyt carots whyt
Wood to Cleaue
Buy any persneps
Buy any cocumbers
O yis. Any man or woman that
Can tell any tydings of a little
Mayden Childe of the age of 24.
Yeares. Bring worde to the Cryar
And you shalbe pleased for
your labor:
And Gods blessinge.
Quick periwinckels
Buy any Whyting
Birds and hens.
Whyt scalions.
Fyne pomgranats.
Pins of the maker
Hot Codlings hot.
New thornebacke
Rype Chesnuts.
Buy any bone lays
Hote podding pyes
Rype walnuts.
Hote eele pyes.
Buy any Russes.
Any scuruygras
Buy all my soales
Fyne oate Cakes

The earliest extant London series of Cries *includes 'Buy any Pompions.' The 'pompion' or pumpkin was a new type of cooking gourd introduced from France. The poor baked them stuffed with apples; the well-to-do enjoyed them in elaborate pies*

more advanced. In the Low Countries market gardening had been well established near Amsterdam, Bruges and Ghent since at least the early fifteenth century and Flemish garden produce, especially onions and salad vegetables, regularly exported to south-east England.

As a result of religious persecution under the Spanish, in the mid-sixteenth century some of the Flemish Protestant gardeners settled as refugees in East Anglia and south-east England, setting up gardens in Norwich, Colchester, Yarmouth, Sandwich and Deal. They began market gardening, and in particular the intensive production of root crops. At Norwich *c.* 1575 they were said to 'dyge and delve a grete quantitee of grounde for rootes which is a grete succor and sustenaunce for the poore'.

In 1577 the Rev. William Harrison noted the greater variety of fruit and vegetables then available for the poor, who were eating 'melons, pompions, gourds, cucumbers, radishes, skerrets, parsnips, carrots, cabbages, naevewes, turnips, and all kinds of salad herbes'. While the coarse gourd of medieval times had been stewed in pottage, Harrison's 'pompion' or pumpkin represented the new cooking gourd introduced from France. Poorer people stuffed apples with pumpkin seeds and pith, then baked them. The better-off cooked elaborate pumpkin pies. Cucumbers were being grown more extensively in the sixteenth century, both for summer salad and pickled for winter use. Perhaps the only item which surprises in Harrison's list is the melon, newly introduced from France. Although becoming more common in this country, and cultivated

Traditional pease pottage was
a national dish until the end of
the seventeenth century. From
then on the middle classes ate
green peas avidly in the
summer season

on a limited scale, it is unusual that Harrison saw it as a food of the poor.

The earliest (*c.* 1600) extant version of the 'Cries of London' – an illustration of street sellers with their various commodities – shows that pompions, as well as a curious round cucumber, were being sold in the street markets by the end of the sixteenth century, together with the more usual parsnips and carrots. In the 1580s Thomas Cogan wrote of carrots and parsnips, 'The rootes are used to be eaten of both first sodden, then buttered, but especially Parseneppes, for they are common meate among the common people all the time of Autumne, and chiefly uppon fish daies.' The high sugar content of parsnips also made them a favoured ingredient for cakes.

The turnip was another favoured vegetable. In the 1590s Gerard, famous gardener and barber surgeon, wrote in his *Herball*, 'The small Turnep groweth by Hackney, in a sandy ground, and those that are brought to Cheap-side market from the village are the best that ever I tasted.' Perhaps he had in mind the French turnip from Caen, but grown from seeds here, which others considered the superior type. Smaller and longer than the big round English turnip, they were considered much tastier. (The use of turnips as a winter fodder crop in the field for animals was introduced into England from the Low Countries in the mid-seventeenth century, but was not well established until the following century.)

This greater supply of vegetables appears to have had its effect on the food of some Londoners at least. A schoolboy's diet in the 1570s,

recorded in Hollyband's *The French Schoolmaster*, reflects this change:

> Our breakfast in the morning, is, a little piece of bread not bulted [sieved] but with all the bran in it, and a little butter, or some fruit, according to the season of the year. For diner we have herbs or everyone a mess of porridge. Sometimes turnips, colewarts [cabbage], wheat and barley in porridge, a kind of delicate meat made of fine wheat flour and eggs. Upon fish days, fleeted [skimmed] milk, in deep porringers (whereout the butter is taken) with some bread in it. Some fresh fish in fish Street can be had at a reasonable price. If not salt fish, well watered. After, peas, or fitches, or beans, or lupins.

One institution's frugal menu thus provided a reasonably balanced diet in today's terms. Unfortunately, other London institutions were less enlightened, fruit and vegetables not being generally included in such menus until the eighteenth century.

The benefits of a variety of cheap produce from market gardening were to some extent countered by other concerns, however. It was felt that gardeners were putting profit before hygiene of produce. In 1593 it was feared 'a number of poor people, living by roots, turnips, herbs, and such like are infected by the evil juice of such roots and herbs as are grown upon those corrupt laystals [rubbish heaps] and

Strawberries remained small and unimproved until the eighteenth century when they were crossed with a Chilean type. Finally, in 1806, a plant was produced which bore large, red, well-flavoured berries, comparable with those we know today

grounds which many gardeners and others of late have practised to sow, before they have lain a convenient time to rot and be fit for manuring'.

Such cases were probably rapidly forgotten during the terrible dearth years 1595 to 1597. With the shortage of grain as a result of poor harvests, and hence of bread, root crops inevitably played a larger part than before in feeding London's poor. To supplement local produce, root crops, mainly carrots, were shipped from the East Anglian ports of Norwich, Yarmouth and Colchester. As Appleby records, between October and March 1593–4, 281 tons and 600 bushels were shipped from Yarmouth to London, in 1597–8, 812 tons and 60 bushels were sent and in 1598–9, 639 tons and 1 last were shipped. These were small quantities in comparison with the 111,075 quarters of grain received in the Port of London in the seven months ended 26 May 1597, yet obviously a welcome addition to London's food supplies.

It would appear from the comments of contemporaries, such as Richard Gardiner of Shrewsbury, that suppliers were not guided by philanthropic concerns even in these times of hardship. Gardiner's pamphlet (1599) 'Profitable Instructions for the Manuring Sowing and Planting of Kitchin Gardens. Very profitable for the Commonwealth and greatly for the help and comfort of poor people' was the first such work on vegetables to be written. Gardiner exhorted his countrymen to grow carrots and cabbages in that time of dearth. He gives the fair price for good seed, which predates prices in any seedsman's catalogue (as quoted above) and is shocked by the 'great summes of money' spent on importing carrots into the City.

Gardiner considered carrots the most important vegetable for relief of hunger and gave a number of recipes for them. 'Carrots in necessitie and dearth, are eaten of the poore people after they be well boyled, instead of bread and meate. Many people will eat carrots raw, and doe digest well in hungry stomachs. They give good nourishment to all people, and not hurtful to any, whatsoever infirmities they be diseased of, as by experience doth prove by many to be true.' To be able to eat food raw, with minimum preparation, was obviously a great advantage in times of extremity, especially to townsfolk who might have no hearth for cooking.

The first pamphlet to be produced as a result of the dearth was one in 1596 entitled 'Sundrie new or typical remedies against famine, written by H.P. upon the occasion of this present dearth'. The author, Sir Hugh Platt, son of a wealthy brewer, was educated at Cambridge and Lincoln's Inn and chose to live in and near London. Platt includes several recipes for famine meals, including one for parsnip cakes, 'Sweete and delicate cakes made without spice or sugar'. Unfortunately some people ate so many vegetables that they developed hunger-oedema, a condition characterized by water-logged tissues and swollen limbs; as Parkinson recorded, the 'moist and loose flesh' which a London apothecary noted as a result of turnip eating in 1629.

Both Platt and Gardiner thus recognized the potential part roots and other garden vegetables could play in feeding the poor, and in doing so they reflected increased consumption of these foods in London and elsewhere in England in the late sixteenth century. But other shrewd observers, such as the Flemish immigrant gardeners, were also impressed.

Market gardening

In about 1600 many Dutch and Flemish gardeners moved to the Surrey bank of the Thames, particularly in Battersea, Wandsworth and Bermondsey. Some fifty years later old men in Surrey could still recall 'the first gardeners that came into those parts, to plant Cabages, Colleflowers, and to sowe Turneps, Carrets, and Parsnips, to sowe Raith [or early ripe] Peas', as Sir Richard Weston records.

This marked the beginning of intensive market gardening in the London area. The immigrants were even said to have introduced the practice of thoroughly digging the ground before planting: William Lawson, writing in 1617, reported that gentlemen who had leased their land to refugees feared 'they would spoil the ground because they did use to dig it'. 'So ignorant were they of gardening in those days,' he added scornfully. Presumably, the landowner felt the new intensive cultivation methods could ruin the land.

In suburban Middlesex, too, local husbandmen and gardeners were finding that market gardening proved lucrative, such was the demand of London's growing population (now numbering some 200,000). In 1605 the Gardeners' Company of London was incorporated to fend off this competition (although records of gardening in London are known from at least 1345). The Charter stated that its members had to live within six miles of the City of London, and to follow the trade, craft or mystery of gardening, planting, grafting, setting, sowing, cutting, arboring, rockery, mounting, covering, fencing and removing of plants, herbs, seeds, 'fruit trees, stock sett and of contriving the conveyances to the same belonging'.

The trades of gardener and fruiter were thus carried out by the same company, although the Fruiterers, also of early origin (possibly 1292), had their own charter as early as 1463. By 1616 the Gardeners' Company claimed to be employing 'thousands of poor people, old men, women and children in selling of their commodities, in weeding, gathering of stone' etc.

London was growing at such a fast rate in the late sixteenth and early seventeenth centuries that it needed all the food it could get. John Norden in 1607 mentioned Fulham in a list of carrot-growing areas, and by 1616 the husbandmen and gardeners there were in legal dispute with the Gardeners' Company, since their large-scale root production threatened the trade of the Company, being so extensive in terms of garden size and numbers of employees. The Company was sarcastic about the apparently untrained 'husbandmen' also of the neighbouring Kensington and Chelsea, producing their turnips, carrots and other vegetables in their common fields, although appearing to tolerate the sale of produce by 'foreyners' in the City.

The dispute with the private gardeners continued until 1633, when it was found that the Middlesex producers 'by this manner of hus-

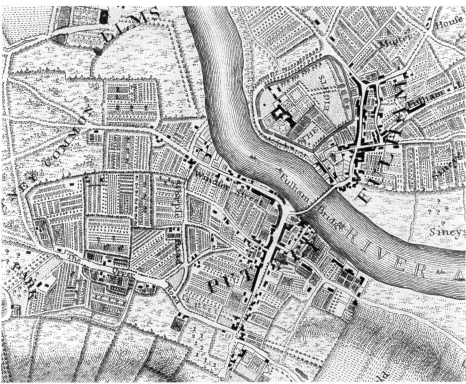

Above: *Gardeners in the fields at Millbank, with Westminster Abbey in the background. The Thames-side market gardens supplied London with asparagus, artichokes, beans, berries, carrots, melons and other produce*

The eighteenth-century maps of John Rocque introduced an extraordinary level of sophistication into the use of land symbols. For areas of open space, he distinguished between marsh, market garden, orchard, ploughland, park and common. It therefore becomes easy to identify London's market gardens, and Putney is but one example in West London

bandry and employment of their grounds [furnish] the city of London, Westminster and places adjacent with above four and twenty thousand loads yearly of Rootes'. And so the Gardeners' Company lost their bid to control the independent horticultural enterprises.

When Busoni, Chaplain to the Venetian Ambassador, visited the market gardens in 1618, he reported that they produced very large cabbages (some up to 28lb according to his ambassador), potatoes, cauliflowers, grapes, and carrots, as well as artichokes, 'large' with a red 'tinge', grown on hot beds during ten months of the year, and rootstocks for fruit trees and roses. Interesting points to note from this list are the inclusion of cauliflowers (a recent arrival from Holland, and also included by Gerard in his *Herball* of 1597) and potatoes (presumably the sweet potato, since the 'Virginian' potato remained a novelty for most of the seventeenth century). Hot beds were used to extend the season, and were especially practical for early plantings of salad vegetables and other seedlings. Hot beds consisted of piles of fresh manure over which a covering of several inches of soil was spread. Heat produced by the fermenting manure warmed the soil, and encouraged plant growth. (This use of hot beds, together with that of large glass bell jars or 'cloches' for forcing, was the most significant feature of English vegetable gardening until the nineteenth century and contemporaries noted how foreign gardeners had thus influenced gardening techniques.)

The intensive market gardening introduced by the Flemings demanded such treatment, and yields and profits were high. Despite the high rents, it was said an able man could keep a family and even employ extra labour on a holding of only three acres.

England was very gravelly, Busoni reported, often to more than seven feet below the surface. London market gardeners dug out the gravel, however, sold it for ships' ballast, for mortar, or street repairs, and filled in the holes with the 'filth of the city', which excellent manure Busoni said, was 'as rich and black as thick ink'. Some of this would already have served on the

hot beds and had come by cart, or was later shipped as part of a regular trade from the aptly named Dung Wharf (established in 1665) near Puddle Dock in the City, the boats taking back produce by return. (Access to the river, as well as the natural advantage of the level ground along its banks, and the high water table, explains why so many market gardens were sited near the Thames.) Once manured, the land was then enclosed with palings, deep ditches or walls made of soft mud mixed with rotten straw and thatched on top, a traditional type of cheap walling now seldom seen.

Which market gardeners did Busoni visit?

From the gardens to the market: a less efficient means of transport than boat which probably indicates local transport for small-scale produce

The Gardeners' Company records show that John Markham (a warden) was a market gardener in Clerkenwell about 1605, and his sons, Moses and Tobias, carried on the business. Thomas Oaker was at Shoreditch, and eleven others in Stepney, Fulham and St Martin's-in-the-Field, Westminster. The Cherry Garden, Bloomsbury, belonging to the Earl of Southampton, was a landmark, as was the Liquorice Garden near by on the north of High Holborn, while Short's Gardens, St Giles-in-the-Fields – rented by one Short for market gardening – is still recorded by its street name. By the seventeenth century English gardeners had learnt the best skills of the immigrants and were well established, a pattern typical in other crafts and trades at this period.

On the south bank, near Tower Bridge, the Gardeners' Company had a large area of land, which it divided up among members, with a maximum of ten acres each, while other members worked in Bermondsey and Battersea. Such south London gardeners might have paid as much as £6 an acre for their land, yet managed to live comfortably, reports Fuller in his *Worthies of England*, published in 1662. 'Oh the incredible profit by digging of ground!' he exclaimed, adding that, although the spade was

Native, new and imported produce at the close of the seventeenth century. Native cherry growing was then greatly improved to produce larger and sweeter crops, although imported fruit such as China or sweet oranges, were increasingly common, and lemon was the principal garnishing fruit. Asparagus, familiarly known as 'sparrowgrass', was a fairly recent introduction and was enjoyed boiled and buttered. Pickled vegetables like cucumbers were in constant use

Opposite: *With a rise in wages, the diet of townspeople tended to improve after 1860. Among new fruit introduced at this time was the tomato or 'love apple', on sale in most markets*

slower than the plough, it gave much better results. By that date an estimated 10,000 acres of market gardens surrounded London.

Battersea was a prime area for market gardening, especially to the east around Nine Elms (served by its own wharf), and in Battersea Fields. Dog carts, much used in the fields, were thought to have been introduced by Flemish gardeners. Battersea was especially famous for its asparagus, and for 'Battersea Bundles' or sparrowgrass/speregas as it was familiarly known to all Londoners. Pepys particularly enjoyed a dish of buttered asparagus, and it is one of the few vegetables he mentions in his *Diary*.

Massinger, in his play *City Madam* (1632), refers to 'the neat houses for musk-melon, and the gardens where we traffic for asparagus!' The Neat Houses in Chelsea, so called from their former use as cow houses, lay across the river from Battersea, and had developed into a market and pleasure garden by the seventeenth century. Samuel Pepys visited them several times in 1666, where he 'sat in a box in a tree and sang' on one occasion, although he professed disappointment with the catering on another visit! The market gardens, clearly described by John Strype in his edition of Stow's *Survey* (1720), existed until the beginning of the nineteenth century, when they were obliterated by soil extracted from the site of the new St Katherine's Dock. Little is known of the Neat House gardeners, although one Jewell is recorded as being the first man in England to send 'young salad herbs' for winter marketing, and force kidney beans on hot beds.

Although these low-lying areas near the Thames may have had natural advantages as market gardens, land to the north and east of the City had traditionally produced London's food, as Stow reminds us in his *Survey*. Hoxton, north-east of the City, was noted for its market gardeners and nurserymen. In 1633 a market gardener, John Noble, left money for two ser-

mons against gambling to be preached annually in Hoxton. Produce from the Hoxton market gardens, and those at Blackheath and Greenwich, would have been sold at the new market in Spitalfields, established in 1681 to serve the growing East End population.

To the west of London the developing residential area of Covent Garden (originally Convent Garden, supplying Westminster Abbey), laid out by Inigo Jones in the 1630s, needed new market areas for the rich inhabitants of the new houses. Market gardeners gathered on the south side of the Piazza along the Earl of Bedford's garden wall in increasing numbers, and in 1670 the Earl, owner of the development, obtained a charter to hold a market within the Piazza. Inevitably the thriving market caused complaints from inhabitants of the highly rented new houses. But there was no stopping London's premier fruit and vegetable market once established. Rival markets at Hungerford set up in 1678, and proposals for Dowgate in the City in the mid-eighteenth century, never succeeded in

taking much trade away from Covent Garden. Indeed Covent Garden was rapidly replacing Stocks Market in the City as the chief fruit and vegetable market. Within the City of London the Great Fire of 1666 stopped just short of the market at Leadenhall, and Aldersgate Street herb market was able to continue, although the Gracechurch Street and Newgate markets were destroyed. Rebuilt after the Fire, there would appear to have been enough business left to occasion a petition to the Lord Mayor in 1720 complaining that the space once occupied by

M. Grosley, stated. English vegetables were expensive and of indifferent quality:

> All that grow in the country about London, cabbage, radishes, and spinnage, being impregnated with the smoke of sea-coal, which fills the atmosphere of the town, have a very disagreeable taste ... I ate nothing good of this sort in London, but some asparagus.

butchers at Newgate was by then taken by 'gardeners, fruiterers, carts and pannayers all the morning at the market days so that there is hardly room to stir'.

Billingsgate remained the chief river port for landing vegetables for the City markets, and also handled large quantities of Kentish cherries. Regular sailings left Queenhithe with manure for Maidenhead, Windsor, Chertsey and Kingston. Coming home the boats brought fruit and vegetables for the London markets. The hygienic conditions of such transport might well have been questioned, but serious observers such as Evelyn in his *Fumifugium* (1661) concentrated more on the evils of coal dust from chimneys, a condition which did not improve in the eighteenth century as a French observer,

With so much horticultural activity it is perhaps surprising to learn that schemes were considered necessary to have cheap food available for the needy poor. In 1664 Fellows of the newly founded Royal Society encouraged a scheme to cultivate potatoes, by that date grown only in a few kitchen gardens. Corn harvests had been disappointing for some twenty years (hardly surprising, perhaps, given the state of civil unrest of the period), and it seemed appropriate to make the potato as popular among the poor as it was in Ireland. The traditional belief that potatoes were 'windy' and indigestible was not yet overcome, and potatoes were not fully exploited until the eighteenth century. For a labourer earning one shilling per day in the mid-seventeenth century, asparagus cost six-

Far left and left: *A produce market had been officially established in Covent Garden in 1670, the owner Earls of Bedford putting the empty space of Inigo Jones's piazza to profitable use*

pence per bundle, but globe artichokes nine-pence-halfpenny each, with basic vegetables like cabbage and carrots costing much less. Although gooseberries might be as little as two-pence per quart, cherries were prohibitively expensive at 8lb for five shillings and fourpence. This high price for fruit must have put it beyond the purse of the ordinary inhabitant. By the early eighteenth century common vege-tables were very cheap: potatoes at fourpence to sixpence a peck, a cabbage for a halfpenny. 'Legumes' were particularly cheap in Soho, home of numerous Huguenot immigrants. According to Tucker, writing his *Tracts on Political and Commercial Subjects* in 1748: 'But the price of Garden Stuff is prodigiously sunk to what it was in former Times.' He doubted whether 'any Town of note ... can now vie

The first coster cry heard in the morning in the London streets was that of 'Fresh Wo-orter creases!' In earlier times thought of as a cure for toothache, watercress was widely cultivated as a salad in late Georgian times

Opposite: 'Covent Garden, the Heart of the Town' (Steele). While all the vegetables in the picture would have come from the local market gardens, there was a tendency during the eighteenth century for Covent Garden and other London markets to receive increasingly large supplies of fruit from foreign sources

with the Common Markets of London in That Respect'. It was certainly deplored by Sir Richard Weston in 1742 that the name of gardening and hoeing was scarcely known in the north and west of England at that date 'in which places a few gardeners might have saved the lives of many poor peoples, who starved these dier years'.

The changing diet

Although there may be ample evidence that market gardening developed rapidly during the seventeenth and eighteenth centuries, what proof is there of its having any effect on the diet of the average citizen of London during that period?

Unfortunately, it is not easy to obtain a clear picture of the popularity of fruit and vegetables by the mid-seventeenth century. Pepys certainly mentions the topical asparagus, which he enjoyed buttered, but otherwise it appears that vegetables were still used in their traditional way, as ingredients of soups rather than as an accompaniment to meat. At least this made such 'windy' food digestible. This, of course, may well have been due to the attitude, prevalent even among the servant class, that vegetables were mainly the standby of the poor.

In exile in France in the mid-seventeenth century, Sir Ralph Verney revealed the contempt of the English maidservants in his household for the 'potages' and 'legumes' which were the ordinary fare of the working people in France. His 'Luce' and 'Besse' demanded meat. 'I know noe English maids will ever bee content ... to fare as the (French) Servants faire ... Noe English maide will bee content with our diet and way of liveing ... I rost but one night in a weeke for Suppers, which were strainge in an English maide's oppinion.'

By the end of the seventeenth century, however, vegetables were beginning to be used as an accompaniment to meat. A French visitor, M. Misson, describes the English tradition at the close of the century: 'Another time they will have a Piece of Boil'd Beef, and then they salt it some Days before-hand, and besiege it with five or six Heapes of Cabbage, Carrots,

Turnips or some other Herbs or Roots, well pepper'd and salted and swimming in Butter.'

When Ned Ward in *The London Spy* (1703) speaks of a 'calves head with cabbage' or a 'large neat's tongue with greens' and 'Fetch your mistress and I three hap'worth of boil'd beef, see first they make good weight and then stand hard for a bit of carrot', or when Thames watermen could scoff at a boatload of Lambeth gardeners with being 'You ... who can't afford Butter to your Cabbage, or Bacon to your Sprouts', it was indeed a sign of changing habits.

At a time when serious questions are being asked about the entire food chain in Britain, we might do well to consider the advice of the earnest reformer Jonas Hanway in 1767, that 'The food of the poor is good bread, cheese, peas and turnips in winter, with a little pork or other meat when they can afford it.' Sage

Still life – an acescent diet! By the eighteenth century contemporaries were beginning to classify food as either acid (acescent) or alkaline (alkalescent). All fruit and most vegetables were considered as 'acid'. Health depended on a balance of acidity and alkalinity

words, and with the possible exception of the reference to pork, a diet to be recommended for today's rich as well as the remaining poor.

Perhaps the improved crops were less 'windy' by this date. Traditionally vegetables were also eaten well seasoned with oil in salads. Evelyn in his volume *Acetaria* (1699) favoured a dressing of three parts of olive oil, one of vinegar (or lemon or orange juice), dry mustard and the mashed yolks of hard-boiled eggs. The range of salad vegetables was still very wide, and while it was important to promote their use in this 'natural' way, his work was intended to convey a far more important concept, one which helped change the population's attitude to eating fruit and vegetables during the eighteenth century.

The notion had taken root that the health of the body was governed by a balance between acidity and alkalinity. Foods came to be clas-

sified according to whether their influence was acid (acescent) or alkaline (alkalescent). Fruit and most vegetables were placed in the 'acid' class of food. Meat was placed in the 'alkaline' class, so it was very acceptable that its excessive 'alkalescence' was cured with a proper portion of 'acescent' vegetables. Similarly, the old theory that fruit caused fevers was gradually discarded, and fruit came to be regarded as beneficial and even necessary for health. Diets from then on were ideally a balance between the two different types.

This new attitude to fruit and vegetables, with the ever increasing supply from the broad belt of market gardens around London, the improved output of Kentish orchards, and the lowering of prices (at least during the first half of the eighteenth century), resulted in fruit and vegetables being used daily by every stratum of society.

All in full bloom

The Georgian Period

People of leisure met in parks and entertained in gardens.
Elaborate pavilions, seats, retreats and summer-houses
were dotted around the larger gardens, while flowers and plants
not only came into the house but also invaded all forms of interior
design, as well as Londoners' own costume and accessories.
In the words of Flanders and Swann, 'The house is full of plants
and the garden full of furniture.' From the gardens of the great,
duly recorded by the mapmaker John Rocque, to the
burgeoning back gardens of the middle classes, the eighteenth
century is remarkable for the sheer quantity of
new gardens in the capital.

Opposite: *The London street seller Anatony Antonini carries*
his showboard of artificial flowers constructed of silk and paper
with wires for their stalks

'A grand design of an ichnographical survey'
A TOUR OF LONDON'S GARDENS WITH JOHN ROCQUE

When the great cartographer, John Rocque, made his survey *Twenty Miles Round London* between 1741 and 1745 (first published in 1746) he could hardly have chosen a better moment. The landscape revolution of Lancelot 'Capability' Brown was still a decade away, and only William Kent had begun to soften the geometric divisions. In consequence, Rocque has preserved an astonishingly rich record of formal gardens, ranging from Tudor to the Kentian semi-formal style, that had not yet been remodelled. In particular his achievement is a monument to the formal gardens of the Williamite and early Hanoverian reigns, roughly between *c.* 1680 and *c.* 1740, during which period the genius of our garden designers in London was pre-eminent. However, Rocque surveyed half a dozen gardens in a new style that has recently been described as Gardenesque. In them England made a great advance in the treatment of walled gardens of small scale. They display a combination of perspective effects, ornamental features in sculpture, serpentine walks and an attention to the display of flowers. Pope's garden at Twickenham (by 1730), Kent's Carlton Garden (*c.* 1735), and Westcombe, Blackheath (*c.* 1729) were *loci classici*. Rocque shows notable ones at Acton, Whitton and Hackney.

Greater London incorporates not only the City of London and Westminster, but beyond the old borough boundaries, what were once the suburbs of London (such as Acton, in Middlesex), and even farther afield, the Home Counties. As a political entity it has nothing to do with gardens. Nevertheless, Rocque's survey, covering 19 miles from west to east and 13 miles from north to south, provides a frame-

At Chiswick House the Orange Tree Garden and adjacent canals and bason belong to the second phase of garden design, executed about 1722 following Lord Burlington's marriage. All these parts are by Burlington unassisted by Kent, and are interesting for the garden archaeologist

work by which to judge the gardens of Greater London. As a land surveyor who described himself as '*dessinateur de jardins*' Rocque pays minute attention to their configuration. In order to appreciate the force of the landscape revolution that created the Brownian garden, and obliterated nearly every formal garden in London, Rocque's survey can revealingly be compared with J. Cary's *Survey of the Country Fifteen Miles Around London* (1786). His green parks show up well and provide a conspectual assessment of change as well as demonstrating how estates tended to congregate in favoured localities: in the south-west around Wimbledon Common, Richmond and the Thames, extending up to Twickenham; in the south-east taking advantage of the broken forests and woodlands of Sydenham and Chislehurst; in the east around the lush meadows of the Lea Valley; in the north-east and in an arc to the north-west around the Waltham and Epping Forests to the

Enfield Chase; and at the western extent of Middlesex, along the banks of the rivers Frays and Colne.

This history of the change in garden design between 1745 and 1786 becomes a matter of garden archaeology when the gardens of Rocque and Cary are located in the built environment mapped by the Ordnance Survey for the *Geographia Greater London Street Atlas* published by Geographia Ltd with the Automobile Association (amended with revisions up to September 1987) on a scale of 3.17 inches to the mile – referred to for short as 'Geographia'.

By this comparison history from paper documents can be translated into the excitement of physical exploration – the archaeological 'dig', so to write. Reconstruction begins by laying an earlier road system upon a later one, or by tracing the line of rivers or streams, or by relating a Rocque or Cary park with a surviving area of green, whether recreation ground, school play-

ing field or football field. A fragment of a water garden can be identified with a pool isolated in concrete, or time and again cemeteries and hospitals conform to the old garden-park. The perimeter of the old manor house of Belsize with its late seventeenth-century formal wilderness, seems to fit in to the surrounding streets today; or the estate of Stamp Brooksbank at Hackney, with its house and garden designed by Colen Campbell and Stephen Switzer, fits the area covered by Homerton Hospital. Abandoned country houses frequently became poor

south to Waltham Cross (Hertfordshire) in the north, was an unmitigated disaster, now aided and abetted by the historically ignorant decision taken by the editor of the *Buildings of England London* to conform with the unwieldy volumes that are no longer a traveller's tool. For sensible historians Cranford Park will always be in Middlesex, as will Hanworth, Dawley and Osterley. Of course, all essential topographical studies of Greater London conform to the old Home County boundaries. There is *The Ambulator* in a useful 11th edition of 1806, James

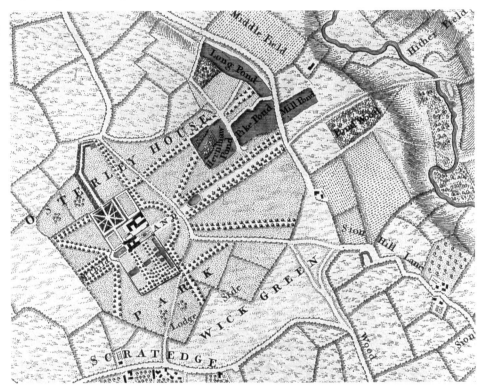

Rocque's Osterley is the Elizabethan house surrounded by late seventeenth-century formal gardens attributed to the ownership of Nicholas Barbon. The tree planting is unusual in that it conforms to the trio of avenues and patte-d'oie of Hampton Court as perfected in the 1680s

houses, and then hospitals, just as Lord Shaftesbury's famous house and garden on the Fulham Road turned into the late-lamented St Stephen's Hospital. What is so striking about this garden archaeology is how rarely our borough administrators bother to commemorate a house, garden or family by naming streets that now cover the site. It is quite different in an enlightened Europe.

For historians the local government reorganization in 1965 that made the vast conurbation of Greater London, extending from Uxbridge (Middlesex) in the west to Upminster (Essex) in the east, and from Coulsdon (Surrey) in the

Thorne's *Handbook to the Environs of London*, 1876, reprinted; and naturally all the county histories. Only *London 2: South* of *The Buildings of England* (1983) has appeared so far, and unfortunately garden archaeology, even when there is ample evidence on the ground, is not taken into account.

It is significant that by 1745 the gardens of the City of London and Westminster were by and large those that have survived today. Many of the gardens of the great mansions had already been built over, and the later gardens that are such a striking feature today are those of the urban squares. What is also obvious, for reasons that are self-evident, is the survival of the royal parks and gardens. That of Buckingham House by Henry Wise became Buckingham Palace by Brown, Nesfield and others; St James's Park with André Mollet's long canal was turned into a Picturesque park by John Nash; and so it is with Kensington Palace Gardens, Hyde Park and Green Park. The most notable loss by 1745 was the great Privy Garden of St James's Palace, built over as Carlton Garden developed into Carlton House Terrace. As far as Greater London is concerned, Bushey

park of Hillingdon Court, that the house is still there, and the park one that may well have been remodelled by Capability Brown? It can still be enjoyed, which is more than can be said of Dawley, near London Airport, where a fragment of a brick wall and Pinkwell Playing Fields is the only memorial to one of the most magnificent formal gardens in the Home Counties next to Canons and Wanstead. They were laid out first by George London followed by Charles Bridgeman, and Pinkwell Park seems to be on the site of Bridgeman's huge

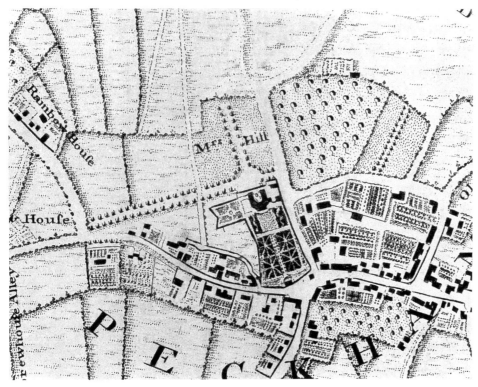

Framed by Hill Street, Peckham High Street and Commercial Way was the grand garden of Sir Thomas Bond in a sophisticated George London style. Indeed, William Talman, London's architectural partner, is known to have designed for the Bond family, so this garden may well date from the 1680s and 1690s. Nearby is the ancient moated site of Hatcham House, Tudor in date

Park, Hampton Court, Richmond and Kew and Greenwich must be taken into account, and Rocque provides invaluable evidence of their configuration by 1745.

Hand in hand with Rocque and Geographia: Uxbridge to Kensington

More than Rocque, the green parks of Cary are the beacons of this trip of discovery. The western fringes of Greater London are beyond Rocque, so initially Cary and Geographia must come to our aid. Who would guess from Geographia that RAF Uxbridge occupies the

Wilderness. Amazingly, Stanwell Place, or at least the long canal and outline of the Bridgeman–James Gibbs garden, is to be discovered under the flight paths; and east of the airport is Hanworth Park, identifiable with the vast Tudor hunting park shown by Rocque and Cary.

Not far away is Cranford House, whose stables are such a prominent feature pressed up against the M4. Despite its bisection by Parkway Cranford, the park is as Cary shows it, watered by the river Crane and naturalized by Thomas Wright for the Berkeleys in the 1750s. His crescent-shaped pond is also gone.

Also against the M4 is Tudor Osterley,

Hampton Court: looking to the Broad Walk from the Privy Garden which boasts the famous Tijou screen on the side overlooking the Thames

Opposite: *Syon House and Kew from the air: this demonstrates the contiguity of Richmond Gardens (George I and II) and Kew Gardens (Frederick, Prince of Wales) separated by Love lane, a public way. Only in the 1770s were the two under one royal ownership, and only after the creation of the Kew Botanic Garden were they physically combined. Today the famous Pagoda remains a focal point, and the golf course covers most of the old royal domain, upon which Chambers built his Observatory in 1768*

shown before rebuilding in the 1750s framed by a system of avenues based upon the *patte-d'oie* at Hampton Court. These may be seventeenth century in date, as is the fragmented T-shaped long canal. The main avenue points to Boston Manor House, on Rocque surrounded with orchards, and today with many of the yews and cedars for which it was celebrated. Neither Rocque nor Geographia prepare us for Cary's surprise of the green park of Sion Hill House. By 1758 Capability Brown had made for Lord Holdernesse one of his best small gardens. It extended from the present London Road, across the Great West Road, and into Wyke Green Golf Course. In 1786 the southern half belonged to the Duke of Marlborough, and the northern half to a Mr Robinson.

Had we exited from the gates of Sion Hill, opposite would have been, as today, Robert Adam's north entrance to Sion (or Syon)

House, like Osterley a Tudor house surrounded by enclosed formal gardens. These were as yet unaffected by the landscape taste introduced between 1767 and 1773, when Capability Brown erased the lot – and more's the pity.

From Sion, the voyager with Rocque could go in two directions: the pleasant one, as today, towards Isleworth, once so fashionable with the gentry. Here were smaller gentry gardens, and apart from the large formal one of Kendal House around Hartland Road, none of great distinction. There is Gordon House near here (now the Marion Gray Training College), and a ferry would have taken Rocque across the Thames by Isleworth Ait to the Richmond side of the river. This route must have been his, because he would have been fascinated by the three magnificent gardens laid side by side across what we know as the Old Deer Park, roughly extending from the river's edge inland

to the site of the Old Observatory. Mr Justice Salwen's and Mr Jeffries's were almost as one, both in the grandest formal manner, the latter with a baroque house and parterres in the style of George London. They were approached by Sheen Lane across what is now the Old Deer Park Recreation Ground, skirting the even grander garden of Sir Matthew Decker. This ranked with Chiswick, with geometric wildernesses, basons, canals and winding paths. The designer ought to be known if it is not Stephen Switzer.

The alternative route from Sion returns to Boston Manor, taking Windmill Road (the old road to Ealing), passing Ealing Park (shown as a large landscaped garden by Cary), and finding on the corner of South Ealing Lane the small semi-formal garden of Charles Lockyer. Folly Lane (now Pope's Lane) would bring us to Gunnersbury House, in Rocque's day still as

built by John Webb in 1658 as a Palladian villa. Its garden was singular in having parallel canals aligned on to a square parterre. Today we may be confused by what we find, for in 1801 the Webb house had been replaced by a Copland one, and in 1835 Nathan Meyer Rothschild built a second house, both now within a predominantly nineteenth-century garden. However, in 1743 William Kent had effected some work (after Rocque), and at an undisclosed date Sir William Chambers made a miniature Kew here for Princess Amelia. His is the Round Pond and the Doric Temple.

From Gunnersbury Rocque found Acton an attractive suburban village with three major gardens. On the site of the North Thames Gas Sports Ground was Sir Joseph Ayloffe's, laid out as a part formal, part wiggly wilderness when the house (The Elms) was built in 1735. More interesting was Derwentwater House in

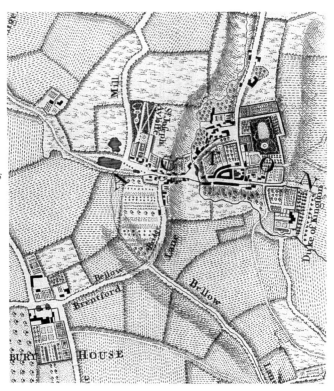

The village of Acton around 1750 could boast around three gardens in an evolving style from formal to informal. The Duke of Kingston's had two lateral canals; Derwentwater House had a Pope-style perspective with mount and wiggly paths; and Sir Joseph Ayloffe's contained a part formal, part wiggly garden. This last was on the present site of the North Thames Gas Sports Ground

Opposite: *The artist Jacques Rigaud was working at Chiswick in 1733, and he shows the north front wilderness that by the end of the year had been swept away by William Kent in what was then termed the 'modern' landscape taste*

the angle between Norn Lane and Acton High Road and centred by the school on Newburgh Road, with a rare Pope-style garden of the perspective sort with mount, central lawn and wiggly perimeter paths. The third garden, Berrymead, belonged to the Duke of Kingston, made between 1706 and 1731 when the two lateral canals were dug.

From Acton to Chiswick, Turnham Green, as it now is, was partly taken up by a house with complex geometric gardens, once Lord Lovat's. South are the three almost conjoined estates of Sutton Court, Grove House and Chiswick House. They fall over the edge of Rocque's map and only Chiswick is precisely mapped and is all that remains today in an area once rich in gardens. Towards Shepherds Bush, Ravenscourt Park is still an open space, and can be identified with the Elizabethan house shown by Rocque as a main block with a pair of lodges to the entrance court, and a symmetrical parterre garden with central fountain and avenue beyond. At Hammersmith the Metropolitan Line station has snuffed out Captain David de Charms's wiggly garden made after 1730. Although Brook Green was a fashionable area, the many gentry gardens there were probably

too small for Rocque to map, and his nearest large garden is Holland House, surprisingly lacking any trace of the expected great formal gardens. Rocque preceded Kent's work of 1747 and Charles Hamilton's tree planting of 1753. However, Cary seems to show a formal wilderness north of the house. The eye of Rocque moves very quickly to the huge formal garden of Norland House, more or less across Holland Park Road, laid out by Thomas Greene in the early years of the eighteenth century. The parterre is almost the size of Wilton, and in the style of George London's Dawley House. It can only have been designed by the London and Wise partnership working from the Brompton Nursery that Rocque surveys across the site of the present Victoria and Albert Museum.

Had we followed the Thames from Chiswick, our first stop would have been the Bishop of London's famed gardens at Fulham Palace, probably little altered since George London gardened here in the 1670s. Rocque shows the old moats before they were filled in in the 1760s. Today something of the walled character of the gardens can be recaptured, unlike the almost complete obliteration of the vast magnificent gardens laid out by Lord Peterborough

soon after the Restoration. Parsons Green and Eel Brook Common lie across them, and they survive on Rocque in a disused condition, but still with avenues, parterres and traces of mounts and canals. Even in 1745 this area between Chelsea and Fulham was being broken up into small estates and suburban gentry gardens. Samuel Foote's Hermitage on the North End Road was a typical but late example of a rococo semi-formal garden laid out around 1767.

South-west:
Bushey Park, Twickenham, Richmond, Wimbledon

The royal gardens of Hampton Court are well known; less so Bushey Park with its avenues planted by George London from 1689, and the remarkable survival of its system of conduits formed out of the Longford River in 1638. A cascade made about 1710 survives by Water-house Pond. Within the park are Upper and Lower Lodges, built for the keepers. Rocque's Upper Lodge has a water garden made out of the conduits, and his Lower Lodge shows the survival of a perfectly symmetrical formal

garden laid out when the house was built for Edward Proger by William Samwell in 1664. What is not shown by Rocque is the small garden and house built on the southern edge of the park for the second Earl of Halifax's mistress. His rare rococo garden by Thomas Wright 1757–69 survives with its restored grotto, and is one of the wonders of its kind.

Downstream from Hampton Court, the villas that once fronted the Thames at Teddington were a post-Rocque development, an extension of habitation from the fashionable reaches of Twickenham. All the celebrated gardens of Twickenham have gone: Pope's, except for a fragment of his grotto; the fascinating group of rococo town-house gardens on Heath Road; and just a few fields left of Horace Walpole's Strawberry Hill. It is likewise north-east towards Whitton. Rocque shows the Duke of Argyle's Whitton Place with its speciality of an ornamental nursery garden by James Gibbs and Roger Morris, but supervised by the gardening Duke. East of this and just south of Murray Park, Rocque maps another perspective garden influenced by Pope's, and this may have been Whitton Park. Northwards, on Hounslow High Street and Lampton Road, is a moated

*The Flower Garden at
Strawberry Hill. In 1765
Horace Walpole became
possessed of Mr Frankland's
cottage on the north side of the
Twickenham to Hampton
Court road. Here he laid out
a Flower Garden by 1769 that
seems to have contained
mixed flowers arbitrarily
arranged in the manner of
Dickie Bateman's 'Kingdom
of Flowers' at Old Windsor*

Tudor garden of the manor house of Hounslow built after the Dissolution.

Richmond provides two opportunities: to explore what is now Kew Gardens, or take the hill road to Richmond Park. Rocque strikingly shows the separation between Kew House of Frederick, Prince of Wales and Richmond Gardens of George II. Kew was then not even the Kew Gardens that were to develop under Augusta, Dowager Princess of Wales, from 1757, but a small formal garden attached to the house built by William Kent in 1730. Richmond Gardens comprised the older formal layout by George London, and the semi-formal parts by Charles Bridgeman, with buildings by Kent. Near the Dutch House behind Kew House, a ferry crossed to the Brentwood–Sion side of the river.

To take the alternative road to Richmond Park is to discover park (enclosed in 1637) rather than garden, although there has been no study of the gardens of individual lodges or royal residences within the park, such as White Lodge, where Repton worked for Lord Sidmouth in 1805. The fringes of the park beyond the walls were favoured for villa development from the eighteenth century (Parksted, now Manresa House, or Mount Clare etc), but their gardens have mostly gone. It was likewise with the nearby Wimbledon Common, and with Roehampton.

Twickenham downstream has more to offer: on the town bank York House, Rocque's lost garden of Lord Strafford, Orleans House, and Marble Hill. Only the last-named with open lawn to the river can be identified with Rocque. Towards Richmond and beyond the present bridge, Rocque surveyed the vast expanse of Twickenham Park with avenues on a scale comparable to those of Bushey Park. In 1606 the Countess of Bedford made a mannerist garden here with four mounts, one of which had survived for Rocque to record. It was fully landscaped in the Brown manner by the 1780s and is now built over.

Beyond Twickenham Park was Isleworth, so with Rocque we might have crossed the river by either the Richmond or the Isleworth ferry,

and could return, as we may today, upstream on the opposite bank. Rocque's Lord Harrington's garden is to be identified with New Park Lord Rochester's house built 1692 but burnt 1721, where the gardens were one of London's greatest achievements. We can still sense their scale and position by standing on Henry VIII's Mount and seeing the flat depression of the

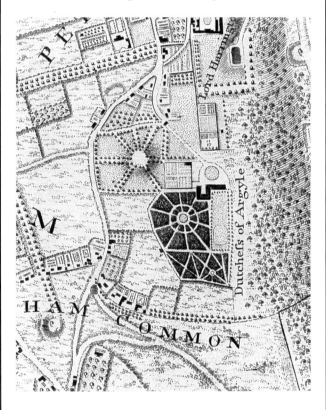

huge hanging parterre that was cut into the hillside. After New Park is the golf course of Sudbrooke Lodge, built by James Gibbs for the Duke of Argyle in 1717. The 'Wilderness' still commemorates Bridgeman's. Finally, before crossing the ferry back to Twickenham, Rocque shows the simplified parterres of Ham House, now restored (although recreated would be a better description).

Rocque can be joined at Upper Richmond Road, walking to Roehampton Golf Course and attempting to slot in Rocque's gardens with what survives today – even if only a pair of gate piers. Thomas Cary's Roehampton House by Thomas Archer is no problem because it is still there, enveloped by Queen Mary's Hospital. A little north-east Rocque shows the hunting seat of Putney Park approached from the south by its long avenue that is followed today exactly by the line of Putney Park Lane. On Putney Lane was the complex baroque garden Percival Lewis designed for James Bateman before 1718, with its Archer connections. However, the most fascinating garden recorded by Rocque stood nearly opposite Queen Mary's Hospital. It too was called Roehampton House (later

Campbell in 1720, and set in an exedra-ended parterre; then a formal garden belonging to Mr Rush; and thirdly the Duchess of Marlborough's house built by Roger Morris and Lord Pembroke in 1732. The garden was by Bridgeman, although more properly a park. From Geographia it can be seen that the estate extended over Arthur Road and Home Park

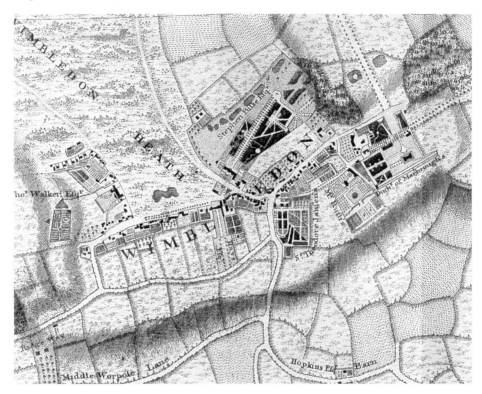

Opposite: *Rocque's Ham shows a simplification of the parterre garden first laid out in the early seventeenth century; then altered for the Duke of Lauderdale in 1672. Erased in the nineteenth century, Ham's first parterre has recently been re-created*

Around Wimbledon village was clustered a fascinating group of gardens: that of Stephen Bisse in a Bridgeman style, and very grand and sophisticated; then Sir Theodore Janssen's, with a villa begun by Colen Campbell in 1720 and an exedra garden in his style; the small formal garden of Mr Rush and the very grand garden of the Duchess of Marlborough, laid out by Bridgeman with the house (by Morris) from 1732. This was partly on the site of old Wimbledon Palace

Grove House) and the huge square enclosure filled with groups of parterres must surely be the surviving garden of Sir Richard Weston made in the 1630s, probably by Isaac de Caus of Wilton fame, where John Evelyn saw the equestrian statue of Charles I now in Trafalgar Square, and a huge painted *trompe-l'oeil* perspective at the end of the vista, shown by Rocque in the 1740s as a separate garden.

Wimbledon village was another magnet for a feast of gardens, and here Geographia is invaluable. Lying across Parkside Avenue, Marryat Road and Somerset Road, was the vast Bridgeman-style garden of Stephen Bisse, unsung in garden history. Then on the south side of Wimbledon Hill, about Grosvenor Hill and Drax Avenue, Rocque maps three gardens: Sir Theodore Janssen's with a villa begun by Colen

Road, across the site of old Wimbledon Palace. The Duchess extended her avenues into what is now Wimbledon Golf Course and Wimbledon Park. This park with its lake is a remarkable survival of a Capability Brown landscape made for Earl Spencer from 1765.

Wimbledon eastwards through south London to Peckham and Dulwich

East of Wimbledon, by Colliers Road Station, across Clive and Warren roads, a playing field marks the parterres of Peter de St Loy's Colliers Wood House, with an unusual grid of canals. Immediately south of Tooting Bec Station was the garden of Joseph Salvadore's house of the 1720s. Just off Rocque's map, and not on Cary's

either, we can still enjoy the mainly eighteenth-century gardens of Morden Hall.

In general the gardens to the north-east seem principally of the nineteenth century and later. For example, south of the Oval Pond on Streatham Common is the Rookery, and there is Norwood Grove and the picturesque green lung of Brockwell Park. North is one early garden of Tudor date, belonging to Loughborough House and covered by the Stockwell Park Estate. In Dulwich, off Gallery Road, is the exceptional survival of Belair, a house of 1785 in a designed parkscape.

As a contrast, moving with Rocque to Peckham, and framed by Hill Street, Peckham High Street and Commercial Way, is the garden of Sir Thomas Bond, for whom William Talman made designs for a house in 1688. The lateral parterre, lawns with wildernesses, and the sophistication of the design are in the language of Talman's partner, George London. In contrast, we can note that Hatcham Park Road, just east at New Cross, follows the line of a diagonal avenue that once led to the moated garden of Hatcham House.

Beddington to Beckenham, Eltham to Greenwich, to Sidcup

In this rather favoured area of south London, Cary takes over from Rocque, and the parks are principally of the landscape kind, although Carshalton has the remains of two formal layouts. At Beddington Place (now Carew Manor School) not much survives to remind us of the famous seventeenth-century gardens. At Carshalton House (Daughters of the Cross) Sir John Fellows called in Bridgeman for the garden 1716–20, and Henry Joynes designed the

William Curtis's Lambeth garden, acquired about 1777, was opened to a subscribing public in 1779 as the 'London botanic garden'. The Festival Hall lies across the site. In 1789 Curtis moved to Queen's Elm, Fulham Road

their later garden of Langley Park, by Humphry Repton, *c*. 1790, with the overlay of buildings north of West Wickham; and imagination is also needed to recreate the park of Hayes Place to Chatham Avenue and the green of Pickhurst School Recreation Ground.

South of here, still in Greater London, parks remain to be enjoyed. Holwood Park, south of Hayes, has a Decimus Burton house of 1823 in gardens made by Repton for Pitt about 1791. Northwards is Sundridge Park (Golf Club), a Nash–Repton house and garden of 1796 in a well-bunkered but beautiful park.

North again, to Eltham, imagination will have to associate the Royal Blackheath Golf Club with the very grand formal gardens of Eltham Lodge laid out for Sir John Shaw in 1664; and it is the same south of Greenwich Park, where Foxes Dale, South Row and Eltham Road lie over the avenues of Sir Gregory Page's grand Palladian mansion of Wricklemarsh. Rocque is invaluable here, and at Westcombe confirms the pioneering gardenesque layout of Lord Pembroke's villa *c*. 1729. It was on the site of the East Greenwich Pleasaunce next to Greenwich District Hospital. Of Greenwich Park itself, it is worth observing that Rocque's late seventeenth-century Great Wilderness is commemorated on the site by the Wilderness Deer Park in the south-east corner of the park. Finally, moving with Rocque to his eastern extremity, the geometric enclosures of Charlton House are the 1607 ones modified in the late seventeenth century.

The fringes of Greater London south-east are mapped by Cary: Lesness Abbey, wooded as today; the belvedere demolished, but its park now Franks Park; Danson Park with a villa by Sir Robert Taylor and a very municipalized park by Brown and Richmond in the 1760s; and a group of parks around North Cray: Lamorbey, still clearly designed in the eighteenth century, but cut up by schools, sports grounds and Sidcup Golf Course set around naturalized lakes; Foots Cray Place now no longer, but a park that may be by Brown; and the unknown landscape park of Mount Markell. Then, for the archaeologist, Queen

Water House. South of Ruskin Road, the open green of Carshalton Park, still with the remains of formal canals and a grotto is all that survives of the huge house that was begun 1722 but never completed.

Today landscaped estates survive around here, almost more than anywhere else near London. A mile south of Carshalton is the big Brownian park of The Oaks, where Robert Adam and Sir Robert Taylor worked for Lord Derby. At Addington Place (Royal School of Church Music) is a Brown park of 1781 around a Mylne house of 1773. Near Beckenham it is difficult to relate Kelsey Park with its natural lake to Peter Burrell's ambitious geometric formal gardens. The process of transition from one style to the other is perfectly accomplished by Rocque and Cary. Indeed, as far as the Burrells are concerned, it is likewise difficult to identify

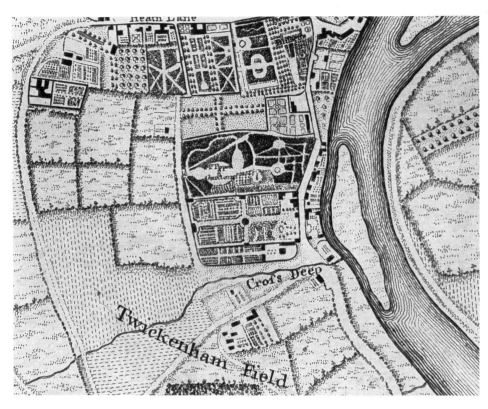

As one of the most popular villages in the environs of London, Twickenham could boast many fine gardens, the most famous (and so most published) being Alexander Pope's. However, more interesting for their variety are the smaller gardens of Heath Lane, mostly in a semi-formal early eighteenth-century style

Below right: *As a village Clapton was favoured for its proximity to the City and its border on the river Lea. The grandest house was Stamp Brooksbank's, designed by Colen Campbell in 1728 with its Switzerian wiggly garden. Nearby is the rare survival of two Tudor gardens: Clapton House with a square parterre and Bromley House with three parterres descending to the river*

Mary's Hospital off Frognall Avenue, Sidcup, incorporated Lord Sidney's Frognall where the outlines of its late seventeenth-century formal garden are perfectly preserved.

North-west London, from Hillingdon to Enfield

The small gentry seats around Ruislip and Ickenham have gone; something remains at Harefield overwhelmed by hospitals; noble Swakeleys is still with us, but its trio of avenues has gone; and there is just a walled garden and a bason to remind us of the axial garden with two long canals of James Dagnia. More survives north-east around the Stanmores, but this is RAF country, and inaccessible. Stanmore Park RAF station was once the Drummond family seat, and the old park, possibly by Brown, can be retrieved in the south beyond Gordon Avenue, where it has become a golf course. The great formal landscape of Canons can be experienced by looking along the vista from St Lawrence's church, Whitchurch. 'The Lake' was the Great Bason, and the North London Collegiate School marks the site of 'Princely' Chandos's huge continental house. North-east is Bentley

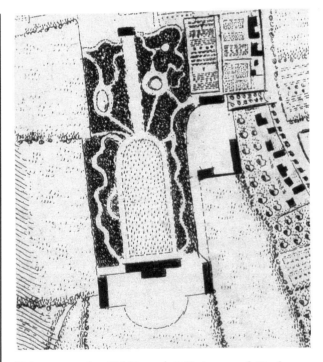

Priory, again RAF and Ministry of Defence. The layout was, and is still, of late eighteenth-century natural character, where one commentator reported that the 'landscape laughs' around the trees fronting the plantations. North-east again, we enter the Enfield Chase with its keepers' lodges: the present Trent Park

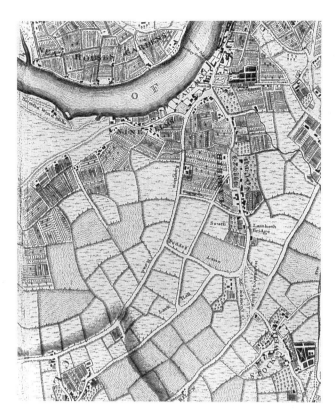

Rocque shows Vauxhall as Spring Gardens, served from the Thames by boats stopping at the Vauxhall Stairs, also serving Ranelagh Gardens a short distance up-river

(Middlesex Polytechnic) still of 1780s and early nineteenth-century Reptonian, but with twentieth-century gardens near the house. South Lodge was Lord Chatham's famous landscape park where he designed a natural lake. It can be located south of Enfield Road, its lake squeezed in between Lonsdale Drive North and East. Enfield Park is south of Enfield proper, once called Bush Hill Park, its gardens have been traditionally attributed to the famous French designer André Le Nôtre. Town Park and Enfield Golf Course cover the site. From Canons, a final group of gardens or parks are to be found in the vale north of Southgate: Arnos Park, Broomfield Park and Grovelands range from early eighteenth to early nineteenth century. As Southgate Grove, Grovelands was built by John Nash in 1797 and retains the best surviving Repton parkscape in Greater London.

East London to Leytonstone, Wanstead and Romford

As a generality, the gardens of West Middlesex and south-west London were aristocratic. On the other hand, Enfield, the Epping Forest, the Lea Valley and the Hainault Forest attracted the merchant and banking classes because of their accessibility to the City. Rocque surveys a plethora of gardens.

Clapton was extremely favoured: near the City, but still a village. Stamp Brooksbank's house designed by Colen Campbell in 1728 has a perspective garden focused upon a temple and with wiggly perimeter paths. If Campbell employed Stephen Switzer elsewhere, so here. Homerton Hospital covers the site. Just north, at the angle of Lower Clapton Road and Lea Bridge Road, was Clapton House with a square Tudor parterre garden. Tudor also is Bromley House below Bow church, with three descending parterres to the river. South of Bow Church Station the garden of Mr Pirhus is of simplified late seventeenth-century style with an avenue, and the long thin parterre of another house is shown by the side of the present Fairfield Road.

The River Lea acts as a boundary. Rocque would have crossed from Bow Road. East of Stratford he found Sir Robert Smith's Tudor moated garden with two parterres, now the site of West Ham Park. Then around Leyton he mapped a group of distinguished gardens all of

Spring Gardens opened in the seventeenth century, but by the mid-eighteenth century had gained European fame as Vauxhall Gardens. This bird's-eye view illustrates two of the most important features of Georgian pleasure gardens: walks and groves. Music and food would complement the evening's promenade

complex, grand, late seventeenth- and early eighteenth-century type, and all unknown to garden history. John Phillipps's Leyton House was watered by the Mill River. In front of the house built for David Gansel *c.* 1706 was a grass terrace, a group of flower parterres, two large square wildernesses, and a lateral canal broken in the middle by a convex protrusion that is echoed by a further convex-shaped canal beyond. Playing fields by the Orient Industrial Park mark the site. A little to the south-east,

other, has a sophistication that speaks of George London. The recreation ground at Fletcher Lane is the only remaining green of this distinguished garden. Finally, east of Leyton Station was Rickholts, or Ruckholes, House where building and gardening works were done for Benjamin Collier in 1721–8. Finally, south of Leytonstone High Road Station, Rocque maps an old-fashioned garden with a six-division parterre.

At this point Rocque has taken us to the edge

In the 1740s Kensington Palace Gardens was a case study of the gardening styles of London and Wise followed by Switzer and Bridgeman, then Kent. Already, George London's complicated topiary parterre south of the Palace has been eliminated and the areas grassed, and on the eastern perimeter of the gardens, Kent's landscaping to the edge of the Serpentine water with his Queen's Temple is evident

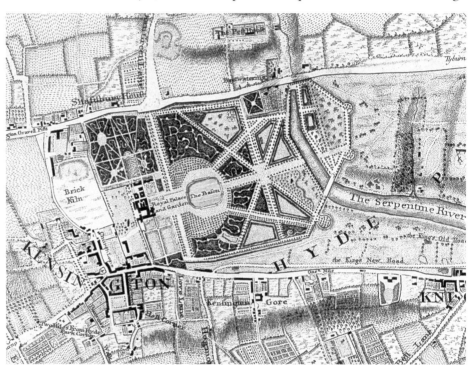

Phillipps's neighbour at Leyton Grange was Sir John Strange. His were vast formal gardens of the Bridgeman kind with avenues, plantations, a wilderness and a lateral canal. The house was also built by Gansel, but in 1715, and was demolished in 1861, following which Leyton Orient Football Club grounds and Coronation Gardens were built over the site. Yet another magnificent formal garden was to be found on the other side of Leyton High Road. This was The Great House, built in 1712 for Sir Fisher Tench, owned by Mr Soresby in the 1740s, and demolished in 1905 following development in 1881. In style the garden with a T-shaped canal, a square of nine trees at the ends of the short stroke of the T and an octagon pond at the

of Wanstead. Whipps Cross Hospital is on the site of one parterre garden, and a green adjacent to James Lane was the site of Boreham House. In the village of Wanstead itself was Rocque's garden of Matthew Wymondesold, a house built for Sir Francis Dashwood about 1690, and later rebuilt as Wanstead Grove. The plantations struck through with diagonal avenues, the thin long canal, and the details, are in the Bridgeman style. By 1885 all had been built over in Grove Park and The Avenue.

Wanstead was the largest private formal garden in London, covering an area nearly two miles square. George London laid it out for Sir Richard Child from 1707 and it was vastly enlarged with rococo ornamental serpentine gardens, grottos and eclectic buildings through the 1720s and 1730s. Relating Rocque with Geographia is to discover just how much survives among playing fields, golf course and fishing grounds. London's Great Bason, his two spiral mounts, the 'Streight' or terminating long canal, an amphitheatre – all are there; and of the rococo period are the blurred outlines of Fortification Island, the Mount of William Kent's grotto, and from a later period, the ruins of the grotto-boathouse. The great vista up to

to the exciting discovery south of Gants Hill Station of Valentines, with long canal, rock-works, cascades and grotto made by Robert Surnam during his ownership from 1724 to 1754, although the house was rebuilt by Sir Charles Raymond in 1769. East of Valentines, less intensive development makes the old parks easier to locate. Pyrgo is still agricultural, the house of *c.*1740 gone, but decayed Italianate gardens designed by Edward Kemp remain; Bedfords has been a public park since 1933, its

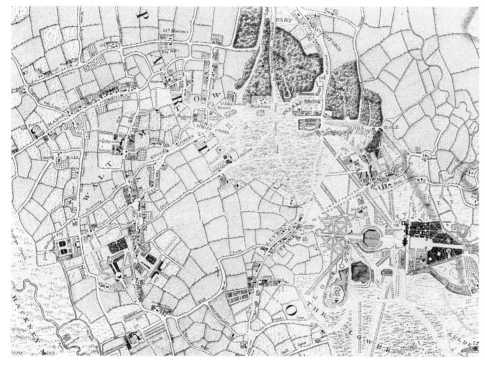

Wanstead was England's Versailles, and the reason for the sobriquet earned by George London as the 'English La Nôtre'. Laid out for Sir Richard Child from 1706, it equalled the scale of Versailles in the 1660s. Rocque shows the rococo exteneions of the 1730s, probably partly by Kent, and even by the 1740s, proving too complexly ornamental to maintain

the summit of the hill where the huge Palladian house no longer stands, is on the scale of Versailles.

For the garden historian, just as the Dash-wood–Wymondesold garden is a fascinating discovery to the north-east of Wanstead, so to the south-east, south of Aldersbrook, is Smart Lethieullier's. Although the house was sixteenth-century, Smart 'made a very pretty improvement' in his gardens before 1748. The style, with a canal of complex shape, is in the late Bridgeman manner, and at Rocque's visit the garden may have included Mrs Lethieullier's 'beautiful hermitage in a wood, with lawn, waters, a mount, parterre etc'.

Eastwards we pass from Rocque to Cary, and

house demolished in 1938; Dagnam Park was built in 1772 and demolished in 1948, and playing fields are all that survive from Repton's landscaping in 1802 and 1816; and Barking Park and Parsloes are just ghosts of old estates. An exciting ground exercise is to reconstruct Gidea Park out of Raphael Park and School and Romford Golf Course with housing in between. James Wyatt's three-arched bridge of 1781 still spans the lake. Then, almost at the eastern extremity of Greater London, there is James Paine's Hare Hall of 1769 with a small park and lake that may have been landscaped by Richard Woods, and south of this Hylands Park, a Labouchère house of several periods, but the park made by Repton before 1803.

'The modest terms of rebuilding and gardening'
GARDENING
AND THE MIDDLE CLASSES
1700–1830

During the eighteenth century the ownership or use of a small private town garden became, for the first time, a common expectation and a popular recreational amenity of London's urban middle classes. Daniel Defoe described the material aspirations of both the country squire and the London merchant when he wrote, 'Every man now, be his fortune what it will, is to be doing something at his place, as the fashionable phrase is, and you hardly meet with anybody who, after first compliments, does not inform you that he is in mortar, and having of earth, the modest terms of rebuilding and gardening.'

The emergence of town gardening as a commercialized leisure activity was one of the manifold products of the consumer revolution of eighteenth-century England. Many London-

In the 1770s the artist Paul Sandby enjoyed a small courtyard garden sandwiched between his studio and his house in St George's Row, Bayswater; he also benefited from prospects into both neighbouring and distant rustic scenery beyond his garden wall

Opposite: *The tradesman gardener became the champion of free enterprise in the competitive world of town gardening. Such self-employed operatives catered to the middle classes*

ers who found themselves benefiting from the rising tide of national wealth converted their capital into material belongings which improved their household surroundings. The small urban garden figured pre-eminently among the elements which elevated the average household from a level of subsistence to one of comfort and style, and an increasingly commercialized garden industry promoted the activity of gardening as an affordable and viable urban recreation.

During the eighteenth century more Londoners than ever before enjoyed the experience of acquiring material possessions – many of which had previously been denied to them. Growing purchasing power was being laid out on a greater range of consumer goods, beyond mere necessities. What were once luxuries became 'decencies', and what were once 'decencies' became necessities. The desire to consume was not unique to eighteenth-century English society; but the ability to do so, however modestly, by most classes of people was new. As the century unfolded the prices of many staple commodities dropped and real wages for skilled labourers increased, making the consumption of material comforts attractive. These factors, combined with easy credit,

In the eighteenth century gardening became a popular national pursuit and recreational pastime which nurtured new and evolving notions of the roles and responsibilities of the individual and the family

Below right: *The frontispiece to Thomas Fairchild's* The City Gardener *(1722). This book was largely responsible for the gardening mania which swept across eighteenth-century London. It was a pioneering account of problems and peculiarities of town gardening*

low interest rates and lack of legal security for bank and friendly society savings, encouraged spending rather than saving.

Nowhere in England was the full force of the consumer revolution more pervasive than in London. The eighteenth-century capital developed into a prodigious cosmopolitan hub, where citizens mixed comfortably in their new surroundings, readily adapting to a geography that was once worldly and diverse. By 1750 over 11 per cent of England's population was resident in London – and it has been estimated that given the seasonal migrations in and out of the metropolis, one in six of the total adult population of England had the experience of living in the capital for some stage of their lives. With such a high proportion of people acquainted with London's fashions, markets and lifestyles, the city exercised a considerable influence over national taste and consumer behaviour.

Among the most significant contributions London made to the provinces was the sophisticated exploitation of leisure; this was made possible through the development and commercial organization of the press. Through the instrument of the press consumer taste and material

aspirations became truly national – or more frequently emulative of the latest fashions of the capital. From the early eighteenth century, newspapers carried extensive quantities of increasingly diversified advertisements and information which promoted nearly all forms of recreation. Thomas Fairchild's *City Gardener* (1722) was largely responsible for the town gardening mania which swept across eighteenth-century London. His efforts were not unique, but they were pioneering. Fairchild galvanized seedsmen, nurserymen and horticulturists to cater to the wants of the urban bourgeoisie, recommending town gardening as an affordable and seductive leisure activity.

A number of other factors abetted the expansion of urban gardening in the eighteenth century; among them were the availability of cheap urban garden labour, a widening variety of cheap plants, abundant accessible garden and horticultural literature, and a highly sophisticated nursery trade.

Jobbing gardeners

Although many Londoners were happy to pursue gardening as a recreational or leisure activity, they were seldom prepared to do all the work involved in gardening. The urban middle classes more frequently employed the services of jobbing gardeners for cheap, practical and quick gardening services. Self-employed, itinerant garden operatives, or tradesmen gardeners (those freed from professional indenture) were the champions of free enterprise in the sphere of town gardening; they solicited their own custom (door to door, or at times through advertisements in local papers), used their own tools, and occasionally supplied their own plants or seeds (frequently from their own small gardens) to make, mend and manage small to medium-sized town gardens and garden squares. Their common contractual agreements were negotiated on one-off commissions, or on hourly, daily, monthly, quarterly or annual contracts. Jobbers catered to an urban clientele that wanted gardens, needed occasional 'professional' gardening services and advice, but had neither

the quarters nor the inclination to keep a full-time gardener.

There was well-founded scepticism in the abilities of many jobbers, who were branded by the true professionals as 'rude people, Northern lads and higglers' or 'audacious Empiricks' who were eager to exploit the expanding market for urban gardening services. The so-called 'Empiricks' were claimed to debase the business of town gardening by opting out of professional apprenticeship and dodging the code of ethics upheld by tradesmen and serving gardeners who subscribed to the Worshipful Company of Gardeners of London. Stephen Switzer (1718) especially decried the scores of 'ignorant pretenders' who called at houses where they knew there was a slip of ground, 'let it be in season or out, and tell the owner it is a good time to dress and make-up their gardens; and often impose on them that they employ them, by telling them their everything will do . . . this is a great discouragement, which makes those Persons, who delight a little in a garden, neglect doing anything at all; thinking that their Labour and Cost thrown away'. Despite such imputations, most Londoners at some time found themselves employing itinerant operatives for perfunctory chores of watering, mowing, turning gravel walks, or the laborious tasks of initially setting out a garden, shifting rocks, topsoil or waste.

By the late eighteenth century, jobbers who had previously found their commissions lucrative and plentiful felt the squeeze of the commercialized services provided by large, organized contracting firms and their retinues of professional garden operatives. The business of commercial gardening trade and services had by the 1790s swollen to such an extent that Middleton described the environs of Middlesex as follows: 'From Kensington, through Hammersmith, Chiswick, Brentford, Isleworth and Twickenham, the land both sides of the road, for seven miles in length, or a distance to ten miles from the market, may be dominated the great fruit garden, north of the Thames, for the supply of London. In this manner, much of the ground in these parishes is cultivated.' He went

on to note: 'at Chelsea, Brompton, Kensington, Hackney, Bow, and Mile End much ground is occupied by nurserymen, who spare no expense in collecting the choicest sort, and the greatest variety, of fruit trees, and ornamental shrubs and flowers, from every corner of the globe, and which they cultivate in a high degree of perfection; the latter to a very great extent, and to almost endless variety . . .'

The nurserymen

Virtually every corner of the capital could boast celebrated nursery grounds, many of which had long been in existence and were carried on by descendants of the original owners, or by successors; among them Thomas Fairchild's (c. 1691–1734) was at Hoxton; Robert Furber's (1700–1846) in Kensington Gore; Davey's (1791–1833) in Camberwell; Christopher Gray's (c. 1720–1881) in Fulham; James Gordon's (c. 1740–1837) at Mile End; Kennedy and

Lee's (1745–1894) at Hammersmith; and Loddiges' (1760–1860) at Hackney. Each establishment had its own particular distinction, and list of horticultural triumphs which were publicly promoted through sophisticated advertising campaigns. Some nurserymen took advantage of the press, while others advertised through catalogues and pamphlets, flysheets, cheap pocket manuals and gardeners' calendars. More ambitious and successful nurserymen launched advertisements in the form of periodicals: Robert Furber's *Twelve Months of Flowers* (1730), The London Society of Gardeners' *Catalogus Plantarum* (1731), and Loddiges' *The Botanical Cabinet* (1817–33).

The combined efforts of London's botanists and commercial gardeners ensured that the city maintained its centuries-old distinction as the cynosure of all garden improvements. Nothing serves better to reinforce this claim than the publication of John Claudius Loudon's first

Left: *The Chinese Pavilion (c.1740) of Montagu House, Whitehall, is a unique survival of a temporary garden pavilion. It was, until the late nineteenth century, annually erected in the spring and stowed away in the autumn*

Below: *Detail of the roof of the Chinese Pavilion of Montagu House*

Opposite: *This view of the tidy front garden of Ranelagh House, Chelsea, is a particularly charming example of the use of potted plants around the house and garden*

volume of the *Gardeners' Magazine* in 1826. Compiled in Bayswater and launched in London, it was England's first popular gardening journal. The object of the magazine was 'the dissemination of useful knowledge, its subjects inexhaustible as the vegetable kingdom, and among the most interesting that concern domestic life; its plan calculated to procure information from every possible source at home and abroad; its contributors belonging to every department of gardening and botany'. It was proclaimed by its author to be a vehicle which 'will put Gardeners in distant parts of the country on a footing with those about the metropolis'.

Loudon admitted that not all gardening improvements were forged in London, 'but more are made there than anywhere else, and most of those made elsewhere are soon heard of in the metropolitan district'. He alleged that almost all new importations and introductions of plants were made through the capital's nurseries and market gardens; and these were the most numerous and advanced in the entire kingdom. Only they could reasonably advertise the latest in garden and vegetable culture, production and technology, and the management of the foremost and most accomplished of the country's 'first-rate' gardeners. London was also the undisputed source of the largest outpourings of garden and horticultural literature, and the scene of the country's most celebrated emporium of garden 'intercourse and novelties' – the London Horticultural Society, and its extensive gardens.

The initiatives of London's eighteenth-century nurserymen were timely in as much as during that period there evolved an avid secular curiosity in the natural sciences. The fascination was not, however, exclusively theoretical; plants, planting and gardening became popular urban recreations for people of moderate affluence who had time for leisure activities. Urban gardening flourished due to the ferociously energetic commercialization of the leisure industry which was developed for all classes of consumers, from the botanist to the amateur and even children. For instance, in the third quarter of the eighteenth century there occurred a revival of herbaceous gardening, which made available a wide range of cheaper medium and small hardy flowering plants. The new produce was well within the reach of middle-class consumers who owned and occupied small gardens in town; and fast maturing, easily managed flowering herbaceous plants promised immediate and abundant results encouraging gardening as a recreational pastime for women and children.

The garden, like most household accoutrements, was improved, created anew and designed to delight, amuse or exhibit one's taste, status or wealth, with the avowed intention of proclaiming one's ability constantly to improve on the old and the inherited, and to swell the demand for what is new and exciting and modern. The rise of specialized plant contracting and gardening from the second quarter of the eighteenth century did much to promote the evolving consumer ethic.

James Cochran (1763–1825?) has the distinction of being one of London's more successful commercial nurserymen about whom we know a great deal due to the survival of perhaps the earliest thoroughly documented accounts of a florist and plant contractor operating in the metropolis. The documents are invaluable for their records of plant and garden accessory leasing inventories, which give us insights into the creation, costs, constituents and display of imaginative temporary indoor and outdoor London town-house gardens.

Cochran went into business in 1800 as a nurseryman, seedsman and land-surveyor oper-

ating from Paddington. His business, although successful, might have gone undistinguished had he not bought out a flourishing plant contracting partnership around 1815. He immediately set up a retail shop in Duke Street, Grosvenor Square – the hub of fashionable London – where in the span of four years he saw the fruits of his enterprise increase his

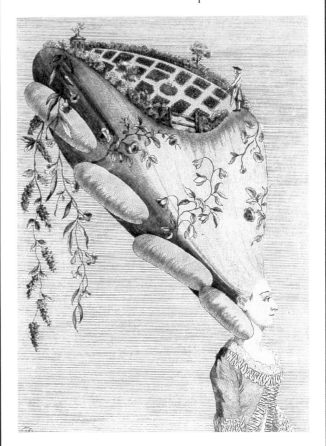

profits seventeen-fold. Cochran's astonishing success was due to a combination of his location, and more importantly his business of supplying flowers and shrubs for hire to the *beau monde*.

Plant contracting and leasing services developed to relieve the town gardener of trouble and uncertainty. 'The difficulties which beset the amateur florist in London are great, and almost irremediable; day and night he has to contend incessantly with a poisonous atmosphere – no skill or art – no assiduity or care – will protect his plants from the destructive infection of the pernicious blacks, their withering influence will baffle all his precautions.' It was commonly agreed that 'all plants, after flowering in London, will inevitably die, unless taken the very greatest care of by a practised gardener; they therefore, if purchased, become very expensive.' The only way to counter such discouraging pronouncements was to ensure a perpetual supply of vigorous and robust plants through a gardening contract. Contracts entailed weekly, monthly, quarterly, or annual

and parlours in order to heighten and exaggerate the 'vitality' of the current season. Spring was above all the most celebrated and popular garden season, as lawns were pulled up and re-turfed, gravel paths were turned or replaced, and hundreds of spring-blossoming shrubs and flowers were planted out for instant effect. Few concessions were made to natural sequential

inspection by professional and jobbing gardeners who through pruning, syringing, and replacing wilted specimens, brought renewed freshness to clients' plant displays.

Cochran engaged in short and extended contract plant hire for both the indoors and the outdoors, specializing in the leasing of 'plants for the night'. He had at his disposal a variable number of gardeners whom he in turn subcontracted for the building of new gardens, alteration or maintenance services at his clients' premises. If people had the means and the enthusiasm they delighted in the greatest benefit of contract gardening – large seasonal contingents of flowers, shrubs and small trees were plunged into gardens, balconies, sitting rooms

Opposite: *A pouffe au sentiment of* 1777. *This sky-scraping confection portrays a fashionable flower garden at its summit*

Above: *Joseph Salway's* Plan of the Road from Hyde Park Corner to Counter's Bridge *(1811) shows carefully rendered houses and their respective front gardens. Street drains, horse troughs, bollards, lamp standards and other details are shown with clarity*

blossom – almost everything was forced. Since spring was celebrated as 'perpetual', nothing was displayed to portend the subsequent seasons. A small and somewhat limited variety

Left: *The garden of the celebrated Regency collector Mr Upcott in Upper Street, Islington (c. 1820), captures the character of a small urban garden and depicts a contemporary* nessay *in the increasingly informal composition of town gardens*

Right: *'May' is one of a series of imaginative prints devoted to illustrating the plant stock of the nurseryman Robert Furber who ran a fashionable nursery at Kensington Gore*

of favourites were displayed and sustained through constant replacement to keep the garden in a state of suspended climax (and this was kept up for weeks, and even months). If customers wanted perpetual spring then nurserymen were happy to oblige; nothing was easier and cheaper for commercial nurserymen than growing enormous quantities of a limited assortment of blooms.

Just as it was fashionable to hire long-term

boxed displays, or to lease almost entire seasonal gardens, so it was – perhaps more so – to hire plants for the night. Floral caprice reached its heady climax with the creation of ephemeral Elysiums: vast living landscapes which straddled the indoors of the townhouse and its small garden; fantastical scenes which surpassed the alleged excesses of Elagabalus; 'fairy wildernesses' which were pulled down almost five times as fast as they were erected. These creations were perhaps the greatest inventive accomplishments of London's talented nurserymen, and undoubtedly the most potent advertisement of conspicuous consumption in the art of urban gardening.

Of course the fruits of Pomona and Vertumnus were but one ingredient in the theatrically

Bedford Square was the first uniform square to be built in London (1776–86). It was designed to accommodate members of the wealthy merchant middle classes. Various houses on the square had small gardens behind them, most notably Lord Eldon's

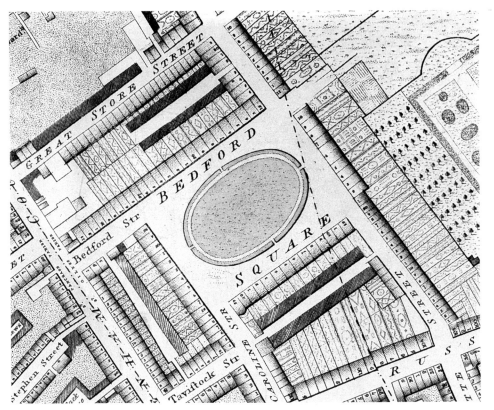

indulgence of the rich had by the early 1810s percolated to the middle classes, who delighted in creating equally effective but less costly indoor garden spectacles. There was, however, by this time a noticeable withering in taste for such exuberant displays of floral caprice. The tide of consumerism which had kindled and nurtured

staged spectacles which took place in Regency London's townhouses. At 'the Fashionable World's' fêtes, masquerades, balls and *ridotti*, few expenses were spared, as everything – chandeliers to geraniums, console tables to jardinières – was hired so as to convey the utmost refinement of taste, and a familiarity with the latest and the best. Everywhere indoor rooms were transformed into garden caricatures where walls were decked with hundredweights of cut ivy and laurel interwoven with flowers, hundreds of potted plants formed *allées*, hedges and wildernesses, and fishponds, grottos, springs and temporary pavilions were thrown up to make guests believe that they were rollicking *en pleine campagne*, if not acting on the stage of Louis XIV's *Théâtre de Verdure*.

These fanciful scenes which began as the

these fanciful expressions of urban gardening also quashed them. Material motivations overwhelmed, and ultimately irrevocably dulled the novelty of the scenes.

The private garden

There were, of course, many other instances of the widespread repercussions of consumerism and evolving material motivations. One significant change was the decline of the importance attached to prospect. By the early nineteenth century Londoners were increasingly insensible to the psychic gratification of the urban 'prospect' – specifically, the visual appropriation of nature. There was no longer a place for Addison's citizen of 'Polite Imagination' who often felt a greater satisfaction in prospect than another did in possession. People no longer saw a kind of 'property' in everything they saw – they demanded the satisfaction of appropriation and ownership. Urban tenants, and especially the rich, were by the mid-eighteenth century obsessively acquisitive. For instance, where the wealthy had previously condescended to share the amenity of a key-holders' garden (i.e. a garden square, or a subscription garden), they now often found the

The garden designed in Gower Street (1791) by Richard Twiss is the best surviving account of a small London garden of its period

notion unattractive. People preferred small private garden enclosures for 'flower gardens' to shared open spaces; they wanted secure and defensible private garden retreats to insulate themselves from their neighbours, and from the inconveniences of the public realm.

The material motivations of late eighteenth-century Londoners might suggest that objects such as houses and gardens were increasingly invested with properties which in themselves gratified their possessors' psyche – that they achieved this through being purveyors of privacy and social distancing, and through rupturing the work setting from the scene of domesticity and family-nurtured morality. One popular misconception is that the evolving cult of privacy and domesticity did not blossom until the appearance of the semi-detached and detached house, each with its own garden. The terrace house – as a single family house – was by no means inimical to the germination of the

suburban ethos; it was, in fact, the terrace house and garden which nurtured the evolving suburban spirit to the point where it could develop independently in the suburb.

The town garden was in many ways a precursor to the suburban plot. The eighteenth-century garden introduced the possibilities of privacy and seclusion in a very straightforward manner: the garden was tangible evidence, however small, that the dream of being a townsman living in the country was not just an illusion. A well-kept garden was a measure of economic comfort and success. The garden was the essential ingredient of the single family house: the front garden displayed to the outside world a picture of neatness, propriety and pride of ownership; and the back garden served as the exclusive and unadvertised domain of the private family.

The increasingly ubiquitous development of city houses, each with its own garden, emerged in the third quarter of the eighteenth century. This trend coincided with the promise of a respectable, virtuous and natural lifestyle within easy reach of the metropolis. The proposition became all the more appealing to the middle classes as the well-off found the notion of *rus in urbe* attractive. It is, however, not enough to claim that the aristocratic lead in Nash's Regent's Park terraces, or the upper-middle class's colonization of the Park Villages triggered a latent middle-class nostalgia for the near countryside. In London's developing suburbs the immigrants from the countryside or small rural towns and villages were likely to outnumber the immigrants who fled from London and Westminster. Additionally, the notion of *rus in urbe* had long been incubating in London culture awaiting the appropriate stimulus to awaken; this stimulus arrived in the form of the commercial revolution and its consequences. What is undeniable is that by the early nineteenth century the small garden was integral to both the urban and the new suburban ethos and lifestyle. The garden was just as much an attribute of the city as it was of the country; it was the medium which bridged country and city, public and private, culture and nature.

'Ornamented with leaves and blossoms'
LONDON GARDENS
AND THE DECORATIVE ARTS
1680–1800

London had become the leading centre for conspicuous consumption in England by the mid-eighteenth century. The new materialism took many forms, but included the aspiration that a working life devoted to gaining wealth should have a reward in the form of a rural retreat.

Some privileged citizens were able to enjoy a semi-rural existence in the grounds of their own London homes, and such London gardens could be enjoyed all the year round by using specially designed garden buildings. In the first decade of the eighteenth century, an orangery was built to the designs of Hawksmoor and Vanbrugh at Kensington Palace for Queen Anne; by the 1720s Lord Burlington had built a series of garden buildings in the grounds of his villa at Chiswick and Alexander Pope's friends were invited to view his grotto at Twickenham. In the 1730s Queen Caroline, George II's consort, commissioned from William Kent 'Merlin's Cave' at Kew Gardens, where several decades later Queen Charlotte enjoyed a newly built thatched cottage for picnicking.

Most middle-class London merchants and businessmen only had small yards to their houses. But they could indulge in their fantasies of a future rural existence by decorating their homes with floral designs. Those with higher incomes might create an atmosphere of relaxation with porcelain figures representing country pursuits. Such interior furnishings could be enjoyed in comfort at all times of the year and in all weathers. By the 1720s many households used plants indoors to soften the urban environment.

Londoners and visitors to London became increasingly aware of the pleasure to be gained from enjoying not just their own gardens, however modest they might be, but of visiting public pleasure gardens (bowling greens, skittle alleys and ball courts were attached to many taverns) or even of looking out over the secluded garden of a residential London square.

This new fashion went hand in hand with a philosophical awareness of the merits of 'nature' in contrast to 'artifice' which, according to that arbiter of taste the third Earl of Shaftesbury (1671–1713), was epitomized by the formal garden. Joseph Addison (1672–1719), writing in the *Spectator* in 1712, promoted the pleasures to be derived from 'a confusion of Kitchen and Parterre, Orchard and Flower Garden'. The emphasis lay increasingly on individual specimens rather than the overall effect, although the debate on the relationship between Nature and Art continued throughout the eighteenth century. Thus gardening and the cultivation of

'These beautiful flowers lack nothing but the scent they seem to exhale.' One of a series of furnishing pictures painted by Jean Baptiste Monnoyer for Montagu House, Bloomsbury, in about 1690

plants were seen not just as an indication of social status, but as a reflection of the latest school of philosophy. It was fashionable to take the time to indulge in this growing outdoor leisure activity.

Aristocratic Londoners already had the benefit of gardens in both town and country, and a glance at the gardens of Ralph, Duke of Montagu, early in the century reveals a standard for emulation by the middle classes. At Montagu House, Bloomsbury, the garden covered seven acres and was situated to the north of the house looking towards Hampstead and Highgate. The garden at Montagu House appears to have been a miniature version of Montagu's country seat, Boughton in Northamptonshire, where the Duke spent much time and energy on the landscape, creating in an area of 118 acres, elaborate water gardens and a large 'wilderness'. At Boughton, with the exception of bay trees, the planting was deciduous, for the Duke was mainly in residence during the summer months, whereas at Montagu House the formal planting of yews, hollies, laurels, bays and box was evergreen and could be enjoyed during the winter months as well.

Interior decoration

The green outlook at Montagu House provided a foil for the interior decoration, which included over thirty 'flower and fruit pieces' by Jean Baptiste Monnoyer (1636–99), a painter of Franco-Flemish origin who came to London in about 1687 at the invitation of Ralph Montagu. The flowers in these paintings served as a substitute for flowers in the garden. In the Drawing Room upstairs which looked out over the garden, '1 oring tree by Baptest' reproduced a popular garden plant. This may have been a chimney board inserted into the fireplace during the summer months when a fire was not needed. These decorative 'furnishing pictures' were placed over doors and fireplaces, but despite the height at which they were seen, they were painted with the greatest botanical accuracy. Indeed, Dezallier d'Argenville, whose treatise on the French formal garden was published in 1709, wrote of Baptiste, 'he brings to

everything he paints a freshness and truth so perfect that one is convinced that these beautiful flowers lack nothing but the scent they seem to exhale ... He reproduces every detail, down to the dew which forms on the flowers at the break of day and lives on throughout the day.' They were built up from studies and incorporate flowers which bloomed at different times of the year. Baptiste's work was engraved by John Smith and the prints were highly influential on all aspects of design. In France, as flower painter to Louis XIV, Baptiste had designed flowers and floral borders for the Gobelins and Beauvais tapestry works. Baptiste's work remained a source of inspiration for the decorative arts for many decades.

These painted flower pieces reflect a new fashion which took two forms. On the one hand there was an instinctive response to natural beauty which stressed the purely decorative quality of flowers; on the other there was a desire to reveal the plant's botanical character. The leading flower painters combined both characteristics, but two-dimensional decorative floral patterns which ignore scientific accuracy are found on much oriental export ware and its London-made imitations throughout this period. At the same time Western artists' attempts to illustrate accurately specimens which were then grown inspired the decoration of a wide range of applied arts, including ceramics, embroidery and furniture.

The taste for exotic stylized floral decoration can be seen in the unusual tile panel depicting a vase full of flowers with oriental birds which was probably made in London early in the eighteenth century, and is typical of contemporary chair and settee covers. From the mid-century, porcelain from the London Bow Manufactory was often decorated in an oriental style and naturalistic flower painting was less common.

Botanical specimens grown for the first time in this country prompted new literature which was often illustrated with coloured plates. Many of these books were published in London by subscription and the illustrations were based on drawings by some of the leading flower

Long case clock with floral marquetry, c. 1690. Emigrant Dutch cabinet makers practised the craft of marquetry in other European capitals, London included

painters. *The Flower Garden Display'd* (with twelve plates illustrating *The Twelve Months of Flowers* 1730 and *The Twelve Months of Fruit* 1732) was illustrated with engravings based on drawings by the immigrant Antwerp painter Pieter Casteels (1684–1749), a follower of Baptiste. They were published by Robert Furber, who from 1700 ran a fashionable nursery at Kensington Gore. *The Flower Garden Display'd* illustrated (see page 131) 'Four hundred Curious Representations of the most Beautiful Flowers; regularly dispos'd in the respective months of their Blossom', and was described as, 'very useful not only for the Curious in Gardening, but the Prints likewise for Painters, Carvers, Japaners etc also for the Ladies, as Patterns for Working and Painting in Water-Colours; or Furniture for the Closet'. The London Society of Gardeners' 1730 catalogue and John Martyn's *Historia Plantarum Rariorum* (1728–32) incorporate plates based on drawings by Jacob van Huysum, the younger brother of the more famous Dutch flower painter Jan van Huysum (1682–1749). The latter volume includes some of the exotic new Central American plants in the Chelsea Physic Garden in London. Jacob, who imitated his brother, spent the last twenty years of his life working in England and died in London. According to the antiquary George Vertue, he lived with 'A Mr Lockyears at the South Sea House'. His landlord had '6 curious paintings of fruit & flowers painted in Holland by Jan Van Huisen' and Jacob 'Has painted some pictures in the same Manner that comes very near the perfection of his Brother Jans'. Jan van Huysum's paintings are remarkable for their technical virtuosity and are executed in the Dutch tradition of still life, not, as in the case of Baptiste, as furnishing pictures for an interior decorative scheme. In 1730 Jacob van Huysum copied the Baptistes in Montagu House to furnish Sir Robert Walpole's new country seat, Houghton in Norfolk.

The finest marquetry furniture from the late seventeenth century is usually decorated with flowers. The leading exponent was the Dutch cabinet maker Jan van Mekeren (1658–1733), who was based in Amsterdam. However, emigrant Dutch cabinet makers practised their craft in other European capitals, and London was fortunate to attract Cornelius Gole, son of Pierre Gole (1620–84), distinguished cabinet maker to Louis XIV. In 1691 Gole supplied Queen Mary with 'a large table of Marketree the sides drawer & supports carved with ornaments & flowers & finely lackred also a pair of stands carved and lackred suitable for her Majtys service at Whitehall' for £20. Marquetry of a similarly high quality can be seen on the cases of long-case clocks and even on the fingerboards and tail-pieces of the finest viols by Barak Norman of the 1690s.

There is tantalizingly little information on flower arrangements in interiors, although artificial flowers were certainly used. The 1688 inventory at Burghley records 37 bunches of

Below left: Panel of sixty-six tin-glazed tiles decorated with a vase of stylized exotic flowers and birds in imitation of oriental export-ware, probably made in London, early eighteenth century

Below: Silver roses and poppies from thirty-seven bunches of silver flowers which were used as table decoration at Burghley in the late seventeenth century. These are in a later ormolu vase

silver flowers which were used as table decoration. Some of these survive in a pair of later eighteenth-century ormolu vases and are recognizable as roses and poppies. It is thought that the silver flowers were acquired by John, fifth Earl of Exeter, in Italy. The flower paintings of Jacob van Huysum, Jean Baptiste Monnoyer and Pieter Casteels are certainly more elaborate

Right: Tapestry woven with a vase of flowers in a floral border from the workshop of Joshua Morris, Soho, during the 1720s. The design is inspired by the paintings of Baptiste

and contrived than contemporary flower arrangements would have been but they are a reflection of the increasing interest in naturalism derived from Dutch traditions of still life.

This trend can be seen in contemporary furniture and tapestry. Indeed Baptiste himself painted flowers on mirrors and decorated one for Queen Mary II at Kensington Palace, 'her Majesty sitting by him almost all the while'. A mirror answering to this description, although only traces of painting are visible, can be seen at Cotehele, Cornwall. Floral arrangements lent themselves easily to reproduction on tapestry; indeed, a lack of highly skilled workers in this field in London probably led to the increased production of floral work which was less demanding to execute than 'history pieces'. The main supplier during the 1720s was Joshua Morris (fl. 1700–28) who advertised an auction in November 1726 at his house in Frith Street, Soho. A series of arabesque tapestries which may have been designed by Andien de Clermont (described as 'a disciple of Mr Baptiest') and were executed by Morris can be seen at Hagley Hall, Worcestershire; Grimsthorpe Castle, Lincolnshire; and Drayton House, Northamptonshire. They incorporate exotic birds and vases of flowers which were probably inspired by the paintings of Baptiste and subsequent engravings. A chair cover in the same style was probably part of a suite of furniture intended to accompany wall hangings of this series.

In furniture and woodwork the influence of plant motifs was to be seen in decorative carving throughout the period. Grinling Gibbons (1648–1721) is associated with the finest naturalistic carving from 1680 to 1720, but the tradition of using such forms as decoration was continued and can be found in marble and wooden chimneypieces of the mid-eighteenth century. The carver's and gilder's workshop had more opportunity to use such motifs. The astonishing suite of giltwood rococo furniture supplied by James Pascall, a carver and gilder of Hanover Street, Long Acre, for the Long Gallery at Temple Newsam House, Leeds, in 1746, incorporates garlanded bullrush fronds in the girandoles, which would have looked particularly effective by the light of the six candles which they each support. By the 1770s, vases of flowers in naturalistic vein were used as decoration in marquetry on commodes by John Cobb (d. 1778). In 1772 Cobb supplied 'an extra neat inlaid commode' and a pair of vase stands with similar decoration to Paul Methuen at Corsham Court.

Another aspect of the influence of gardening on furniture design can be seen in some of the rare contemporary pattern books and manuals, which illustrate garden furniture in the rustic style and became fashionable during the 1750s, although very few documented examples of such furniture survive. In *The Cabinet and Chair-Makers Real Friend and Companion* Robert Manwaring illustrated chairs 'executed with the Limbs of Yew, or Apple Trees, as Nature produces them ... ornamented with leaves and blossoms, which if properly painted will appear like nature'. Although the engravings are rather crude, Manwaring asserts that 'he has either executed the designs himself or seen them completely finished by others'. *A New Book of Chinese Designs* by Edwards and Darly, published in 1754, includes etchings of four chairs and a table which are created out of contorted tree roots. By the end of the century an anonymous publication, *Ideas for Rustic Furniture*, which was printed for I. & J. Taylor at the Architectural Library, Holborn, devoted twenty-five illustrations to chairs, stools, settees, tables, basin stands and looking glasses, which, neo-classical in shape, display a rustic surface.

The designs and style of the Adam brothers incorporated naturalistic features where appropriate, although their artistic vocabulary was dominated by classically inspired ornament. A pair of side tables of satinwood made in about 1780 in the Adam style are decorated on the top and frieze with garlands of flowers. They may have been placed as pier tables between the windows, or simply against the walls.

The apogee of naturalism in the decorative arts can be seen at Osterley where Robert Adam provided designs for the interior decoration for the banker Robert Child from 1766.

Rustic chair based on designs for Robert Manwaring in 'Rural Chairs for Summer Houses', 1765, which included chairs executed 'with the Limbs of Yew, or Apple Trees, as Nature produces them'

The State Bed which was designed in 1775–6 was conceived as a Temple of Venus with hangings of green velvet embroidered with flowers in coloured silks. The valances are embroidered in gilt thread with poppy heads, an emblem of sleep, and the domed canopy is garlanded with silk flowers (recently replaced). In 1778, Horace Walpole complained that the bed was 'too like a modern head-dress, for round the outside of the dome are festoons of artificial flowers'. By the late eighteenth century artificial flowers were quite common.

At Osterley the Antechamber or Tapestry

Room is dominated by a set of Gobelins tapestries which were specially ordered from Paris for the room in 1772 and delivered in 1776. They portray scenes of the Elements as personified by the Loves of the Gods from designs by François Boucher and are ornamented with flowers designed by Maurice Jacques and Louis Tessier. In addition, the tapestry chair and sofa backs represent the seasons, using scenes from Boucher's *Les Amours Pastorales*, and their seats are strewn with flowers. The carpet was woven to the designs of Robert Adam by Thomas Moore of Moorfields, and incorporates four great baskets of flowers and fruit. The pier glass is surmounted by a vase of flowers, flanked by female figures and putti supporting further garlands of flowers. The pink foliage on the claret ground of the tapestries creates the effect of a bower, ornamented for a festival with garlands and vases of flowers, in which birds and animals appear together with trophies of sport and love. Here the interest in naturalism is combined with the idyll of rural retreat for intimate home consumption.

Costume and textiles

During the late sixteenth and early seventeenth centuries, flowers and plants were used as decorative devices in English domestic embroidery and on articles of dress. The early eighteenth century saw a revival of the use of isolated floral motifs, often based on earlier sources such as Gerard's *Herball* (1597); Crispin de Passe's *Hortus Floridus* (1614); and Parkinson's *Paradisi in Sole Paradisus Terrestris* (1629). Some sources were pattern books deliberately aimed at the amateur embroiderer. Shorleker's *A Schole-House for the Needle* (1632) includes single flowers, small clumps, pots of flowers and insects, flies, dragon-flies, bees and worms which bring the idea of the garden to life. The tradition of amateur embroidery continued, but by the mid-century it was fashionable to represent sprays or groups of flowers rather than single specimens. An apron which belonged to Rachel Paine was embroidered with auriculas and roses combined with semi-naturalistic forms and probably dates from the late 1730s. A

most remarkable embroiderer of the eighteenth century was Mrs Delany (1700–88). Lady Llanover, Mrs Delany's great-great-niece who edited her correspondence, described the petticoat of Mrs Delany's court dress which she had worked in about 1750 as

> covered with sprays of natural flowers, in different positions, including the bugloss, auriculas, honeysuckle, wild roses, lilies of the valley, yellow and white jessamine, interspersed with small single flowers. The border at the bottom being entirely composed of large flowers in the manner in which they grow, both garden and wild flowers being intermingled where the form, proportions and foliage rendered it desirable for the effect of the whole.

The embroidery was based on her drawings of flowers, many of which were grown in her own garden, Delville, near Dublin.

Amateur embroiderers were able to purchase canvases marked out with a design by a professional, and sold with hanks of wool. They could then be worked in the home. A floral carpet at Hatfield which has been described as 'the finest example of English eighteenth-century wool embroidery in existence' is associated with Anne, Dowager Countess of Salisbury, and was probably executed in the 1740s. The design would have been provided by a professional 'pattern drawer', probably in London. It consists of a riot of naturalistic flowers and leaves on a dark blue ground including chrysanthemums, peonies, tiger lilies and bluebells. The composition is held together by a central poppy flower with radiating leaves. It is framed by a border of naturalistic flowers on a pink ground.

Contemporary designs for silk dress fabrics betray the same renewed interest in natural history. Many of the London designers were closely involved with this increasingly popular hobby. James Leman, who lived in Steward

Street, Spitalfields, had his own small collection of natural history specimens, although the designs he produced in the second decade of the eighteenth century show no special feeling for natural form, for this was not yet the high fashion it was to become. Another silk designer, Joseph Dandridge (1665–1747), built up a collection which reflected his interests as an ornithologist, entomologist and botanist. Dandridge went on botanical excursions to Highgate Woods with his distinguished scientist friends, and he wrote treatises on spiders and caterpillars. Surprisingly his designs are the least naturalistic.

Over one thousand designs for silk by Anna

Right: '*The finest example of eighteenth-century embroidery in existence*'

Below: *The Tapestry Room, Osterley, which creates a rural bower effect and brings the garden inside*

Below right: *Apron embroidered with auriculas, convolvulus, honeysuckle and roses, c. 1736*

Maria Garthwaite (1690–1763) survive. The daughter of a Lincolnshire parson, she settled in Spitalfields in 1730. From the early 1740s, her designs reveal an increasing interest in botany and incorporate specimens of holly, aloe, pinks, strawberries, heartsease, auriculas, honeysuckle, daisies and convolvulus. Unlike Dandridge and Leman, little is known of Garthwaite's interests, but Natalie Rothstein has suggested that she may have seen some of the rarer specimens that she includes in her work in a London garden, such as that at Mill Hill belonging to Peter Collinson, a merchant trading to America with his brother

James, who was also a celebrated botanist.

Garthwaite's style is closest to that of G. D. Ehret (1708–70) the German botanical artist who settled in England in the mid-1730s. Ehret worked with Phillip Miller, Keeper of the Chelsea Physic Garden from 1722 to 1771, on the 1755–60 edition of *The Gardener's Dictionary* which had 300 plates. He was elected a Fellow of the Royal Society in 1757 and regarded the illustration of new specimens as his most important work. His own publication *Plantae et Papiliones Rariores* appeared between 1748 and 1759.

It is not known whether Garthwaite knew

Ehret or ever saw his work, but it is curious that she was incorporating aloes into her designs shortly after the Royal Society had acquired Ehret's drawings of aloes, and her enthusiasm for auriculas coincides with Ehret's studies of that plant in 1742–3. Her designs of the early 1740s incorporate a wide variety of naturalistically rendered flowers; in the later part of the

Detail from the petticoat of a court dress embroidered in about 1750 by Mrs Delany with both cultivated and wild flowers. The lower edge consists of a garden border

Opposite: *Palampore of painted and dyed cotton made for the English market on the Coromandel coast (India) during the 1730s. The floral motifs are taken from Robert Furber's* The Twelve Months of Flowers. *Furber ran a fashionable nursery at Kensington Gore*

chintz bedcover, of painted and dyed cotton made for the English market on the Coromandel coast during the 1730s is decorated with bouquets tied with ribbons in each corner and a central flower arrangement derived from the colour plates for March, April, June, July and August in Furber's *Twelve Months of Flowers.* The designs from the original source have been

decade her work was characterized by a preference for carnations and roses. The resulting silks are regarded as some of the highest achievements of the English silk industry.

Even at the time, Garthwaite's contemporary William Hogarth had favoured copying objects from nature for use in designs for silks and linens. A dress of brocaded silk dateable to 1744–5 is close to Garthwaite's designs in the way in which it combines flower motifs with the serpentine 'Line of Beauty' as advocated later in Hogarth's 'Analysis of Beauty', 1753. This freshness of design contributed to the success of London silks abroad, particularly in the colonies. Sometimes textiles were produced abroad to London designs. A palampore, or

somewhat adjusted, probably by a western hand, to suit the format of the textile.

Likewise, the production of accessories was influenced by the fashion for naturalism, as a paper fan of about 1750, hand-painted with a honeysuckle pattern, reveals. Watch-cases, brooches and enamelled trinkets betrayed the same taste. Amazingly the recurrent tulips, honeysuckle and convolvulus flowers give the impression of having been painted from real flowers rather than from commercial copybooks. An astonishing nest of porcelain toilet boxes painted with roses and convolvulus was produced by the Chelsea Porcelain Manufactory in the later 1760s.

Joseph Talwin, one of the owners of the

textile printworks at Bromley Hall, Middlesex, was one of three hundred subscribers to William Curtis's *Flora Londiniensis* and the illustrations were used as a source by his designers. The *Flora* aimed to cover plants growing wild within ten miles of London and recorded that 'many plants which formerly grew plentifully around us' were now rare as a result of the 'rage

for building ... in the environs of London'. It was published in 72 parts between 1775 and 1798. Two designs dating from the early 1780s combine cultivated flowers, passion flowers and irises, with clusters of berries and grasses. The illustrations were based on drawings by William Kilburn who had previously worked as a designer for other London calico printers.

China and porcelain

The fashion pervaded quality household goods. The proprietors of the Chelsea Porcelain Manufactory advertised in the *Dublin Journal* in July 1758 a forthcoming auction of 'a very fine tureen, in Curious Plants, with Table Plates, Soup Plates, and Desart Plates enamelled from

Sir Hans Sloan's plants'. This notice describes a series of plates which have long been associated with Sloane and the Chelsea Physic Garden. It has been suggested that the decorators at the Chelsea Porcelain Manufactory worked from specimens obtained directly from the Physic Garden, but the decoration of these Chelsea plates was in fact based on illustrations by G. D. Ehret, both those for *Plantae et Papiliones*, published by Ehret himself in 1748–58, and the first sixty plates of the 1755–60 edition of *The Gardener's Dictionary*. They date mainly from the 'Red Anchor' period of the 1750s and often have a wavy rim edged with brown enamel. The plates are decorated with a variety of specimens including acacia, acanthus, bocconia and convolvulus; some however are decorated with a botanical fantasy, giving a false impression of scientific accuracy which would probably deceive all but the best informed. Recent research has shown that very few of the insects on Chelsea plates are accurately represented. The tureen mentioned in the Dublin advertisement was probably one of a series of tureens and covered containers which were modelled on fruit and plant forms including melons and apples.

Other Chelsea productions included custard cups modelled as baskets with lids formed of piled fruit. Finials on porcelain and silver vessels often took plant form – artichokes and pineapples were particularly common. A design for a tureen and cover signed by Nicholas Sprimont, the proprietor of the Chelsea Porcelain Manufactory, incorporates an artichoke as the centre of the cover. A caudle cup and cover produced by the Bow Manufactory in the early 1760s is moulded in the form of a pineapple. However, the use of particular plant forms was sometimes inspired by Continental porcelain, such as Meissen or Sèvres, rather than as a direct influence from the developing interest in horticulture in this country.

The Chelsea Porcelain Manufactory also produced a wide range of ornamental figures initially for inclusion in a table setting, and to be seen from all sides. Later figures were made to be displayed against a wall or on a mantelpiece.

Often these figures or groups of figures were set against 'bocage' work embellished with elaborate flowers which are not botanically convincing, but as a luxurious addition to the furnishings they evoke the new spirit of leisure and the deep-seated urban desire for rural retreat. The figures in the bocage groups of *The Dancing Lesson* and *The Music Lesson* are shown seated in rural bliss. They probably date from the 'Gold Anchor' period of the early 1760s.

In the same vein the Bow Manufactory produced tubs of realistically modelled flowers dec-orated in bright enamel colours and sheaves of flowers sometimes made in a 'flatback' way for display on a mantelpiece. An astonishing table clock with the case in the form of a bunch of re-alistically coloured flowers, with the clock face set in a central sunflower, was made at Chelsea in about 1761. Sometimes the garden effect was heightened by using a basket-moulded surface as in the lobed oval dish made at Bow which is decorated in the reserves with naturalistic flowers and insects.

Botanical illustration was used as a source for

Right: '*The Dancing Lesson*', *Chelsea porcelain, early 1760s. The figures in their flowery dress surrounded by flowers and fruit evoke the new spirit of leisure and the urban desire for rural retreat*

Opposite right: *Sheaf of Flowers, Bow porcelain, 1760–5 made with a flat back to adorn a mantelpiece. The Bow Manufactory specialized in the production of baskets, tubs and sheaves of flowers*

Opposite top: *This Derby porcelain ice pail (c. 1795), is decorated with 'Cistus' and 'China Rose Hibiscus' inspired by illustrations in the* Botanical Magazine, *published by the London botanist William Curtis in 1787*

Opposite bottom: *Iris from William Curtis's* Flora Londiniensis, *1775–98, which illustrated plants growing wild in the London area. Found in marshy meadows, by the sides of rivers and ponds, the iris flowered in July*

decoration on porcelain produced later in the century at the Derby Manufactory. Records show that plates from the *Botanical Magazine* which was first published in London in 1787 by William Curtis were copied in the factory in 1792. Specimens for illustration in the magazine were provided from a botanic garden in Lambeth which Curtis opened to subscribers in 1783. A yellow ground ice pail of about 1795 is decorated with named botanical specimens taken from engravings in the *Botanical Magazine*; these are 'Strawberry Blite', 'Virginia Ling-

wort', 'Beautiful Cistus' and 'China Rose Hibiscus'.

The influence of the new philosophy and interest in horticulture made itself felt on many aspects of the decorative arts produced in London. Sources of inspiration ranged from native wild flowers to newly imported botanical specimens. It is significant that through London's overseas trade, this fashion affected taste and manufacture as far afield as the American colonies and the Indian sub-continent.

The Victorian Period

The two most enduring hallmarks of Victorian gardening have remained little known. They are the parks created for the people which were a great source of inspiration to their visitors; and the sudden availability of plants and gardening materials to a much wider public than in previous times.

As a result of these two factors, domestic gardens became increasingly prominent in people's lives – as is demonstrated by the works of the artists discussed in 'A Picture Gallery'.

Opposite: *A view of the Palm House at Kew, designed by Decimus Burton and Richard Turner, built in 1844–48 in a functional style intended to suggest neither classical nor Gothic influence. The parterres and lake surrounding the Palm House were designed by William Andrews Nesfield*

'Charming vistas'
VICTORIAN PARKS

Cyclists at Alexandra Palace. Within a decade, reported Colonel Sexby, the Parks Superintendent for the London County Council, 'cycling has become part of the national life', and Battersea Park in particular played host to the craze

Opposite: *These three views by Joseph Maccoby illustrate features of Victoria Park – most notably the Victoria Fountain, designed in a muscular Gothic style by H. A. Darbishire, and presented by Lady Burdett-Coutts in 1862*

During the two decades following the end of the Napoleonic wars, London experienced a building boom. It removed from public use many areas of open space that had formerly been available to the inhabitants, and by the early 1830s it was threatening to usurp Hampstead Heath. Especially from the point of view of foreign visitors, Lon-don boasted an astonishing degree of public open space, in the form of the central royal parks, where there had long been a tradition of public access for walking and – in Hyde Park – for riding; but the less fashionable areas of the metropolis were beginning to acquire their reputation for overcrowding and insalubrity. In 1833 a Select Committee on Public Walks was

convened, and reported a substantial loss of open space in London, the effect of which had been to 'shut out the humbler classes from being able to take...healthy exercise'; it recommended the provision of open spaces which would provide an alternative to 'drinking houses, dog fights and boxing matches'.

In 1822, John Claudius Loudon wrote that 'Till lately, Hyde Park, at London, and a spot called The Meadows, near Edinburgh, were the only equestrian gardens in Britain; and neither were well arranged.' The new factor was the laying out of Regent's Park, a project not completed until the 1820s. John Nash's original design for this park was not fully carried out. He had envisaged the Prince Regent's house occupying an inner circle, from which a grand avenue led to the periphery of the park, intersecting a broad walk and parallel canal. By the time works got under way, the Prince Regent had become King, and had taken over Buckingham House as his residence; so the inner circle, its carriage drive and the broad walk emerged as design features without a house defining an axis and unifying the scheme. The Regent's Park was in part financed by the sale of a ring of new villas which enclosed it, and for whose residents it was to serve as an amenity; it was not until the 1840s that the park was fully opened to the public.

Victoria Park

The Select Committee of 1833 placed special emphasis on the crowded East End of London, where 'there is not a single place reserved as a Park or Public Walk; yet there is no place in London where such Improvements are more imperatively called for'. James Pennethorne, in a report to the Office of Woods and Forests in 1841, cited evidence that epidemics tended to arise in the congested districts of east London and then travel to the West End, and the Sanitary Reports issued by Edwin Chadwick confirmed the East End as a source of disease for the capital. Partly because of these sanitary arguments, partly as a means of dissipating potential social unrest in the days of the Chartist agitation, but largely because the campaign was led, for whatever motives, by prominent MPs of both parties, two Acts were passed, in June 1841 and May 1842, without debate in Parliament, to enable the Commissioners of Woods and Forests to create a royal park in the east of London. As with Regent's Park, great attention was paid to the development of profitable villas overlooking the park, and a portion of its land was reserved for future building.

The design of Victoria Park, for which James Pennethorne, a protégé of John Nash's, was largely responsible, was a haphazard affair and at first the phrase 'open space' would have been a sufficient description of its qualities. In 1845 Samuel Curtis was appointed as superintendent for the park, and, probably as a result of his

prompting, the plans began to show a proposed lake, filling an area of ground already excavated for brickworks, with islands created by depositing the excavated earth; in 1847 a Chinese summer-house was acquired and placed on the larger island. At the time of the park's opening, however, the dominant impression was one of muddle and underachievement; John Lindley, the botanist, attacked the result in his magazine, the *Gardeners' Chronicle*:

Forty-four thousand pounds is a large sum to expend on 290 naked acres of land, and under the most unfavourable circumstances, is capable of producing beautiful results. With such a fund the most level surface may be broken into picturesque forms, charming vistas may be produced, water may be lavishly introduced, even in Spitalfields thriving plantations may be rapidly established, and beautiful vegetation may in a few years be made to decorate the scene.

This is what the public expected when Victoria Park was formed . . . Let the reader consider an undulating space of 290 acres, entered by a lodge which can be compared to nothing better than a modern ruin in some Cockney garden . . . Having entered, let him imagine a road bending through the place till it finds its exit at the other side, another unfinished road, overgrown with Grass leading to the left, a few others curving in different directions; unmeaning masses of little miserable trees and shrubs, evidently the sweepings of some neglected nursery ground, and a great piece of water on the right, having in its middle an island looking more like an old naval

A view of the Royal Horticultural Society's garden in Kensington, designed by William Andrews Nesfield and opened in 1861 to great acclaim. In 1888, after a long dispute over the lease, the Society vacated the garden, which is now the site of the Science Museum and Imperial College

Carpet bedding – the use of dwarf foliage plants to create a decorative pattern – in the garden at Cleveland House, near Balham, as illustrated in the Gardeners' Chronicle *in 1876. Mr Ralli, the proprietor, opened his garden to the public in the summer when the carpet beds were on display*

cocked hat than anything we can call to mind, and he will have as good an idea of Victoria Park as we have the skill to convey.

Battersea Park

Victoria Park was only part of the Commissioners' grand plan for London, however. Pennethorne envisaged a series of three new parks: Victoria in the east, Albert in the north, and Battersea in the south. An Act was passed in 1846 to allow for the creation of another new royal park in Battersea Fields, and its creation dragged on through the 1850s, with Pennethorne being assisted this time by John Gibson, a protégé of Joseph Paxton's. A more resolute design was selected early on, centred around a grand avenue which bisected the site; at the eastern end were a lake and islands, which in the 1870s were further ornamented by the creation of rockworks, erected in part to hide the view of Clapham Junction. The rockworks were made by the firm of James Pulham and Son, using their characteristic 'Pulhamite' method: masses of brick and clinker were gathered together, a Portland cement mixture poured over them, and the wet cement fashioned into the appearance of boulders, arranged with geological accuracy to suggest a sandstone fault. ('The rocks represent a mountain-side, as if it had been rent asunder by some volcanic eruption, and the water meanders between the rugged walls into the lake below', wrote Col. Sexby in 1898.) The Battersea rock-

A view of the Crystal Palace, Sydenham Hill, painted in 1854, somewhat in anticipation of the completed scene, for the fountains were not turned on until 1856. In the foreground is the lake with Waterhouse Hawkins's models of prehistoric animals; note the great formal axis bisecting the slope

work quickly became the most famous rockery in a public park in the country, although the Pulham firm carried out another London commission in the 1890s – the 'rocks' in the eastern end of the lake in St James's Park. Battersea also became renowned, in the late 1860s, for John Gibson's 'subtropical garden' – an area in which he experimented with bedding out tender foliage plants during the summer months; his experiments were soon followed in other parks,

Botanic gardens

and the Dell in Hyde Park came to rival Battersea for its display of large and ornamental leaves.

The *Gardeners' Chronicle*, looking back in 1866, recalled that 'the London parks were large prairies, fairly wooded, and pleasant enough at all seasons of the year. They are pleasant still, but a little artistic landscape gardening has given them a new character without robbing them of one of their old charms.' 'Artistic landscape gardening', in this context, meant flower gardening; and flower gardening in London was, until the end of the 1850s, a feature not of the royal or municipal parks but of public gardens run by private societies or commercial firms. In 1843, the royal gardens at Kew, having undergone a period of decline, were reorganized as the Royal Botanic Gardens, with a new Palm

House, the area around which was laid out as a geometric garden by the landscape gardener William Andrews Nesfield. The Horticultural Society of London had, from 1821, a garden at Chiswick, on ground leased from the Duke of Devonshire, where during the 1830s the modern flower show developed; but the Society soon faced rivalry from public gardens closer to central London: from 1840, the garden of the Royal Botanic Society, in the inner circle of Regent's Park, and from 1854 the Crystal Palace, both of which staged flower shows. Under the direction of their President, Prince Albert, the

side, creating 'one great geometrical line'; terraces to the sides sported canals, fountains and arbours. No such grand formal scheme had been seen in London since the seventeenth century. Around the periphery of the park lay stretches of lawn, or 'English landscape', with novel educational features such as a model Derbyshire coal mine and a series of lakes and islands boasting models of prehistoric animals, cast by Waterhouse Hawkins under the direction of the biologist Sir Richard Owen.

Crystal Palace Park was not yet a municipal park; one had to pay an entrance fee. But the

During the last third of the nineteenth century, conservatories multiplied in municipal parks as a means of providing displays of exotic plants; most of them, such as this one in Finsbury Park, have been demolished during the course of the twentieth century

(now Royal) Horticultural Society opened a new garden in South Kensington in 1861, designed by Nesfield, and which survived until 1888 on the site between the Albert Hall and the Natural History Museum.

Crystal Palace Park

Crystal Palace Park was by far the most influential of these gardens on the subsequent developments in the parks. Joseph Paxton's original Crystal Palace, built to house the Great Exhibition of 1851 in Hyde Park, had been dismantled; but Paxton had founded a company to re-erect it on a suitable site, and one was found on Sydenham Hill. A bigger and better Palace was erected, and from its terrace a series of steps and cascades descended the hill-

idea of providing a floral display in a park, so that 'the working classes could see a display of summer flowers without going to Kew', was now in currency, and it was put into practice by two successive Commissioners of Woods and Forests, Lord John Manners and William Cowper-Temple. The first expression of this tendency was the appearance of beds, containing more than 30,000 bedding plants, along the eastern end of Hyde Park in 1859. The idea of flower gardens in the parks was contested in Parliament by, among others, Paxton, who feared a decline in the fortunes of the Crystal Palace if people could see a flower display for free elsewhere; but the press was largely in favour, the *Gardeners' Chronicle* remarking that 'Flowers are wanted in the people's parks just because the people's houses have no gardens, and nine-tenths of those who frequent the parks have no opportunity of seeing growing flowers anywhere else.' The flowering of the parks continued, and Nesfield was brought in to advise on improvements, notably the extension of the Broad Walk in Regent's Park into a new Italian garden, designed by his son Markham.

During the last quarter of the nineteenth century, municipal parks followed the lead of the large private gardens, and every fashion in ornamental horticulture that could be found on the ducal estates was put on display for the

Active leisure

More active forms of leisure now began to be catered for as well. As early as 1848 a gymnasium was set up by the Commissioners on Primrose Hill, followed soon after by one at Victoria Park. Cricket and archery grounds began to appear. The Royal Horticultural Society provided the example of bandstands at their Kensington garden (designed by Francis Fowke, the architect of the Albert Hall – one of them survives today on Clapham Common), and Victoria Park soon followed; by the Edwardian period most London parks had a

An Edwardian postcard of Ruskin Park, designed for the London County Council by Colonel J. J. Sexby and opened in 1907. The park was created by knocking together the gardens of three villas that had come on the market and were purchased by public subscription

public in the centres of towns. Rock gardening, wild gardening, glasshouse cultivation, changing flower-bed styles, Gibson's sub-tropical gardening and its spin-off, carpet bedding – the use of dwarf foliage plants to create flat panels of intricate patterning – all of these were available in public parks for study and emulation. The function of parks as showcases for currently fashionable styles helped to speed up their adoption in the smaller domestic gardens. Carpet bedding in particular survived in public parks long after it had fallen from favour in private gardens; and in the early twentieth century, three-dimensional displays, in the form of floral clocks or wire-frame constructions like crowns, became a horticultural feature unique to the parks, not emulated in private gardens.

bandstand, the available styles ranging from cast-iron and Italianate to wooden and rustic. Drinking fountains and refreshment kiosks followed during the 1860s, with Regent's Park and Victoria Park in the lead; and during the last third of the century glasshouses also began to proliferate. Most of these have now vanished, but by the Edwardian period Victoria Park had a palm house, Battersea Park a chrysanthemum house, and most large parks a glasshouse of some sort.

McKenzie's parks

Meanwhile, Pennethorne's plans for Albert Park in the north of the metropolis had not come to fruition, but a portion of the intended ground was eventually to open as Finsbury

Park; and this park introduces us to London's next major park designer, Alexander McKenzie. Two of his parks, Finsbury and Southwark, opened the same year (1869); both had lakes, edged with thickly planted shrubberies, as central features. In social terms, both parks mark a change of focus for London: although Finsbury Park, like Victoria Park, had a portion of its area reserved for building purposes, it was no longer seen as being an amenity primarily for its immediate neighbours; it was intended as an amenity for the Finsbury area, quite a distance away. Southwark Park was originally intended to have an area set aside for building, but this

idea had to be abandoned under popular protest; the carriage roads already made for the park were broken up and reduced to paths. McKenzie insisted that the primary purpose of a park was to provide grass for walking upon, and denounced the provision of flower-beds as a waste of money; but successive superintendents made the flower-beds at Finsbury Park one of the most popular features of an extremely well-used park.

The year after Finsbury and Southwark Parks were opened, the Victoria Embankment Gardens, designed by McKenzie with the assistance of Joseph Meston, were opened, and

In contrast to the High Victorian decorative ironwork of the Clapham Common bandstand is the rustic bandstand, adorned with climbing plants; this version in Brockwell Park is no longer extant

promptly led to a public debate over the propriety of informal design in an urban setting. McKenzie had designed the gardens to contrast with the rectilinear character of the surrounding streets, but the architectural press condemned his undulating paths, and the *Building News* complained:

> All attempts at rural landscape-gardening should have been avoided, and the whole attention of the designer directed to urban embellishment. Rural landscape-gardening and urban embellishment are very different things. A central avenue of Plane trees, the only trees which thoroughly withstand the London smoke, terminated at the Charing Cross end by a handsome architectural entrance ... would be infinitely preferable to the meaningless paths, leading from nowhere to no whither, which at present puzzle the public. A central basin of sufficient dimensions, or an architectural mound of masonry or terra-cotta to contain flowers, would be quite enough in the way of floriculture. The ground should be, in fact, treated as an arboretum, not as a parterre.

McKenzie's principal work, however, was none of these, but Alexandra Palace, of which he was made superintendent. Intended as the north London rival to the Crystal Palace, it boasted a great exhibition building – its lower storey encased in a masonry construction as a means of fireproof building, for one wing of the Crystal Palace had already burned down in the 1860s, and Alexandra Palace itself, in its first incarn-

The old walled kitchen garden
of the Brockwell estate was
not demolished when the
estate became a municipal
park in the 1890s, but was
laid out as an old-fashioned
garden, and in the Edwardian
period boasted all the flowers
mentioned in Shakespeare

ation, burned down little more than two weeks after opening. But the treatment of the landscape could not have been more different from that of Paxton's extravaganza; instead of a great formal axis leading from the Palace, McKenzie laid out a carriage drive that swept down the hillside in a long curve, cutting directly across the main vista. McKenzie published proposals for a vast increase in the number of suburban parks, and for the creation of a network of major, tree-lined avenues through London, with Oxford Street and Whitechapel Road among its major thoroughfares.

Concurrent with the creation of the first municipal parks in London was the protracted agitation over the treatment of its best-known open space, Hampstead Heath. In 1831 Sir Thomas Wilson, Lord of the Manor, tried to begin building on the Heath in an attempt to meet the increasing demand for suburban housing, and met strong popular resistance; in 1853, as yet another nearby estate was bought up for building, Charles Robert Cockerell published a plan for turning the Heath into a public park with a grand avenue leading from Primrose Hill, a series of terraces, and the planting of conifers and American trees. In 1858 the Hampstead Vestry applied unsuccessfully to Parliament for power to purchase the Heath as a public park; finally, in 1872, it was taken over by the Board of Works and dedicated to the use of the public for ever. In a similar venture, Epping Forest, after protracted debate, was purchased by the Corporation of the City of London; Alexander McKenzie was made superintendent. Thus a pattern was set for the acquisition of heaths and woods throughout outer London during the latter part of the century.

The London County Council

It had long been apparent that the space for large-scale park development in the central boroughs could be made available only by the acquisition of private estates, and by the 1890s the size of estates coming on to the market was diminishing. That decade saw the arrival of a new trend, toward the conversion of existing gardens with their basic design unaltered, rather than new creation; this was signalled by the takeover of a Regency villa, the Brockwell estate, near Brixton, in 1892; even the kitchen garden, a walled structure at a distance from the house, was retained. The LCC went on to annex private estates to be turned into such

Below: *A view by John Crowther, looking across the churchyard of St Botolph's, Aldersgate, now known as Postman's Park, and showing a more elaborate treatment of a disused burial ground, with shrubberies and sub-tropical planting*

Above: *The exodus of London's population to Hampstead Heath on a summer's day. At the time this was painted, the fight over preserving the Heath was raging: the local inhabitants fought a long series of legal battles between 1831 and 1871 when the Heath was finally saved from building development*

parks as Valentines Park (1899); Springfield Park, Hackney (1902); Ruskin Park, Camberwell (1907) – these last two being formed by knocking several gardens into one; The Rookery, Streatham (1913), to which the adjacent Norwood Grove was added in the mid-1920s; and Danson Park, Bexley (1925). The process continued after the Second World War with the acquisition of Cannizaro Park by Merton Council in 1948.

The LCC's first superintendent of parks was Lieut-Col J. J. Sexby, who described his field of responsibility in his book *The Municipal Parks, Gardens, and Open Spaces of London* (1898). Sexby was responsible for the arrival in the London parks of the arts and crafts style, and of horticultural revivalism: the planting by preference of 'old-fashioned flowers', those that had been popular before the introduction of the nineteenth century's immense range of garden hybrids. When he converted the Brockwell estate into Brockwell Park, he had the old walled kitchen garden planted as a 'Shakespeare garden', containing all the flowers mentioned in Shakespeare's plays – although it also contained a range of modern bedding plants, a fact complained about by Alicia Amherst in her book *London Parks and Gardens* (1907). The walled garden proved surprisingly popular, and Sexby made the provision of formally designed flower gardens with vernacular-style furnishings a feature of the parks he subsequently designed. One

One of the bandstands from the Royal Horticultural Society's garden at Kensington was relocated on Clapham Common after the closure of the garden in 1888. The bandstand was designed by Francis Fowke, architect of the Royal Albert Hall

Right: *In the nineteenth century, the use of Royal parks for fashionable meetings and promenades shifted from St James's Park to Hyde Park. This view near Stanhope Gate well illustrates some of the glamour of Edwardian outings*

of these, in Peckham Rye Park, was called the 'Sexby garden' in his honour. In Ruskin Park, he erected the first pergola in the London parks system; and the façade of one of the houses that had occupied the site was retained, because it sported what was then reckoned to be the largest wisteria in London.

Burial grounds

A further strategy for increasing the proportion of open space was that advanced by the Metropolitan Public Gardens Association, founded in 1880: the clearance of the older, more derelict burial grounds in London for use as public gardens. These were either churchyards and chapel grounds – closed for further burials after the Burial Acts of 1850 and 1852 – or small commercial graveyards which had closed after becoming too full for further burials; but one of the original eight London cemeteries of the 1830s and 1840s, Victoria Park Cemetery, had already filled up, and was cleared to form the present Meath Gardens. Gravestones might be retained somewhere in the grounds if of sufficient interest, but the main procedure was total clearance, refurbishment of paths or creation of new ones, and planting of shrubberies and flower-beds.

Probably the most interesting of the Association's ventures was one which did not reach fruition: the proposal in 1909 to turn the burial ground of the Chapel of the Ascension, Bayswater Road, into a park for women only. The proposal was described in *The Times*: 'We are convinced that it would be a great boon to many women to know of a place where they could walk, sit down, rest and saunter at their ease, under other conditions than obtain either in the streets or in the parks ... This provision would be greatly appreciated by women who hesitate, not without reason, to make use of the free seats in the parks.' The design of the garden would have been more formal than most of the Association's works: 'The garden that we suggest would be essentially a place for rest and ease – not a playground – a garden rich in flowers with shady and with sunny walks, and with broad spaces of lawn between the flower walks.'

Recreation

As the phrase 'not a playground' indicates, the emphasis on active leisure pursuits in parks was increasing, and by the Edwardian period smaller parcels of land were being adapted for use purely as recreation grounds, with little in the way of horticultural display. Some of the sports facilities within public parks coexisted comfortably with ornamental gardening; bowling greens, for example, were usually surrounded by herbaceous borders or dry-wall gardens, but other activities were greedier for simple open space. Football was, by the 1880s,

becoming a respectable sport, in large part because of promotion by church groups, and tracts of flat lawn were required for this purpose. And the Edwardian period also saw the arrival, around the fringes of London, of golf courses, at first operated by private clubs, as with Sundridge Park (from 1902), but appearing under municipal auspices during the interwar years. The golf course provided a model of lawn and trees, unadorned with flowers, that was taken up by later designers, until by the 1960s a writer in the *Gardeners' Chronicle* could recommend the removal of flower-beds from park lawns and their replacement by 'an invigorating sweep of grass': a return to the pre-Victorian 'large prairie, fairly wooded'.

Postscript

After World War I, the pace of park-making slowed, although the provision of recreation grounds continued apace. The most significant new trend was the linear park, the London prototype of the genre being Southfields Park (later King George's Park, Wandsworth), laid out in the early 1920s by Percy Cane: a long glade partially enclosed by trees. In more recent times, the linear park has been enthusiastically promoted as a means of linking different areas by channels of open space; Burgess Park, in Southwark, and the redevelopment of Mile End Park, have both followed this model, partly from policy and partly because of the piecemeal way in which parcels of land have been acquired for them. Mile End Park has been planned as a deliberate contrast to Victoria Park in style: instead of broad expanses of lawn with avenues or clumps of trees as features within them, it is intended to form a series of grassy glades within a well-wooded periphery. The Canal Way Parks project, begun in 1978, is an analogous attempt to create a continuous ribbon of open space running through part of London.

The trend towards encouraging 'active recreation' came to dominate park planning in the post-war years, so that sports facilities have multiplied in parks while the glasshouses, bandstands and flower gardens that remained the

Alexander McKenzie's landscaping of Alexandra Palace is in deliberate contrast to the formal terracing of the Crystal Palace; the grounds slope informally away from the building, and where Paxton would have placed a grand axial avenue, McKenzie's carriage drive sweeps across the main vista

Below: *In the wake of the Disused Burial Grounds Act of 1884, many derelict churchyards were converted into gardens. This example is the south churchyard of St Botolph's, Bishopsgate*

characteristic features of municipal parks into the inter-war years have declined or been destroyed. In recent years, there has been much agitation in the press about 'green deserts', parks that have outlived their usefulness, parks that are out of tune with the demands of the twentieth century; but it has been argued that active recreation is always a minority interest, and that it is the elimination of a focus for 'passive recreation' that has led to a decline in park usage. Current proposals for the rethinking of parks range from the demand by the 'ecological' movement that the emphasis on high maintenance and exotic planting be abandoned in favour of native species planting and the encouragement of wildlife, to Brian Clouston's proposal that parks be commercially farmed for biomass production. An alternative in the case of some parks, however, is recognition as historic landscapes; over sixty of the

municipal and royal parks, squares and cemeteries of London now appear on the Register of Parks and Gardens of Historic Interest compiled by the Historic Buildings and Monuments Commission. Extensive restoration works are being undertaken in Crystal Palace Park, and plans have been announced for Victoria Park. Not everything that is promoted as 'restoration', however, properly deserves that name – as is shown by the treatment of the Pulham rockworks in Battersea Park, vaunted as a 'restoration' by Wandsworth Council; is 'restoration' the proper word when the resulting structure can no longer be recognized as a work by Pulham and Son? The replanting of the historic parks of London in the wake of the great storm of 1987 may help to focus public attention on this issue, and promote a greater interest in the historical value of the London parks.

'Nurseries, seedsmen and market gardeners'
COMMERCIAL HORTICULTURE IN VICTORIAN LONDON

The nineteenth century saw an enormous increase in the number of horticultural establishments in and around London. As the spread, first of suburban villas and then of urban housing, swelled the confines of London, creating large numbers of new gardens, large and small, so the nursery trade expanded also, a multitude of new firms springing up to compete with each other throughout the middle years of the century.

The established giants of the eighteenth century one by one gave way to new firms. The Kensington Nursery, made famous by Robert Furber in the 1730s, had a last period of activity under Richard Forrest, better known as a landscape gardener, from 1835, but closed little

A bird's-eye view of the nursery of Wills and Segar, Onslow Crescent, South Kensington, from one of the firm's catalogues. Palms and ornamental foliage plants, the firm's stock in trade, required protected cultivation: hence the large proportion of the site given over to glasshouses

Opposite: *The Loddiges nursery in Hackney closed in 1852 with a general sale of its stock. The Crystal Palace Company bought its collection of trees and shrubs for planting in Crystal Palace Park, then being laid out*

more than a decade later. The Brompton Nursery – known in its latter years as Gray, Adams and Hogg – closed in 1852. The following year the Exotic Nursery of Knight and Perry in Chelsea was bought up by James Veitch, to achieve new fame under its new ownership. The Fulham Nursery, once Christopher Gray's, was operating as Whitley and Osborn in the 1830s, and being praised by John Claudius Loudon for offering 'the most complete catalogue of hardy trees and shrubs that was ever published in this or in any other country'; it lasted until 1881. The Vineyard Nursery of Lee and Kennedy, in Hammersmith, continued to flourish under the management of Charles Lee into the 1860s and 1870s, but eventually closed in the 1890s, having moved its main offices out to Feltham.

The new nurserymen

By far the most important of the new firms that grew up to fill the niche occupied by the decaying giants was Loddiges. The founder, Conrad

Loddiges, a German immigrant, had leased fifteen acres in Paradise Fields, Hackney, around 1790, and developed a successful nursery. It was his son George, who became a director in 1826, who was responsible for the firm's years of greatness. He developed an arboretum within the grounds, in the form of a walk twisting around the periphery, passing through one category of trees after another – a design concept that was imitated at Chatsworth; more importantly, he adopted the recent innovation of the Wardian case. This was a sealed glass case in which plants could be packed with some soil and water; water could not escape through the close glazing, so a cycle of evaporation and condensation took place throughout the day. Loddiges reported that whereas previously his firm was lucky if one specimen out of twenty imported from abroad arrived safely, it was now a misfortune if one out of twenty was lost. The general adoption of Wardian cases was to make the number of new plants introduced into England during the Victorian period increase beyond any previous expectation.

Loddiges, in addition to their general nursery stock, developed a thriving line in orchids and palms for the new market in conservatory plants, in effect becoming the first of the major specialist nurseries. Throughout the 1820s and 1830s they were promoted by Loudon and issued catalogues that, annoyingly for the botanist, are simply checklists of names without descriptions. This is a problem also with their major publication – for, following the example of William Curtis and his *Botanical Magazine*, they produced a magazine devoted to the

Commelina tuberosa.

depiction of new plants: Loddiges' *Botanical Cabinet*, published in twenty volumes between 1817 and 1833. They were far from the only imitators of Curtis's publishing success. Robert Sweet, an employee of James Colvill's nursery in Chelsea, illustrated plants new to cultivation in a series of books published during the 1820s and 1830s; growers would often send him new plants in the hope of getting them illustrated. (This unofficial commerce was nearly Sweet's downfall: he was tried in 1826 on a charge of receiving stolen plants. He was acquitted, but the charge could have brought the death penalty.)

Edward Beck, a nurseryman at Isleworth who became important in the development of bedding pelargoniums, started a successful magazine, *The Florist*, in 1848; it long survived his death, and under the title of *Florist and Pomologist* ran into the 1880s. E. G. Henderson, of the Pine-Apple Nursery on Edgware Road, published *The Illustrated Bouquet* between 1857 and 1864; this was the last of the colour-plate works associated with London nursery firms, until B. S. Williams's *Orchid Album* in the 1880s.

George Loddiges died in 1846, and the firm thereafter declined; part of this decline could be traced to the increasing air pollution of the surrounding suburbs. The stock of the nursery was sold in 1852 to the Crystal Palace Company and put to use in planting their site in Sydenham. Loddiges's successor as the leading exotic nursery in London was James Veitch, who took over Knight and Perry's site in Chelsea in 1853, having already established a successful business in Exeter. Veitch employed various collectors to collect plants in Asia and the Americas, most notably the Lobb brothers, Charles Maries and John Gould Veitch. They brought seeds of the

A coloured engraving of Commelina tuberosa, *a perennial from Mexico, reproduced from the second volume of* Loddiges' Botanical Cabinet *(1818). This periodical, illustrating plants grown in Loddiges' nursery, ran to twenty volumes between 1817 and 1833*

monkey puzzle into commerce and introduced a wide range of plants: exotic conifers like the wellingtonia, pitcher plants, foliage plants like crotons and dracaenas, *Lilium regale* and many orchids. *Hortus Veitchii*, an immense book published in 1906 to record the firm's achievements, listed 422 plates in Curtis's *Botanical Magazine* based on plants provided by the Veitch nurseries. The first orchid hybrid to be raised in cultivation was grown by the Veitch foreman, John Dominy, in 1856; he and another Veitch employee, John Seden, were among the principal orchid hybridists of the century.

Other large firms employed their own collectors; one of the earliest to do so was Rollissons of Tooting, a firm famous for its hybridization of Cape heaths in the early years of the century, and which developed a prominent line in New Zealand plants towards mid-century; there is a story that the first specimen of *Begonia rex* to arrive in England was found by accident in a box sent back by their collector. Another such firm, William Bull and Sons, with offices on the King's Road, Chelsea, from 1861, helped to popularize orchids by their annual exhibitions; during the 1870s, Bull employed two collectors, Edward Shuttleworth and John Carder, to import orchids from Colombia. (These two later formed their own rival nursery, which was eventually absorbed into the longer-lasting firm of Charlesworth.)

Show houses

An important requirement for the big London nurseries was a glasshouse where their stock of plants could be represented on display. Loddiges had had an important early glasshouse, and had published a pamphlet on the steam heating of glasshouses as part of the *Botanical Cabinet*. At mid-century, the display house of Rollissons of Tooting was 'reckoned at the time the finest show house in the trade'; Andrew Pettigrew later recalled it for the *Gardeners' Magazine*: 'The show house, a very large span-roofed structure with ornamental lantern on the top, was entered by a massive door in the end from the public road. It had a gravel walk all round, with a broad bed in the centre...

planted with choice camellias, rhododendrons, aralias, araucarias, tree ferns, and a great variety of plants from the temperate zones... Passifloras, tacsonias, clematis, and many others hanging down in long festoons from the roof ... and the tall, stately tree ferns spreading out their large fronds in graceful form, produced a sight not to be forgotten.' An important rival was Henderson of Pine-Apple Place on the Edgware Road, whose decorative glasshouse was illustrated in the firm's advertisements; Henderson also maintained a library of 700 volumes for the benefit of his workers. During the 1860s, Bull, Veitch and others began to attract notice for their show houses, the climax of this trend being reached with the two nurseries of Benjamin S. Williams in Holloway, the Victoria and Paradise Nurseries, in the 1870s.

Crystal Palace Company, both of which organized shows; and finally, in the 1860s, the now renamed Royal Horticultural Society began holding shows – including the first competitions in flower arrangement – at its garden in Kensington. Amateurs and professionals competed at these shows, and they formed an important means for the nurseries to display their wares. Nurserymen from outside London found them a good means of promotion for the London market; William Paul of Waltham Cross, one of the most prominent rose growers, held a one-man rose show at Regent's Park in 1874. Similarly, regional shows offered London nurserymen a chance to advertise themselves in the provinces; in the 1870s, the Royal Horticultural Society held a series of shows in major cities (Bath, Birmingham, etc.) which attracted

Flower shows

Next in importance to the show house was the flower show. The old florists' societies, which had arranged competitions for new varieties of carnations, pinks and the like, were dying out by the 1830s, to be replaced by the new local horticultural societies, devoted to a wider range of – largely exotic – plants. The Horticultural Society of London pioneered the modern flower show at its Chiswick garden during the 1830s and 1840s; it was followed by the Royal Botanic Society in Regent's Park, and by the

A view of the camellia house in the Victoria Nursery, one of Benjamin S. Williams's two establishments in Holloway

much attention. The Society's great spring show was held in the Temple Gardens from 1888 to 1911; in 1913 it was transferred to the grounds of the Royal Hospital, Chelsea, a change of venue arranged by the then Treasurer, Sir Harry Veitch, director of the great Chelsea firm.

Horticultural auctions were another means of securing publicity for nurseries. Hermann Herbst, who gave up his position as superintendent of the Rio de Janeiro Botanic Garden for the exciting life of a nurseryman in Richmond,

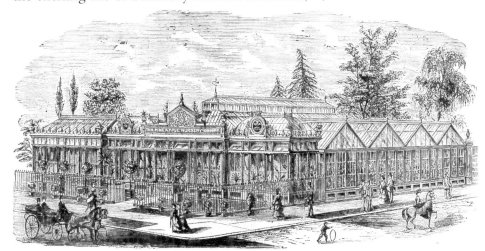

sold 25,000 new and rare plants in 1877, thus attracting great attention for his stock of exotics. The firm that conducted the auction was Protheroe and Morris; Alexander Protheroe and Thomas Morris started their auction house at Highbury around 1830, and by the time their sons took over the business in 1870, they had become the most eminent firm of plant auctioneers in the country. (Alexander Protheroe retired to manage the American Nursery in Leytonstone, which they had acquired in 1840 as a subsidiary enterprise.) In

the latter years of the century, they were particularly famous for their orchid auctions; private estates being broken up, and nurseries closing down, often cleared their stocks of plants through their auction house.

Specialized trades

The increasing domestic use of greenhouses and conservatories, especially after the withdrawal of the taxes on glass and bricks in the 1840s, led a number of nurseries into specialist enterprises. Some nurseries came to be associated with particular fashions in gardening: Barr and Sugden with the vogue for 'sub-tropical plants', i.e. exotic foliage plants used for summer bedding, in the 1860s; Henry Cannell, first of Woolwich and later of Swanley, with that for carpet bedding, i.e. the use of dwarf foliage plants for patterned beds, a decade later; Cutbush of Highgate, originally known for forced bulbs, with the fashion for topiary in the Edwardian period, often importing fully grown specimens (between the wars, a rival was to appear within the London area in the form of John Klinkert's Kew Topiary Nursery).

Some nurseries were noted for their work with particular genera of plants: John Laing, who started his career as the London operative for the Edinburgh firm of Downie, Laird and

Part of an advertisement for Russell's Hotel, showing the upper terrace of Covent Garden Market, built by Charles Fowler in 1827

Below: *Calceolarias reached the peak of their popularity as bedding plants in the 1850s*

Laing, and then took over their Forest Hill site for his own, began hybridizing tuberous begonias in the 1870s; Hermann Herbst of Richmond gave his name to *Iresine herbstii*, an important carpet-bedding plant; John Salter, who had establishments in France and Hammersmith (the 'Versailles Nurseries'), was the major figure in the early Victorian history of the chrysanthemum. The fern craze of the 1860s and 1870s found its leading London nurseryman in Benjamin S. Williams, of the Victoria and Paradise Nurseries in Holloway.

But perhaps the strongest identification of a nurseryman with a category of plant is that of Peter Barr with the daffodil. Barr, a Covent

Garden seedsman, was intrigued by the account of apparently lost daffodil varieties in John Parkinson's *Paradisus Terrestris* of 1629, and, convinced that they must survive somewhere, began a programme of daffodil breeding and collection; in 1884, he was largely responsible for the first Daffodil Conference held by the Royal Horticultural Society, and for the formation of a committee to oversee the naming of new varieties.

Floral decoration, during the 1860s, came to be regarded as a separate discipline from that of the provision of nursery stock. The foremost figure in this business was John Wills, who set up a nursery in Brompton at the end of the 1860s, with subsidiary establishments at Anerley and Fulham, and so was in a position to profit from the sudden vogue for floral decoration that 'came in, if one may say so, with a rush' in 1871, when Sir Edward Scott commissioned the decoration of his house regardless of expense. Wills described some of the subsequent events in an article in the *Journal of the Royal Horticultural Society* in 1893: 'During the following years many and much larger decorations took place, amongst which may be instanced what at the time was called the "hanging gardens of Babylon", on the occasion of a ball given by the Marquis of Bristol, when six tons of cut Ivy alone was used, to give a castellated effect to the bare walls of an improvised ball-room. A few days afterwards one gentleman gave a magnificent entertainment, the flowers for which cost over £500. Various other similarly decorated entertainments followed, the result being that more than £3,000 was paid to one single firm for floral decorations only, in less than one month, and Messrs. Veitch, Turner, Paul, Bull, Lane, and many other great plant-growers were very largely drawn upon, nothing being considered too expensive or too rare. Magnificent Orchids, Roses by the ten thousand in a single day, as well as innumerable Ferns and other decorative plants were used.' Wills himself would buy over a quarter of a million plants in a year for use in decorations. By 1880 the business had become so great that he turned it into a limited liability company under the name of the

General Horticultural Company, but in this guise it was less successful, and eventually reverted to Wills and Segar.

Landscape gardening had long been a service provided by nurserymen in an informal way, but by the 1870s it had begun to be advertised as a special feature of some firms' work. Dick Radclyffe of High Holborn had a practice designing rockeries, but was surpassed in this field by the longer-standing firm of James Pulham and Son of Broxbourne, Hertfordshire, the makers of the celebrated 'Pulhamite' rock gardens, who by the 1870s had opened a branch at Loughborough Junction, near Brixton. Cutbush of Highgate was an example of a firm adding garden design to its skills by the end of the century.

The growth of specialist nurseries was of great horticultural importance, but the greater number of firms remained suppliers of general stock, catering to local buyers. Despite the legends later propagated about the wholesale abandonment of traditional hardy flowers during the heyday of Victorian bedding, and their rediscovery in small cottage gardens by later enthusiasts, a glance at the trade catalogues of the mid-century will show that all the principal genera of older garden plants remained in commerce; as the great gardener Donald Beaton wrote in the *Cottage Gardener* in 1853, 'Go to the seed shops, however, and there you will learn that more than half the people grow annuals, and a great number of perennial plants, from seeds every year; and that the rage for this economy is getting more and more into the fashion every year.'

Seed houses had this advantage over nurseries, that they were less likely to be badly affected by air pollution, which had been noted in the 1850s as a reason for the decline of Loddiges. James Carter set up his seed shop at 237 High Holborn in 1836; William Hurst opened his premises in Leadenhall Street shortly after (eventually moving to Houndsditch in the 1870s). In 1861, Barr and Sugden, probably the most important of the London seed houses from the horticultural point of view, opened in Covent Garden. Watkins and Simpson, founded by Alfred Watkins, a former employee of Hurst and Son, opened in Savoy Street in 1876; by the turn of the century they had premises in Exeter Street, Tavistock Street, and Neal Street, eventually opening their last offices in Drury Lane during World War I.

Barr and Sugden – later Barr and Sons, and during the 1950s absorbed into Wallace and Barr – were the pioneers of a new publishing trend: the illustrated nursery catalogue. Hitherto, nursery publications had been either name lists or expensive colour-illustrated productions for the wealthier market. Peter Barr's first

tial annual volumes employing the latest developments in the technology of illustration. Benjamin S. Williams of Holloway made an attempt to revive the older tradition of the deluxe illustrated periodical; the author of *The Orchid Grower's Manual* which went into seven editions, Williams collaborated with Robert Warner, to whom he had been a gardener at the start of his career, on *The Orchid Album* (1882–97), a work devoted to portraits of orchids in chromolithography. Williams is commemorated by a medal awarded by the Royal Horticultural Society.

An advertisement for the firm of J. Weeks & Co. of Chelsea, manufacturers of glasshouses and heating equipment. The firm erected this conservatory at Hampton Court House in the 1870s; the conservatory also boasted an artificial rockwork by Pulham and Son, which still survives

catalogue of 1862 was illustrated with little woodcuts, and greatly increased the amount of descriptive text devoted to each plant, some of the text being written by the florist H. Honywood Dombrain. The immediate consequence was an attack on 'fat catalogues' in the pages of the *Gardeners' Chronicle* by the great botanist John Lindley, who pounced on botanical errors; but Dombrain's fame survived this episode, and the fashion for woodcut illustration spread throughout the nursery trade, until by the turn of the century, the big seed houses – Carters' among them – were often producing substan-

Market gardening

While the production of ornamental plants was reaching these heights, the production of food crops for the London market was undergoing many changes. In the early nineteenth century the growth of London meant a profitable business for large numbers of market gardeners in the suburban districts, such as Stephen Spooner of Hounslow, one of the first specialist fruit growers in the London area in the 1820s, and William Ronalds of Brentford. By this time, Covent Garden had become the principal market for the London area, and in 1828 Charles

Fowler's covered market building was erected to improve the site. As the London catchment area swelled, rival markets developed to cater for more outlying areas: Spitalfields and Borough markets, established in the eighteenth century, grew and were refurbished during the Victorian period; Brentford market was given a new, expanded site in 1892; Stratford market, catering for the market garden areas in east London and Essex, was established in 1879. The markets, of course, served as a sales point not only for food produce, but for flowers and such special crops as the lavender that was a mainstay of the Mitcham area.

The spread of railways meant that it was possible to send produce to London from greater distances, and gradually the market gardens nearest the conurbation closed down, suffering from the polluted atmosphere, and yielded to suburban building. To some degree the agricultural depression of the 1870s speeded this process, forcing the less profitable firms out of business, and leading to a widespread neglect of orchards – the subject of a series of articles in the *Gardeners' Magazine* in the 1890s on 'The Wasted Orchards of England'. Fruit production tended to become concentrated into the hands of large nurseries in favourable areas – Kent, the Vale of Evesham – and progressively disappeared from the environs of London. Vegetable production continued, especially in the areas around Brentwood and Feltham; the Edwardian period saw a vogue for 'French gardening' – the use of multitudes of cloches and frames to raise vegetables on an intensive scale – which was encouraged on many co-operative farms, and even in an employment scheme by the Borough of Poplar. But the largest trend in market gardening was the replacement of food crops by flower crops in the outer London areas: Feltham and Bedfont, with the examples of the Dean brothers' seed trial grounds and W. Fromow and Son, who moved out from Chiswick in the late nineteenth century, became centres for wallflowers, violets and daffodils. The 1860s and 1870s, in the wake of the boom in glasshouse manufacture, saw the rise of firms which used greenhouse ranges to

ensure more reliable cropping; the Worthing area of Sussex, several areas of Hertfordshire, and, closest to home, the Tottenham and Edmonton districts became centres of glasshouse production before the turn of the century.

This general trend, for growers to be pushed farther and farther out as London expanded, was coming by the end of the century to affect the seed houses and exotic nurseries as well. The big firms like Veitch's had long relied on grounds outside London – in their case at Feltham and Coombe Wood – for the growing of hardy stock in a cleaner environment; and the big seed houses similarly used trial grounds at a distance from the capital. The early years of the twentieth century saw the disappearance from central London districts of the big names in horticulture: James Carter and Co. abandoned their premises in Holborn in 1911, leaving only a couple of shops in central London, and moved their headquarters to a 22-acre site in Raynes Park, which remained in business until the 1960s. Sir Harry Veitch broke up his family business upon his retirement; the seed business was sold to Sutton and Sons of Reading in 1913, and the next year the King's Road premises and the stock of their outlying grounds were sold at auction. Finally came the closure in 1916 of William Bull and Sons, 'the last of the great metropolitan nurseries' according to the *Gardeners' Chronicle*, which gave as one of the reasons for closure 'that the prevalence of London fog prevented the hybrids from attaining to their full development at Chelsea'. As suburban sprawl extended to surround the nurseries of the outer districts, they too gradually had to give way, and the inter-war years saw the progressive disappearance of the remaining nurseries of importance from what would now be called inner London. John Peed and Son, whose initial success in Brixton, catering for the new villas of the area, had forced them to move to larger premises in Norwood, and had been the last of the specialist foliage plant nurseries in London (specializing in caladiums), left the Roupell Park Nurseries in Norwood in the 1930s. The last of the important links with the Victorian past was severed.

The Twentieth Century

London's open space has been preserved by public and private means in the face of ever-increasing odds. In council-built cottage estates influenced by the Garden City movement and in the private speculative housing of Metroland, small individual front and back gardens providing space for domestic activities, creativity and display ensured a lower ratio of houses per acre compared with other European cities. In the post-war era planning legislation further safeguarded the Green Belt, while London's polluted atmosphere was finally tackled by Clean Air Acts. The 1951 Festival of Britain anticipated a brave new world of labour-saving gardens given over to leisure activities, which was gradually realized by means of the consumer revolution. At the same time the appeal of 'old-fashioned' gardens has never been greater, a nostalgia encouraged by the National Trust revival of historic gardens in London.

Opposite: *London Underground's poster extolling the attractions of Golders Green emphasized its semi-rural character at the turn of the century, far removed from the roar of the great Babel*

'To fulfil the need for an affinity with nature'
GARDEN SUBURB,
GREEN BELT AND WINDOWBOX

In 1908, a poster was produced by London Underground extolling the charms of the Northern Line to Golders Green: 'A Place of Delightful Prospects'. The artist portrayed a mock-Tudor semi-detached house surrounded by a beautifully kept garden; it had a neat lawn and flower-beds replete with old-fashioned flowers which were being watered by the owner, while his wife sat in a deckchair and their child on the grass, winding a skein of wool between them. The background to this domestic idyll was formed by a road lined with young trees receding to the underground station in the distance. Beneath the scene there was an extract from William Cowper's poem 'Sanctuary':

'Tis pleasant, through the
    loopholes of retreat,
To peep at such a world; to see
    the stir
Of the great Babel, and not feel
    the crowd;
To hear the roar she sends
    through all her gates,
At a safe distance, when the
    dying sound
Falls a soft murmur on
    th'uninjured ear.

If this advertisement for the Underground might provoke hollow laughter in commuters

attempting to travel by London's notorious 'misery line' today, the dream it encapsulates has proved over the years sufficiently potent to draw millions of people to work in the great Babel, provided that they can escape to well-tended suburbs and the privacy of their own homes every evening and weekend. The history of the twentieth-century London garden can largely be seen as the attempt by public and private means to keep this ideal alive, in the face of ever-increasing odds. The more the capital expanded and the larger the population grew, the greater the need for privacy and the more people clung to remaining patches of green.

The Garden City Movement

The unrestrained growth of London had long been the object of attack. Ruskin and Morris contrasted the ugliness they saw in the modern city with an idealized vision of smaller communities harmoniously in tune with the surrounding landscape. The development in the 1870s of Bedford Park, on the fields between Chiswick and Acton, made some attempt to accommodate these feelings. The *Pictorial World* of 1880 reported that in contrast to other suburbs, 'the pretty houses are dotted among the trees, and even when there is the least approach to a hard line of frontage, there is always some group of greenery to break the ugliness of the

mere thought of a dead level'. Though the layout of the houses was conventional, the old trees that had been planted by Dr John Lindley, curator of the Royal Horticultural Society gardens at Chiswick in the early part of the century, were retained and a selection of different specimens – limes, poplars, willows and fruit trees – planted in the new gardens. The light filtered through the foliage on houses designed in the 'Queen Anne' revival style by E. W. Godwin and Norman Shaw and featuring dormer windows, balconies and verandas; they opened on to gardens filled with traditional flowers – sunflowers, lilies and standard roses – the overall effect of a small country town being further enhanced by the use of white wooden fences.

A more far-reaching attempt to create a better-planned environment was initiated in 1902 when Ebenezer Howard founded the Garden City Movement, which set to work building the first garden city at Letchworth, Hertfordshire. As one of the Movement's principal advocates, A. R. Sennett, rhapsodized in 1905, 'A Garden City! To the summer toilers in our smoke-beshrouded towns, half-suffocated in their narrow stagnant streets ... how refreshing the name!' The concept of a balanced community in harmony with nature lay behind the plans of the reformer Henrietta Barnett for

The gardens of Lord Leverhulme's residence, The Hill, on the edge of Hampstead Heath, were laid out in a series of terraces to facilitate entertaining on the grand scale and to make the most of the extensive views

Hampstead Garden Suburb. Each house was to be surrounded by its own garden; every road was to be planted with trees and care was to be taken that no house should spoil another's view. Planned by Raymond Unwin and with the Central Square incorporating two churches designed by Edwin Lutyens, the Suburb was laid out with greater freedom and variety because of the suspension of the local building regulations when the private Hampstead Garden Suburb Bill was pushed through Parliament in 1906. New features such as culs-de-sac, internal courts and closes could then be introduced, further safeguarding the peace of the houses (built at the unusually low density of eight per acre) – threatened, it was already recognized, by the advent of the motorcar. Mrs Barnett envisaged a social mix and like Unwin appreciated the rhythm and harmony of alternating open and enclosed space, 'the larger gardens of the rich helping to keep the air pure, and the sky view more liberal; the cottage gardens adding that cosy, generous element which ever follows the spade when affectionately and cunningly wielded as a man's recreation'.

The green tranquillity of Hampstead Garden Suburb, despite the efforts made to incorporate condominiums for old people and working women, scarcely impinged upon London's enormous housing problems. Nevertheless, many of the ideas and plans for such private developments were to influence the cottage estates built by London County Council for the masses. The Housing Act of 1900 enabled local authorities to build houses outside their own territory and, significantly, the Fabian tract *Cottage Plans and Commonsense* (1902) by Raymond Unwin and Barry Parker, whose partnership as

Opposite: *A typical long, narrow London back garden in Camden Town is rendered in the post-Impressionist palette of Spencer Gore. It comprises a central formal bed with urns, coal and potting sheds, a cold frame, vestigial rockery and border*

Metroland guides were produced annually between 1915 and 1932 to promote those historic villages to the north-west of London, served by Metropolitan Railways, as Arcadian suburban developments

183

Osbert Lancaster's drawing of the suburban garden demonstrates the degree to which every household could adapt the uniform plot layout to cater for individual tastes and hobbies

architect-planners was already gaining a reputation, was specifically addressed to these bodies. The first London County Council cottage estates, constructed before World War I at Totterdown Fields, Tooting, White Hart Lane, Tottenham, Norbury near Croydon and Old Oak, Hammersmith, gradually assimilated – despite their much higher density – the lessons of Hampstead Garden Suburb, particularly after the passing of the Housing, Town Planning &c. Act in 1909. Unwin's appointment in 1914 as Chief Planning Inspector to the Local Government Board and in 1918 as Chief Architect for Building and Town Planning to the Ministry of Health placed him in a powerful position to influence the direction of post-war housing. While the LCC's vast estates in Lewisham and Becontree lacked the architectural individuality of the pre-war developments, their density was lower and the overall planning guidelines – screening through the use of greens and shrubberies, culs-de-sac and closes, the preservation of trees and other natural features – remained unchanged. It was a condition of the tenancies that the front gardens had to be kept cultivated, except for the hedges which were looked after by the Council. Competitions were organized to encourage cultivation, while windowbox contests were held in the block dwelling estates.

Private gardens

If the majority of Londoners were expected to get on with cultivating their own gardens, a few could afford to commission others to do the work for them. Where space was available on the outskirts of the city, the more spectacular examples of private garden design could be found. The Edwardian age was the last time the rich could afford to build country houses and gardens on any scale, assured of the labour for their upkeep and unhampered by bureaucratic restrictions. Thus the grounds of Lord Leverhulme's residence, The Hill on Hampstead Heath, were laid out in the years before World War I by one of the leading landscape architects of the day, Thomas Mawson, in the grand Italianate style. The formal terraces, covered pergola walks and loggia, curved flights of steps and stone balustrades, urns, statuary and water gardens were poised above the Heath and afforded prospects to the west as far as Harrow and Windsor.

Space restrictions in central London help account for the paucity of work resulting from the famous partnership between Gertrude Jekyll and Edwin Lutyens (not for nothing known as the Surrey School of garden design). Where they can be traced, the gardens were usually attached to houses dating from the late seventeenth or early eighteenth centuries, precisely the period which had inspired Lutyens's own domestic architecture. And the geometry of Lutyens's schemes echoes those of the formal gardens so carefully delineated on Rocque's 1746 map of London and Westminster, urban versions of the 'gardens for small country houses' beloved of Miss Jekyll. In 1895, Lutyens was employed by Lord Wynford to plan the small rear garden and make minor alterations to 12 Grosvenor Square. He produced a centralized design with paved paths leading to a round pond, and two rectangular flower-beds against the end wall. The drawing is inscribed in Miss Jekyll's hand, 'Irises, orange Lilies, Solomon Seal, hardy Lilies'. (The listed 1727 Colen Campbell mansion with Adam interiors was demolished along with the garden by Charles Clore in 1961.) In 1910 Lutyens produced a similar design for Sir Hugh Lane at 100 Cheyne Walk (currently being restored). The following year Miss Jekyll was asked by George Williamson, an expert on portrait miniatures, to design terraces and a sunken garden for Burgh House, a fine free-standing red-brick house in New End Square, Hampstead, dating from 1703. Here the hallmarks of the partnership – contrasting textures of stone and brick in herringbone and millstone patterns – can still be seen on the remaining terrace.

New houses, usually built in the suburbs, afforded more scope. In 1906, Miss Jekyll produced a planting scheme for Caesar's Camp, Wimbledon Common. In 1920, she designed the gardens of Caenwood Towers, Highgate,

for the architect L. Rome Guthrie. Three years later, she worked with Oliver Hill on the gardens for Wilbraham House, D'Oyley Street off Sloane Street, built in the somewhat effete Lutyens-influenced style that was wickedly dubbed by Osbert Lancaster, Vogue Regency. The plans adopted to make the most of the awkward, long, thin garden site could also have been drawn up by Lutyens: a series of terraces, a pool and millstones of York paving edged with tiles leading towards a formal turfed vista.

The lure of open spaces on the outskirts of London was not confined to the wealthy. Speculative builders followed the tracks made by the Underground and the railways into the surrounding countryside; building societies offered cheap mortgages to potential house buyers and the government gave tax relief. The annual guides to Metroland – an invention of the Metropolitan Railways public relations department in 1915 to describe the districts north-west of London in Middlesex, Hertfordshire and Buckinghamshire served by the railway – were full of property advertisements which exploited the rural connotations of hitherto undisturbed towns and villages. Although the new private estates were planned at the low density of twelve houses an acre, each purchaser received very little else for his money. Sometimes the roads had been named and the verges were landscaped; unusually, the builder John Laing gave a fruit tree to every household who bought from his firm. But the majority of owner-occupiers had to make the most of a bare patch of land front and back (with enough space for an as yet unconstructed garage at the side), thinly spread with top-soil to disguise the builders' rubble beneath.

They succeeded brilliantly, displaying in front gardens an imposition of order, flights of imagination and a profusion of colour not otherwise evident in their lives. The crazy paving leading to the front door was bordered by neatly planted flower-beds, perhaps a modest wilderness in the form of a rockery, an ornamental pool enlivened by a dwarf or a stork fishing. At the back was a more private domain devoted to family life. Near the house

was a lawn where the housewife could keep an eye on the children from the kitchen and sit out herself when the weather was fine and enjoy the scent of the roses; farther away and partly screened were the vegetable patch, compost heap and orchard. Of course everyone suffered the major and minor irritants of suburban outdoor life: flecks of bonfire ash on the washing, the neighbours' children's ball crashing through the cold frame, the cat stuck up a tree chasing a bird, chickens slaughtered by an itinerant fox, the regular clatter and wheeze of a thousand lawnmowers on Saturday afternoons, overgrown trees blocking the sun, fruit disappearing overnight, greenfly in the roses, slugs in the Brussels sprouts. . . . But to be able to observe on the way to the station the regular pattern of the seasons – from the flowering Japanese cherries, the lilac and laburnum and chestnut candles to the dusty green of high summer and the crush of autumn leaves in the gutter – added considerably to the pleasures of living in Metroland.

The Green Belt

Before World War I, the radius of London from Charing Cross averaged between six and eight miles; by 1939, it averaged twelve miles. There had long been schemes to limit London's growth for reasons of health and sanitation, recreation and amenity, besides the need to provide the capital with an adequate supply of fresh food from adjacent agricultural land. Now they took on a new urgency. In 1924, the London County Council asked its Town Planning Committee to consider and report on whether a 'Green Belt' round London was desirable or practical, but only after the

STAINES
BY MOTOR BUS
FROM HOUNSLOW
GENERAL

Opposite: *Harry Bush records the hidden world of back gardens in the south-west London suburbs during the inter-war period, the network of fencing and young trees as yet affording little privacy from the eyes and windows of neighbours*

London Underground and Bus posters competed to attract passengers out of the city into the more salubrious suburbs and the Green Belt, as in this example of 1921

establishment of the Greater London Regional Planning Committee in 1927 was further action taken. With Raymond Unwin acting as technical adviser, its first and second reports, issued respectively in 1929 and 1933, drew attention to the shortage of recreational land round London and the increasing pace of its loss. In the second report Unwin went further and proposed the designation of a parkland belt as near continuous as possible. When the Labour party won control of the London County Council in 1934, his proposals gained the enthusiastic support of Herbert Morrison and Richard Coppock; the following year the London County Council Green Belt scheme was launched. In order to reserve a supply of public open space for recreational use round London, it offered neighbouring county councils and boroughs up to half the cost of an approved land acquisition. The re-

sponse was immediate; within fourteen months 28.5 square miles had been acquired in this manner and its future was ensured with the passing of the Green Belt (London and Home Counties) Act in 1938, which prohibited the sale and development of Green Belt land, without the consent of the government and contributing county councils.

These efforts were in sympathy with the spirit of the times. The essentially German tradition of hiking arrived in Britain via America around 1927, and by the 1930s it was all the rage. Posters encouraged Londoners to 'Go Out into the Country' – to the Downs, the Chilterns or farther afield – and out they went, sporting Basque berets, open-neck shirts, shorts and rucksacks. The railways, competing with the buses, ran Hikers' Mystery Expresses from mainline stations and even slowed trains

Hoeing the roof garden on top of Adelaide House, a fine Art Deco office block next to London Bridge. April 1946

Opposite: *Princess Margaret, deputizing for Queen Elizabeth The Queen Mother as Patron of the London Gardens Society, toured gardens in Stoke Newington in July 1953*

specially when proceeding through areas of natural beauty.

The Modern Movement

The importance of open space was also part of the Modern Movement's philosophy of living. In his influential writings on gardens in the modern landscape, which first appeared in the *Architectural Review* in 1938, Christopher Tunnard made the point, 'Our modern buildings are simple statements, but our gardens have a new mission – to fulfil the need for an affinity with Nature . . .'. His enlarged sense of purpose reflected the fact that in the face of the diminishing market for luxury private gardens, designers had turned to the landscape itself for work. In 1929, the newly founded British Association of Garden Architects changed its name to the Institute of Landscape Architects with greater spatial ambitions. Architectural considerations of form, texture and composition were emphasized, providing the structure into which plantsmanship had to fit. Tunnard was full of praise for the functionalism and simplicity to be found in Scandinavia and

the lessons to be learnt from the Orient: the breaking down of barriers between in- and outdoors, the restrained use of colour, subtle asymmetrical layouts, grouping and arrangement to evoke sensory and intellectual pleasures.

But it must be admitted there was little evidence of such a philosophy being put into practice in London before World War II. Undoubtedly, the most progressive 'garden' design was provided in 1934 for the penguins at the Zoo by Lubetkin, Drake and Tecton: an elegant concrete basin with two interlocking arms swirling down from the upper level to the water. Blocks of flats such as those erected by Frederick Gibberd at Pullham Court, Streatham, in 1935 reserved eighty per cent of the site for open space, in return for a flat density of eighty per acre. Highpoint 1 and 2 constructed on North Hill, Highgate, by Lubetkin and Tecton in 1935–8 also provided for a healthy environment with tennis and squash courts and a swimming pool, as well as a stepped series of patio roof gardens over the garages. Converted by a visit to the Stockholm exhibition in 1930,

Oliver Hill started to work in new international style, designing Hill House in Hampstead for Gerald Schlesinger in 1936–8; here the sloping garden was laid out to the design of Tunnard in a series of encircling grass walks between parallel beds of shrubs. More typically British, perhaps, was the use made of the roof garden incorporated into the design for the new Derry and Tom's department store in Kensington. Roof gardens were fashionable features of the Modern Movement, having been advocated and executed by both Frank Lloyd Wright and Le Corbusier. Instead of the integration of man-made forms with nature to be found in Wright's buildings, Ralph Hancock's plans for the store were wholly contrived: a Spanish garden with a Moorish palace, a more intimate Tudor garden and an English 'woodland garden' with running water and a pool which eventually became home for a family of flamingos. From its opening in 1938, the garden's whimsical novelty continued to attract summer visitors well into the 1980s.

'The humblest citizens'

Despite the availability of such escapist fantasies and the arcadian allure of suburbia, it was for most Londoners a struggle to garden in a city whose smoke and smog killed plants by blocking the essential sunlight needed to encourage their growth, choked their pores with soot and slime and turned the soil acid and sour. Efforts were made by the newly formed London Gardens Society to encourage the growing of flowers (especially in areas considered dull and ugly), to provide a 'healthy and civilizing influence' on those who had otherwise little opportunity for self-expression and to give the opportunity to the 'humblest citizen' to perform a civic function by improving his surroundings. Under the patronage of Queen Mary, the Society held competitions and offered prizes for the best-kept garden and so on. In 1938 an astonishing 65,000 entered as competitors, of which 1,611 were judged in the final of the All London Garden Championships. The annual report always contained photographs of the royal tour of inspection, with the

owners standing stiffly to attention beside the Queen, surrounded by blooms. On 10 June 1939 *Picture Post* presented a round-up of this world which was about to be shattered. A caretaker digs his Dockland garden; a woman on Blackfriars Road grows cowslips, dahlias and chrysanthemums on a factory roof; a tram-driver plants his border among the chemical vapours of Canning Town; an unemployed man in Hackney helps children to escape their tarmac environment by teaching them to cultivate plots of flowers; the men from the Inland Revenue in Somerset House stock and tend their neighbourhood garden, the churchyard of St Mary-le-Strand; a solitary old man watches over the tulips growing in his window-box.

Allotments

The War was to see the return of two contrasting forms of horticulture that had long since disappeared from central London. At one extreme, there was the smallholding which combined market gardening with animal husbandry; at the other, there was the totally

fortuitous restoration of the wilderness. The one required intensive care, the other none at all.

Allotments were not new. They had been advocated since the mid-eighteenth century in England as means of providing a living for the poor after the enclosure of common land. But not until 1887 were local authorities empowered to provide land for this purpose, and in 1908 it became their active responsibility to give them to those who asked. During World War I the demand for allotments grew enormously, but the government delayed until December 1916 before granting local authorities the power to take over unoccupied land without the owner's consent. The King played his part by ordering that the royal parks be turned over to cabbages and potatoes. At the start of World War II, the Ministry of Agriculture was better prepared with its 'Dig for Victory' campaign. The Royal Horticultural Society, the Stationery Office and the national newspapers were also ready with guides on how to produce

Above: *Bethnal Green's allotments, here painted by Charles Ginner, were seen to symbolize the will to survive in one of the most heavily bombed parts of London*

Above left: *Derry and Tom's roof garden presents an extraordinary amalgam of horticultural fantasies, the Spanish Garden featuring Moorish pergolas, a Court of Fountains, 'convent walls' and a campanile*

Left: *Adrian Allinson's painting of 1942 shows vegetable-growing in St James's Square, after the Trustees had finally agreed to the removal of the railings to support the war effort. The statue of William III was also removed from its base for safe-keeping*

food from the garden. By 2 October 1939, the *Evening Standard* was able to report that vegetables were being grown in some London squares (Tavistock at least), while the *Evening News* came out with an encouragingly healthy feature headlined, 'Window-box salads. Beans on your bedroom sill. Tomatoes in tubs.'

The Metropolitan Gardens Association had been founded in 1882 to provide open spaces within the metropolitan area, through raising money for the purchase and layout of parks and gardens and encouraging the conversion of disused churchyards and burial grounds into public gardens. The outbreak of war provoked a new sense of mission, chiefly directed towards furthering the cultivation of fruit and vegetables in London. By January 1940, a three-acre site in Wandsworth had been laid out under their auspices, with space for over seventy allotments, and by April this had been augmented by a further six acres. It was decided that prizes would be offered for the best plot. By July, a pig club had been formed and the allotments had proved so bountiful (despite an oil bomb crater ruining some crops) that the Ministry of Information decided to take photographs of the results for publicity purposes.

Occasionally such efforts, particularly during the Phoney War, irresistibly recall Dad's Army. On 11 March 1940, under the heading 'Gun Sites have a "Beauty Treatment" ', the *Evening Standard* reported that Lieut-Col George Urquart Morgan, Commanding Officer, 30th Battalion, Royal Engineers, had instigated an agricultural scheme which would produce 1,800 soldier-gardeners trained not only to grow vegetables but also flowers to beautify the stations. The work would, he thought, provide interest for the men. He only lacked garden tools, seeds and plants, for which he was appealing to the Lord-Lieutenant of Surrey, for circulation to some of the estate and land-owners in the county.

Pigs had become something of a national obsession. The staff of the royal parks asked the permission of their Controller, Lord Tryon, to raise them in Hyde Park, assuring him that they would be secluded from public view.

The 'battle of the railings' provoked many column inches as the Ministry of Works apparently ignored earlier assurances that those of artistic value would be conserved, and smeared the owners who opposed it. The Duke of Bedford's reluctance to sacrifice the railings on his Bloomsbury estate was reported in the *Daily Express* as unwillingness 'to help the war effort'. (Those in Russell and Bloomsbury Squares went, while Bedford Square's were conserved for their 'historical value'.) Predictably, the *Architectural Review* found that the removal of the railings in Berkeley Square (in the teeth of controversy) afforded a new, aesthetically pleasing experience in urban planning.

As soon as the bombs began to fall in earnest, there was a marked change of emphasis in the newspapers: plans for reconstructing London were endlessly debated, harking back to Wren's post-Fire schemes and forward towards building a better world. But the chipper spirit of Londoners could not be crushed or directed solely towards a hypothetical future. The Metropolitan Gardens Association received requests from ARP Wardens' posts and fire-fighting groups for sites near their respective headquarters where they could grow vegetables. By February 1942, Cardinal Hinsley, Archbishop of Westminster, had obliged with some grassland near the Cathedral, which was duly converted into the local wardens' allotment. Later that month the *Daily Mirror* came out with the headline 'Pigging it in Mayfair' and the accompanying report described how the National Fire Service had established a pig farm (and rabbitry) in a basement in that exclusive neighbourhood. The beasts were doing so well that the firemen had started a pedigree stud book. Of all the allotments, the most coverage was given to those in Bethnal Green, laid out on the sites of bombed buildings. Those behind the burnt-out shell of St Jude's Church had been dug out of a bombed school yard, the asphalt having been broken up by pick-axe and removed along with three feet of broken bricks, before the labour of sieving the soil, adding what manure could be found and planting could begin. In June 1943 the Queen came to

The patio has been described as 'estate agent's language for a backyard', a labour-saving space for professional people to recreate the memory of their Mediterranean holidays, in the increasingly confined space of the modern city

visit and also saw a model farm with its pigs, rabbits, chickens, geese, a goat and a pony housed in buildings made from scratch.

Bomb sites

By 1941, there was more open ground within a mile of St Paul's than at any time since the early Middle Ages, with the exception of the Great Fire. In the vast wasteland opened up to the north of the Cathedral, fire-watchers from the Goldsmiths' Company planted a small garden of flowers where the graveyard of St John Zachary (destroyed in 1666) had stood. A dauntless City plane tree outside Stationers' Hall on Ludgate Hill, whose upper branches had been destroyed in the bombing, threw out new shoots from its trunk. There were reports in *The Times* of trees flowering again after having been stripped by the blast of flying bombs. But the most spectacular natural phenomenon to occur was the growth by the end of the War of magnificent displays of wild flowers on the bomb sites.

According to the records made by Dr E. J. Salisbury, Director of the Royal Botanic Gardens, Kew, and J. E. Lousley, the first plant to arrive (in flower by 1941) was the rosebay willowherb, its distinctive purple flowers attracting many elephant hawk-moths. In the nineteenth century, it had remained on the outskirts of London where it was to be found on gravelly banks and in woods, but during the demolition of Wych Street to make way for the Aldwych in the early years of the present century, it announced its arrival in central London. Its tolerance of soil subjected to heat and capacity to produce 80,000 seeds a season dispersed by miniature parachute ensured its rapid spread. The three groundsels were not far behind: Oxford ragwort had flourished on Mount Etna so it is not surprising that it should quickly feel at home, having made its way down the Great Western Railway since escaping from the Oxford Botanical Garden in the early nineteenth century. Members of the daisy family were also borne in on the wind: ring-wort, sowthistle, coltsfoot and dandelion. Eastern rocket and Canadian fleabane flourished,

together with the most notable garden plant airlifted on to the sites, *Buddleja davidii*. Others grew from seed brought in by the horses who helped to clear the rubble, or on workmen's boots – chickweed, shepherd's purse, greater plantain, assorted clovers and grasses – while the moisture and shade of ruined basements provided ideal conditions for bracken spore to germinate. By the end of 1942, some 27 species had been observed, and by 1944, at least 111.

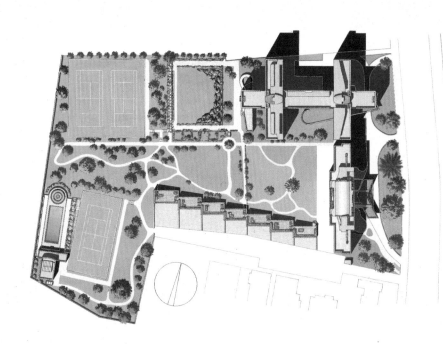

Left: The landscape environment planned for Highpoint 1 and 2 emphasized the Modern Movement's preoccupation with healthy living, featuring a swimming pool, squash and tennis courts

Below: The first garden gnomes were imported from Nuremberg in the mid-nineteenth century to ornament fashionable alpine rock gardens

Opposite: Eliot Hodgkin's painting of St Paul's and St Mary Aldermary from St Swithin's Churchyard was one of a series of works the artist executed at the end of the war which record the variety of wild flowers to be found growing on London bomb sites

After the War

The post-war landscape of London left much to be desired. On the outskirts, the vernacular patchwork of allotments, each with its own idiosyncratically makeshift hut, merged imperceptibly into a no-man's-land of poultry farms and piggeries, gravel pits and scrapped car dumps, airfields, by-passes and filling stations. At least by 1944, forty square miles of Green Belt had been safeguarded. And the planning control recommendations made by Patrick Abercrombie's Greater London Plan, published the same year, were adopted in the 1947 Town and Country Planning Act, which enabled the London County Council to consolidate the Green Belt by turning down planning applications rather than by having to resort to the expensive method of purchasing the land.

But the city itself needed a facelift, still starved of colour, cheerfulness and amusement in the years of Austerity. The 1951 Festival of

195

Britain was a conscious attempt to answer these needs and to promote the idea of a better future. The Homes and Gardens Pavilion looked forward to a new world of leisure, imaginatively utilizing compact spaces for family hobbies. But many of the acoutrements – a handmade picnic basket, a Wedgwood lemonade set, a chaise-longue supplied by Dryad Handicrafts – were decidedly traditional or, in the case of one housing unit of rabbits and poultry, recalled Heath Robinson rather than Le Corbusier.

and Peter Youngman. Here some elements of the Modern Movement's preoccupation with overall design were put into practice, planted with boldly shaped 'architectural' specimens – polygonum, heracleum, rheum, ligularia, bamboo – and set with the distinctive cone-shaped concrete plant-holders that had been specially created for the Festival.

The more progressive ideas about landscaping were only taken up slowly. In the private sector, the partnership formed by G. Paulson

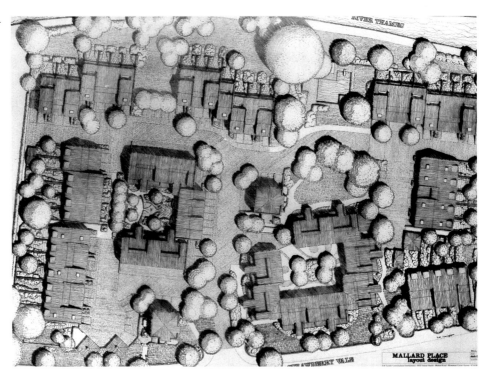

Span Estates layout design for Mallard Place, Twickenham, clearly shows communal landscaping flowing round the buildings and retaining the mature trees on site, while private gardens are reduced to tiny patios

The overall landscape of the Festival was conceived in two parts. The Pleasure Gardens in Battersea Park were designed under the direction of James Gardner with enough hard surfaces, restaurants, buffets and beer gardens (named after the old London pleasure gardens of Vauxhall, Ranelagh and Cremorne) to take the crowds. The Gardens offered a funfair and an array of fantasy elements, including a grotto and the Far Tottering and Oyster Creek Railway, inspired by those most romantically English of artists, Osbert Lancaster and John Piper. In contrast, the South Bank site itself, with its Dome of Discovery and Skylon, was placed in the hands of the landscape architects H. F. Clark, Maria Shephard, Peter Shepheard

Townsend and Eric Lyons with the contractor Leslie Bilsby aimed to *span* the gap between the monotony of many post-war suburban speculative developments and prohibitively expensive, individually commissioned residences. Span Estates completed over fifty schemes, principally in the Greater London area, of well-designed houses and flats set in a carefully designed landscape setting to encourage communal involvement. The landscapes retained the mature trees of the original sites and flowed round the buildings in imaginative and generous new planting schemes devised by the landscape architects Ivor Cunningham and Preben Jakobson. These new 'garden villages' attracted many civic awards. In the public sector, the architects Darborne and Darke incorporated hanging gardens of trees and shrubs on the access balconies to the flats they designed in Lillington Street, Pimlico in 1969 for Westminster City Council, while Preben Jakobson created a series of intricate garden areas for Hounslow City Centre in 1977.

More significant perhaps was the growing number of gardening books specifically directed to the private London gardener: from Lanning Roper's *Successful Town Gardening* (1954) to John Brookes's *Room Outside* (1969) and *The Small Garden* (1977), and *Town Gardens to Live In* (1977) by Susan Jellicoe and Marjory Allen. Despite their differing viewpoints, all concentrated on helping to make the most of small spaces, through careful consideration of the 'bones' of the design, imaginative planting schemes and a variety of ground surfaces and screening devices. Their popularity was symptomatic of what was fast becoming a mass leisure activity, encouraged by the commercialization of the nursery trade.

Standardized John Innes composts were first introduced in the 1930s, chemical weed killers and modern insecticides in the 1940s, systemic fungicides, foliar feeds and grow-bags in the 1960s and 1970s. But the greatest revolution in retailing was brought about through the introduction of container-grown plants, which freed nurseries and their customers from their dependence on the seasons. The promise of instant results was irresistible, an illusion fostered by the well publicized, seemingly effortless displays mounted at Chelsea Flower Show each May, on television gardening programmes and in a bewildering variety of amateur gardening magazines. At the same time, the Clean Air Acts of 1956 and 1968 had helped to rid London of its perpetual pall of smoke. Londoners could now sit out in their gardens and enjoy the fresh, vivid colours round them without getting filthy. White garden furniture set out beneath gaily patterned umbrellas on reconstituted stone patios became for the first time practical, and captured something of the Continental atmosphere many had experienced on package holidays abroad. New

garden centres were quick to supply the tables and loungers, the barques and briquettes.

Although London gardens have proved remarkably adaptable in the twentieth century, yet many traditional usages remain. Gardening is by its nature a conservative occupation, dependent for the best results on cumulative effort and knowledge acquired through experience. Furthermore, the growing realization that historic gardens should be safeguarded was reflected in the formation of the Garden History Society in 1965. The horticultural policy of the royal parks is based on historical surveys, only modified to take account of increased visitors and improvements to plant species. The National Trust has pursued a policy of conservation in its properties, for example replanting a parterre at Ham House, Richmond, with dwarf box hedges enclosing beds of cotton lavender. Jekyll planting and colour schemes have been reintroduced elsewhere and the sophisticated Londoner's partiality for grey and white gardens pays homage to Vita Sackville-West at Sissinghurst. The conservatory that proved so popular in the nineteenth century is also being reinstated, not least because, given the value of London property, it provides a cheaper solution to the perennial problem of space than moving to a bigger house. On a larger scale, the Paxton-inspired glass atrium has been built into some major modern office developments, presumably as evidence that corporate concern for the workers' environment extended beyond a dusty trough of tropical plants in the lobby. City farms in Islington, Stepney and on the Isle of Dogs teach urban children the mysteries of animal husbandry, and since the 1970s allotments have taken on a new lease of life to grow organic fruit and vegetables. The tradition of pocket-handkerchief gardens – often on land where churches stood before the Blitz or the Great Fire – has been maintained by the City Corporation, who now look after nearly two hundred such spaces squeezed in between the office blocks throughout the Square Mile. London may look shabby and unkempt from the outside, but it still has a green heart.

A Picture Gallery

This demonstration of the changing artistic attitudes to the London garden and its surroundings focuses on the role played by paintings, prints and drawings in recording historical gardens. Gradually, instead of being glimpsed in the background to portraits, or documented (like buildings) with proprietorial pride, the garden evolves as a valid subject for the painter in its own right.

Opposite: *This painting, showing the verdant West End in the Regency period, also illustrates an essential theme of the history of London gardens: the interaction between the indoors and the outdoors*

'Your sight is the most perfect
and most delightful of all our senses'
LONDON'S PARKS AND GARDENS:
A PICTURE GALLERY

This essay sets out not only to delight the visual senses but also to give some insight into the historical development of gardens, as perceived by the artist. Some of London's most unforgettable images have been inspired by the unique heritage of the capital's gardens.

Yet two themes emerge to qualify this survey of London gardens in art. First, that the artist was extremely slow to react to social trends, in some cases taking as long as a century. Second, that many of the important breakthroughs came from foreign artists.

Early views of London gardens

Before gardens became artists' subjects in their own right, they could be seen either as 'glimpses' or in plans. Gardens appear in the background to portraits, indicating a special association with the sitter. In the portraits of the Earl and Countess of Arundel, for example, fragments of their garden in the Strand are seen in the background. Similarly, the garden of Whitehall around 1545 is visible in the anonymous portrait of Henry VIII and his family in the Royal Collection (page 15).

At the beginning of the seventeenth century the garden plans of Robert and John Smythson represent a valuable contribution to the visual record on London gardens. They are fascinating historical documents; however they are also frustrating, as by their nature they do not allow the observer to see the three-dimensional appearance of the garden. In some cases, it is difficult to know where specific features were located. The garden of Somerset House, for

instance, was famous for its huge grotto fountain depicting Mount Parnassus. On the plan, we are left to guess a possible location – perhaps the octagonal shape within the circular feature in the east garden. Smythson produced similar plans for Wimbledon and Ham Houses, Northampton House and Lord Bedford's house in Twickenham.

For the earliest painted views of London gardens, we turn to two Dutch works: Jacob Knyff's *Chiswick from the River* and Hendrick Danckerts' *Ham House*. Both painted in the 1670s, they show properties which contrast in style as well as in scale. The garden of Old

design and is on a much grander scale than Corney House.

The anonymous drawing on parchment of Southampton (later Bedford) House, also of the same period, constitutes a fascinating document. It is not only a rare early view of a London garden, but also is the earliest known view of this particular garden, and interestingly it is connected, like the Chiswick painting, with the Bedford family.

The viewpoints adopted by the artists float in the air, or, in the case of Chiswick, hover over the Thames. To adopt a high viewpoint in order to encompass the whole scene is very

This plan shows the garden of Somerset House in 1609. Its most celebrated feature was a large grotto within a pond, the Parnassus, designed by Salomon de Caus, which is probably represented here by the circle marked within the polygonal structure on the right-hand side

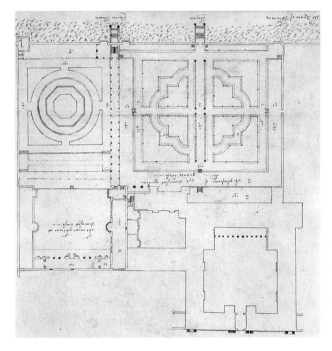

Opposite: *This delicately drawn view of Southampton (later Bedford) House in Bloomsbury not only shows the fortifications that were erected around the property during the Civil War, but is also a unique record of the garden layout in the last quarter of the seventeenth century*

Overleaf: *The garden of No 10 Downing Street with St James's Park in the background. On the terrace the figure on the right is probably George Pitt. The layout of this walled garden has changed comparatively little since those days*

Corney House in Chiswick (page 59) had existed for some time when Knyff painted it; indeed the house dates back to the Tudor period when it belonged to John, first Earl of Bedford, and the little gazebo overlooking the Thames was probably erected in Elizabethan or Jacobean times. This charming feature introduces an element of leisure use into what appears to be a predominantly working garden, with fruit trees growing round the walls and long square beds of unidentifiable produce in the centre.

By contrast the south front of Ham House was painted soon after the completion of the building. It shows the latest fashion in garden

characteristic of this period, and suggests links between the mapmaker's approach and house portraiture. The patterns created by the parterre layouts of seventeenth-century garden design certainly call for such viewpoints, but the artist was also flattering the owner's sense of property by representing the estate in its entirety. The pride of ownership can be detected in the diarist John Evelyn's description of his own estate at Sayes Court, Deptford. Its plan is accompanied by no less than 126 captions. For example:

25) The court with fair gravel
walks planted with Cypress

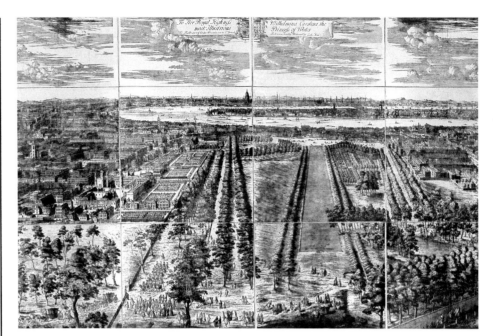

At the beginning of the eighteenth century, St James's Park dominated the newly developed West End. In contrast to the Continental approach of surrounding parks with impressive façades, here it is the rear of the properties with their accompanying back gardens which overlook the park

and the walls with fruit

54) My private garden of
choice flowers and simples

118) The Great Orchard
planted with 300 fruit trees of
the best sorts mingled and
warranted for 3 years upon a
bond of 20 pound.

The painted and engraved work by Jacob Knyff and his brother Leonard fully developed the bird's-eye-view technique and other large London properties of the seventeenth and eighteenth centuries were handled in this way, notably Hampton Court, Kensington Palace, Burlington House and Ashurst in Highgate.

The parks

At the same time that these private gardens were being developed, the royal public parks, pleasure gardens and squares of London were being created. The sixteenth century had witnessed the enclosure of royal hunting land, thus defining Hyde Park, Marylebone Park, Kensington Gardens and Greenwich Park. The seventeenth century saw the continuation of this policy of enclosure, but most importantly, some of the parks were now open to the public, for James I opened up Hyde Park, and Charles I welcomed his subjects into St James's Park –

formerly his private garden. The development of parks as centres of recreation ran parallel to the birth of the first public pleasure gardens: Spring and Mulberry Gardens in St James's Park which, after the Restoration, were followed by the appearance of tea gardens all over London.

The growth of pleasure gardens, parks and squares paralleled the growth of the fabric of London and provided an influential context for the development of the modern private garden. A close examination of a small number of pictures should offer convincing evidence. John Kip's view of St James's Park (*c.* 1710) encapsulates many aspects of the process of converting *rus* into *urbs*, with the preservation of wide open space which seemed to act as a magnet for private gardens to proliferate all around it.

The drawing was executed from the roof of Buckingham House and the panorama remains a key work in terms of the appearance of early Georgian London with its extensive open spaces. The fencing on the left-hand side is a useful reminder of the act of enclosure. At the bottom of St James's Park, on the left, is Spring Gardens, a further enclosure, intended as a reserve for more social activities. Further insight into Westminster's open spaces is afforded by the layout of the surrounding houses. From the grand residence of Godolphin House, St James's

Palace, Marlborough and Carlton Houses to the more modest terracing on the right, all the gardens are turned to the park. Large or small, they are sandwiched between the house and the park.

It is clear when looking at paintings focusing on the gardens that the aim is to include the park in the view. Terraces were built to this effect, and the best illustrated example belongs to the garden of No. 10 Downing Street painted (*c.*1736–40) by George Lambert which shows the way in which walled private gardens appropriated extensive views to enhance their sense of space. The view of St James's Park is not immediately recognizable, as it features the long, straight canal to a French design substituted in 1826–7 by the now familiar serpentine lake.

To the eighteenth-century artist the park was essentially a backdrop framing a whole range of social activities. The most extraordinary example of the eighteenth-century approach is the painting in the Royal Collection entitled *St James's Park and the Mall* (*c.* 1745). Royal and aristocratic figures parade gracefully along the Mall, which is raised above the ground in a broad platform (for the game of paille maille). This seems to form a symbolic barrier between the classes. In the foreground, below, are the 'lower' classes, mothers chatting while breast-feeding, soldiers mingling with foreigners. Less picturesque details can also be detected: a defecating dog and a fat lady pulling up her stockings, both featuring in the foreground. Note, too, that the walled garden of No. 10 Downing Street is visible in the background. In brief, this rich and lively composition is the perfect statement of the use that was made of St James's Park in the eighteenth century by a wide range of London's citizens and visitors.

The river Thames also served to broaden domestic vistas. It is, whenever possible, in-cluded in the view and this is particularly suc-cessful in Canaletto's views of Somerset House Gardens or indeed in Alexander Nasmyth's view of Waterloo Bridge with its charming terracing in the foreground.

The squares

The Bedford and Southampton families who had commissioned the earliest paintings of Lon-don gardens were also involved in the creation of London's first squares: Covent Garden Piazza (*c.* 1638) and Southampton (later Bloomsbury) Square (1665) – the first use of the word 'square' in this context being credited to the circle of the Earl of Southampton.

The use of public views to enhance private

Unlike its paved Continental models, the London square is green. Throughout the eighteenth century it was represented in a steady stream of paintings and prints for which there was a ready market at home and abroad

Left: *This view of Kensington Gardens is an exercise in pure landscape painting and contrasts with the views of parks in the preceding century when they had acted merely as background to social activities*

Opposite: '*The garden of the house at Kew was a great delight to me — from which I painted carefully a background to . . . the conservatory in* The Pet' *(exhibited in 1853 by W.H. Deverell). From the artist's journal*

Below: *One of a series of four watercolours depicting garden buildings in the grounds of Walpole House, Chelsea. The summer house illustrated here overlooked the Thames in a fashion reminiscent of that shown in London's earliest painted garden (see page 59)*

vistas was no longer necessary with the creation of squares, simply because the square actually belonged to the people living around it. If the early prototypes of Covent Garden and Southampton Square were enclosed only by regularly spaced wooden posts, their successors, starting with St James's Square, resolutely adopted railings and locked gates before the close of the seventeenth century. Access was now limited to those with a key (page 23). And this procedure still applies today for the residential squares of Notting Hill, South Kensington, Islington and other areas.

The London square may well have received impetus from Continental models (Leghorn in Italy and the Place des Vosges in Paris) but its character was English from the start. The square became one of London's classic answers to the need for green spaces in the city environment. While squares on the Continent have remained very architectural, in London they quickly became the leafy oases of a constantly expanding capital.

Lincoln's Inn Fields was perhaps London's first true square and drew its inspiration from the landscaping of Moorfields which was the earliest public open space to be laid out 'for the

use and enjoyment of the citizens' (1625). The concept of a grassed area criss-crossed by a network of pathways was originally mooted for Lincoln's Inn Fields in 1617. However reaction to a contentious development of housing on the site led to a royal agreement in 1639 that no further development would take place. The late seventeenth-century painting in Wilton House illustrates the square in its full glory (page 50). Even Covent Garden Piazza, often quoted as London's first self-conscious square and certainly the most architectural of them all, still displayed a token green feature before being taken over by market activities — a central tree

Alongside the grand gardens of the capital, topographers also recorded more humble examples, such as this Hammersmith courtyard of the Regency period – the location for the water pump and for the drying of laundry

just visible in Hollar's view of the West End in 1658 (page 45).

In the Georgian period there are several series of prints devoted to the squares which enable us to survey their landscape. The earliest, engraved by Sutton Nicholls and published in *London Described* in 1731, shows, for instance, that Bloomsbury Square (1665) already had been laid with grass and walks harking back to Lincoln's Inn Fields. Edwards Dayes's series at the close of the century (1780s) enables us to experience the squares at street level through the introduction of carriages and elegantly dressed figures promenading round the gardens. The issue of such series suggests that Londoners were proud of their unique amenity and were happy to promote it abroad.

When in 1792 R. B. O'Reilly proposed to erect a large opera house in Leicester Square, his own design was recorded in a vast painting which shows lavish planting of trees and flowers in the taste of William Mason. Although this scheme was never carried out, it is important to note that the landscaping of Leicester Square is given equal prominence to the architectural project.

Pleasure gardens

Vauxhall Gardens prints illustrating the pleasure gardens were specially created to be experienced by all and the bird's-eye view was no longer a satisfactory rendering. At Vauxhall, the artist Canaletto worked from 'within', thus producing a series of different views for the different features: among them the supper boxes, the orchestra and the walks. This change of artistic approach adopted for what were undoubtedly the most famous gardens in eighteenth-century Europe reflected the concept of garden visiting and was again initiated by foreigners. It had been pioneered at Chiswick House in a series of drawings by the Dutch artist Pieter Rysbrack and the French draughtsman Jacques Rigaud. But the print makers who engraved Canaletto's paintings of public gardens enabled this new approach to reach a wider audience.

The new close-up portraiture of gardens was adopted in the depiction of the grounds of Strawberry Hill, Carlton House, Walpole House and Grove Hill, Camberwell. This trend not only indicates a more widespread interest in gardens, but also highlights changes in garden design. While the intricate pattern of the seventeenth-century parterre was best viewed from a height, the new landscape garden inspired by Lancelot 'Capability' Brown with its focus on the apparent natural arrangement of trees and grass invited promenaders to discover those special effects designed to enliven 'nature'.

Small gardens

There are virtually no drawn or painted examples of more modest gardens before the Regency, when their depiction was partly influenced by the wider development of Romanticism in art (a notable exception is shown on page 123). The interest in nature which was very noticeable in the eighteenth century, but always as the context for social events, gradually developed into the yearning for a more intimate relationship with nature for its own sake. This era sees a great development of landscape painting. One of the greatest landscape artists, Constable, when painting his house and garden in Hampstead, worked to highlight its rural character rather than its suburban aspect by creating the impression that it was in the midst of wild countryside.

This newly acquired communing with nature manifests itself in a spate of pure landscape painting in the commons and parks of London. Hyde Park and Kensington Gardens, once seen bustling with the aristocracy and its followers, are suddenly shown empty, as for instance in the remarkable and little known series of paintings by John Martin.

In this climate, even the depiction of the modest back gardens which were proliferating with the expansion of the capital, became increasingly common. London's two principal exponents of the theme were Jean Claude Nattes and William Capon. Nattes was the more prolific of the two and his drawings range from the small backyard of No. 7 Angel Row in Hammersmith to Mrs Wilson's attempts at basement gardening in her house in Bayswater, and a more spacious town garden, again in Hammersmith. William Capon's drawings of cottage gardens in Westminster are not only charming but informative. They highlight the semi-rural state of many of London's 'villages' at the beginning of the nineteenth century. They constitute an early example of the cottage genre which may seem slightly incongruous in the least rural environment of all: London.

The Victorians

With the Victorians the theme of gardens in art acquired its modern meaning. The Pre-Raphaelites had a powerful interest in the outdoors and had broken new ground in the depiction of the seasons (*An English Autumn Afternoon* by Ford Madox Brown), the parks (*May in Regent's Park* by Charles Allston Collins) and the commons (*The Pretty Baa-lambs* set on Clapham Common). They emphasized the change of light and landscape brought about by the seasons – a trend which would gather momentum at the end of the nineteenth century – and turned gardens into a major artistic source of inspiration. Thus, W. H. Deverell uses his own garden in Richmond Road, Kew, as background in his painting *The Pet*. Furthermore, while the painted gardens of the eighteenth century were largely populated by men (including, of course, that of No. 10 Downing Street), this Pre-Raphaelite painting marks a clear departure from that pattern. Women, very quickly followed by children, became the focus for garden painting.

The French artist James Tissot, who settled in London in 1871, enlivened his *plein air* paintings

with these subjects, using the real settings of Kew Gardens, Holland House Garden, the grounds of Camden Palace in Chislehurst, and the garden of his friend John Bowles. In addition, he produced thirty pictures set in his own garden in St John's Wood including *Holyday*, *Croquet*, *A Quiet Afternoon*, *The Gardener*, *Still on Top*, and *In Full Sun*. The huge conservatory which the artist had built along-side his studio was also given prominence in a number of other works. Tissot's art is so accurately detailed that it has been possible from his paintings and with the help of a few supplementary documents, to reconstruct the layout of his St John's Wood garden. Tissot not only put the nineteenth-century London garden on the artistic map, but his success, both in financial and aesthetic terms, inspired others,

Right: *This late Victorian watercolour is a rare view of the garden of a City house (Austin Friars). It represents the archetypal minimal garden, grassed, but otherwise unadorned*

Left: *This is one of the many paintings the artist James Tissot set in his own garden at Grove End Road, St John's Wood (see also book cover). The colonnade was its most spectacular feature, which was modelled on that of the Parc Monceau in Paris*

Below: *This garden was once that of the actress Sarah Siddons (1755–1831) but it is impossible to say how much of the original had survived by the time this view was recorded in the Edwardian period. Its walled triangular shape is complemented by a simple planting scheme*

thus creating a garden genre in painting. Atkinson Grimshaw is perhaps the most gifted of those who came under Tissot's influence.

John Young Hunter's *My Lady's Garden* also belongs to this garden genre. Hunter used the setting of Holland House garden to create a slightly mysterious scene, parallel with that of Tissot's *The Letter. My Lady's Garden* is, however, fascinating for its use of historical perspec-

tive. The costume is a free interpretation of medieval dress with a Dutch seventeenth-century coif. The 'Lady', who was Mary, the artist's wife, has been placed against the background of the knot-patterned Dutch garden at Holland House which is still there today.

This painting is a good example of the historicist approach to gardening which became fashionable in the second half of the nineteenth

This cottage garden in Westminster is here portrayed just prior to its destruction during the Regency period. Many of the capital's gardens were primarily functional, but this drawing possesses a romantic charm which anticipates the later Victorian idealization of this type of garden

century. The Italianate garden with its terracing and decorative urns was illustrated by Tissot in *The Letter*. Marcus Stone's garden paintings also pick up this theme but we do not know whether he was inspired by London gardens.

On a more prosaic level, two of London's topographers must also be mentioned, John Crowther and Philip Norman. Their recording of a large number of private gardens shows a new appreciation of this aspect of London's heritage. Their professional standpoints bear a certain number of similarities although they were working some fifteen years apart.

John Crowther was employed by Sir

C. E. H. Chadwyck-Healey to make drawings of London from about 1879 to 1890. This appointment was apparently generated by this patron's concern about the destruction of historic buildings. Crowther's drawings therefore focus on London's threatened heritage, recording many of the features that were soon to disappear. Some of his work was accordingly reproduced in E. Beresford Chancellor's *Lost London* (1926).

Similarly many of Philip Norman's watercolours were reproduced in his own book entitled *London Vanished and Vanishing* (1905). In a 1911 letter to the Museum of London, Norman himself describes his work as consisting 'almost entirely of watercolour views of old buildings in London that have disappeared during the last 12 years'.

Both Crowther and Norman were extremely prolific and depicted a wide range of gardens. Both tackled the churchyard garden (pages 162 and 166), small and large town gardens, pubs and almshouses. John Crowther however was a more original artist and a better watercolourist. One of his most vivid works is *Dean's Court* in Carter Lane which, with its paved courtyard and the intricate tracery of two leafless trees, wonderfully captures the sense of a winter's day in London. There is also *Devereux Tower* at the Tower of London, which in 1883 could boast a roof garden with sunflowers lovingly watered by its gardener. One of the best London examples of windowbox display is his view of *The Skinners Alms Houses*.

Two views by Norman of the garden which once belonged to Mrs Siddons illustrate the character of London's walled gardens. The first presents the exterior or public face of the garden, offering the observer a long, high wall with no sight of the garden's contents, while the second shows the interior private aspect of the garden with a viewpoint from the house displaying the garden's attractions.

The work of Crowther and Norman represents the last substantial body of record drawings on the garden theme. Subsequently the camera replaces the pencil and brush. Indeed the impact of photography was already recognized by Norman who based a number of his watercolours on photographs he had taken of the subjects. This is not to say, of course, that there are no painted views of London gardens in the twentieth century.

The twentieth century

The growth of photography inevitably affected artists, and their reaction to the new technology was two-fold. First it influenced their painting technique. There were those artists who, like the members of the Camden Town Group, steered away from the new medium by adopting an impressionist technique and sometimes a symbolic palette. By contrast, no one would fail to label the style of Eliot Hodgkin photographic, although there is an added intensity of observation which gives his works a poetic dimension (page 194).

Second, the existence of photography imposed a new sense of urgency. If we look back to the nineteenth century, the advent of illus-trated magazines in the 1840s had created tight deadlines for the contributing artists. Similarly with the progress of photography this sense of urgency encouraged magazines to switch from drawn to photographic material. It is tempting to suggest a link between this new preoccupation with speed and the artist's wish to capture the constantly changing nature of the outdoors.

This strong sense that the artist is in touch with contemporary and changing trends also manifested itself in the depiction of gardens. Early signs can be detected from the artists' work in the magazine *Punch* which regularly chronicled suburban gardening trends. 'Topiary fever' or 'What can be done with a back garden', to give two examples only, drew strength from their topicality and humour from the pretensions of garden owners. Less reactive and designed to appeal to contemporary taste, poster art promoting the benefits of suburban living was geared to the propagation of the new lifestyle rather than reflecting what had already taken place (pages 178 and 187).

By opting to focus on small-scale domestic gardens the members of the Camden Town Group showed a closeness to their subject which gave immediacy to their paintings. Although deriving much of its impetus from the French Impressionists the group was based in and inspired by London. The parks and gardens they depicted provide indicators to the range of London's open spaces: Mrs Hannay's *Back Gardens*, Spencer Gore's *Down the Garden*, as well as his various views of Mornington Crescent, Malcolm Drummond's *Chelsea Garden*, William Ratcliffe's *Clarence Gardens*, Lucien Pissaro's *Bedford Park* and his *Under the Pines, Kew, Sun*. This Edwardian era sees the triumph of the London back garden and the residential square over public parks and the gardens of the wealthy. It also represents the last great period for garden painting.

With the increasing importance of photography the unglamorous London sights recorded by the Camden Town Group provide a strong contrast to the work of the magazine *Country Life* which at the beginning of the century was pioneering the photographic coverage

*John Young Hunter's picture,
My Lady's Garden (1899),
was painted in the grounds of
Holland House, Kensington.
The walled Dutch garden,
laid out in 1812, is accurately
shown and is still there today*

of noteworthy houses and gardens, with a number of them in and around London. There is no equivalent in painting to surveys such as those of the garden of Alma Tadema who had bought James Tissot's property in 1882 or The Hill garden in Hampstead, or Philip Sassoon's Trent Park in Enfield. The article on Alma Tadema constitutes one of the key documents for the reconstructed layout of Tissot's garden, while the photographs of Trent Park help us to realize just how much of the original scheme has sadly disappeared. Also, the thorough recording of The Hill may now assist with the planned restoration of the pergola, the garden's most striking feature.

This incursion into famous gardens should

not however divert us away from the stardom in the twentieth century of the domestic front and back garden. Artists might even find their own garden a worthy subject, as with Harry Bush's *Laggard Leaves* and *December Sunshine* which were observed and painted in Merton where the artist lived (page 186). Kathleen Allen's *Roof Garden in Holborn* is an example of the post-war answer to some Londoners' search for a little open space they could call their own.

Charming though these records are, one sometimes wishes that the old garden genre could be revitalized. Adrian Berg's vision of the London parks and seasons illustrates the sort of challenge artists should seek. Let us hope others will also be inspired by this unique heritage.

GARDENS TO VISIT IN LONDON

ALEXANDER POPE'S GROTTO *St Catherine's Convent, Cross Deep, Twickenham. Open Sat p.m. by appointment.* A fragment of the grotto survives.

BROCKWELL PARK *Brixton, SE24. Open daily.* When the Regency Brockwell estate became a public park in 1892, the walled kitchen garden was turned into a 'Shakespeare garden'.

CAPEL MANOR GARDENS *Horticultural and Environmental Centre, Bullsmoor Lane, Waltham Cross. Open daily Apr–Oct.* Rich variety of recreated period gardens, plus gardens catering for blind and disabled.

CARSHALTON PARK *Carshalton, Surrey. Open daily.* Remains of formal canals and a grotto survive from Bridgeman's design of 1716–20.

CHELSEA PHYSIC GARDEN *Swan Walk, Chelsea SW3. Open (p.m.) mid-Apr–mid-Oct, Wed, Sun, Bank Holiday Mon; Tue–Fri in Chelsea Flower Show week.* Founded 1673 to grow medicinal plants. Became the world's most richly stocked botanic garden under 18th-century curatorship of Philip Miller.

CHISWICK HOUSE *Burlington Lane, Chiswick, W4. Open daily.* Designed by Kent and Bridgeman for Lord Burlington from 1725. Original features in picturesque landscape include exedra, sphinxes, obelisk and round temple crowning a garden of orange trees.

COLLEGE GARDEN *Westminster Abbey, SW1. Open Thurs.* 'The oldest garden in England', in continuous cultivation for 900 years. Collection of old English herbs within 14th-century river walls.

DERRY & TOM'S ROOF GARDEN *99 Kensington High Street, W8. Open daily.* Original 1930s features include Hispano-Moorish garden, Tudor garden and English 'woodland' with running water and bridge.

FENTON HOUSE *Hampstead Grove, Hampstead, NW3. Open (p.m.) Mar, Sat–Sun; Apr–Oct, Sat–Wed.* Walled garden with raised paths overlooking lawn. Kitchen garden at the side was a common 18th century formula.

GRAY'S INN *Grays Inn Road, Holborn, EC1. Open weekdays 12–2.30 p.m.* Shallow steps at N end and raised perimeter path are traces of Francis Bacon's c.1600 layout. Iron gates and small Purbeck pavings in Field Court date from 18th century.

GREENWICH PARK *Greenwich, SE10. Open daily.* The last 17th-century wilderness is commemorated in the Wilderness Deer Park in the S-E corner.

GROVELANDS *Southgate Grove, N1 .Open daily.* The best surviving Repton landscape in Greater London (pending Kenwood Park's restoration of the Reptonian layout beneath the present design).

GUNNERSBURY PARK *W3. Open daily.* Two ponds and a small temple by William Kent survive remodelling in the style of Capability Brown. 19th-century features can also be seen.

HAM HOUSE *Ham Street, Richmond. Open daily.* Gardens to E and S of house are being restored to their 17th-century appearance by the National Trust.

HAMPTON COURT PALACE *Hampton, East Molesey. Open daily.* Goose-foot plan dates from Charles II's reign. Great Fountain Garden, Privy Garden, Orangery and glorious Chestnut Avenue date from William III. Early 18th-century maze by Henry Wise. Great Vine planted 1769. The garden's golden days belong to the 19th century.

THE HILL *Inverforth Close, North End Way, Hampstead, NW3. Open daily.* Lavish architectural garden designed by T. Mawson for Lord Leverhulme c. 1900. Two distinct sites linked elegantly by long pergola.

HORNIMAN GARDENS *London Road, SE23. Open daily.* Avenue was original drive of Surrey House, home of Frederick Horniman, who first opened house and grounds to public in 1888.

KEATS HOUSE *Wentworth Place, Keats Grove, Hampstead, NW3. Open daily.* Garden partially restored using Garden History Society plans.

MUSEUM OF LONDON: GARDEN COURT *London Wall, London EC2Y 5HN. Open daily except Mon.* A series of beds devoted to the major nurseries from medieval times to the present traces the history of plantsmanship in London.

MYDDLETON HOUSE *Enfield. Open weekdays and certain Sundays each month. Contact Lea Valley Regional Park Authority for details.* Noteworthy since E. A. Bowles began gardening in 1890s. Rock garden, iris beds, rose garden, conservatory and 'Lunatic Asylum' planted with botanical misfits.

THE NATIONAL GARDENS SCHEME A leaflet published annually lists the dates when private London gardens are open to the public.

OSTERLEY HOUSE *Jersey Road, Osterley, Isleworth. Open daily.* William Chambers's Doric temple and 'Roman' bridge across the lower lake and Robert Adam's semicircular greenhouse are 18th-century. The cedars and lake are Georgian.

QUEEN'S GARDEN *Kew Gardens, Richmond. Open daily.* Recreation of a sunken garden of French design; parterre, gazebo, pleached alley and mount. Period planting.

ROCOCO GARDEN *Bushey Park, Middlesex. Open daily.* Rococo design by Thomas Wright survives on S edge of Bushey Park. Its restored grotto is one of the wonders of its kind.

TRADESCANT TRUST *St Mary's Lambeth, Lambeth Palace Road, SE1. Open Mar–early Dec, except Sat.* Replica of a 17th-century garden in St Mary's Churchyard.

TRENT PARK *Enfield. Open daily.* On the S edge of Enfield Chase. Once Elizabeth I's Royal Hunting Ground, remodelled in 1930s for Sir Philip Sassoon; the swimming pool and orangery survive from his truly exceptional layout.

TRINITY HOSPITAL *Greenwich, SE3. Open to public once every 3 years; consult Warden for group visits.* 2-acre back garden; side park; front garden and cloister garden surround building erected 1617 amidst orchards. Ancient mulberry and wisteria. Winner of London Gardens Society's London Challenge Trophy.

LIST OF PLATES

183 Metroland poster (Y/1475). *London Transport Museum*

184 Metroland back garden drawn by Osbert Lancaster. From *The Pleasure Garden* by Anne Scott James and Osbert Lancaster, 1977.

186 'Laggard Leaves.' Oil painting by Harry Bush, c. 1925. *The Museum of London*

187 Staines: 'A Go Out of London' poster (Y/253). *London Transport Museum*

188 Roof Garden at Adelaide House, London Bridge. Photograph, April 1946. *Courtesy of Port of London Authority*

189 Princess Margaret's visit to London's East End. From *The Illustrated London News*, 1 August 1953.

190 Derry & Tom's roof garden. Watercolour, c. 1933. *The Royal Horticultural Society*

191 (Top) Bethnal Green allotment. Oil painting by Charles Ginner, c. 1947. *Manchester City Art Gallery*

191 (Bottom) Allotments on St James's Square. Oil painting by Adrian Allinson, 1942. *Westminster City Archives*

193 Osbert Lancaster drawing of a patio garden. From *The Pleasure Garden* by Anne Scott James and Osbert Lancaster, 1977.

194 St Paul's and St Mary Aldermary from St Swithin's Churchyard.

Tempera on panel by Eliot Hodgkin, 1945. *Private Collection*

195 (Top) Highpoint 1 and 2, Highgate: plan by Tecton (Berthold Lubetkin). Lithograph with ink and gouache. *British Architectural Drawings Collection/RIBA*

195 (Bottom) Gnome, concrete cast, painted, 1950s. *The Museum of London*

196 Layout for Mallard Place, Twickenham, by Eric Lyons Cunningham Partnership for Span Environments Ltd. *British Architectural Drawings Collection/RIBA*

198 'London interior.' Looking across St James's Park from Carlton House Terrace. Oil painting by Louis Pierre Spindler, c. 1834. *Musée des Beaux Arts, Strasbourg*

200 Bedford House in Bloomsbury. Pencil drawing on vellum, late 17th century. *The Museum of London*

201 Somerset House. Pencil drawing by Robert Smythson, 1609. *British Architectural Drawings Collection/RIBA*

202 St James's Park from the terrace of No 10 Downing Street. Oil painting by George Lambert, c.1736–40. *The Museum of London*

204 St James's Park from the roof of Buckingham House. Engraving by Kip, 1710. *Peter Jackson Collection*

205 Bloomsbury Square. Aquatint after Edward Dayes, publ. 1787. *The Museum of London*

206 (Top) 'In Kensington Gardens.' Oil painting by John Martin, 1820s. *(Photo: Bridgeman Art Library)*

206 (Bottom) The garden of Walpole House in Chelsea. Watercolour from the Gulston Collection. *The Royal Borough of Kensington and Chelsea Libraries and Arts Service*

207 'The Pet.' Oil painting by W. H. Deverell, 1853. *The Tate Gallery, London*

208 No 7 Angel Row, Hammersmith. Drawing by J. C. Nattes, 1812. *The Museum of London*

210 'A Convalescent.' Oil painting by James Tissot, c. 1875. *Sheffield City Art Galleries*

211 (Top) 21 Austin Friars. Watercolour by John Crowther, 1881. *Guildhall Library (Photo: The Museum of London)*

211 (Bottom) Inside the garden of Mrs Siddons at 27 Upper Baker Street. Watercolour by Philip Norman, c. 1902. *The Museum of London*

212 'Hovel formerly in Tothill Fields, now destroyed.' Drawing by W. Capon, 1810. *Westminster City Archives*

214 'My Lady's Garden.' Oil painting by J. Young Hunter, 1899. *The Tate Gallery, London*

BIBLIOGRAPHY

GENERAL
Bridgid Boardman, *The Garden in the City* (1990)
Jane Brown, *The Art and Architecture of English Gardens* (1989)
Thomas Fairchild, *The City Gardener* (1772)
John Gerard, *The Herball or Generall Historie of Plants* (1597), facsimile ed., The English Experience, Walter Johnson Inc, Norwood N.J./ Theatrum Orbis Terrarum, Amsterdam (1985)
David Green, *Gardener to Queen Anne* (1956)
Miles Hadfield, *A History of British Gardening* (2nd ed. 1969)
John Dixon Hunt, *William Kent: Landscape Garden Designer* (1987)
John Harris (ed.), *The Garden. A Celebration of One Thousand Years of British Gardening*, Victoria & Albert Exhibition Guide (1979)
David Jacques, *Georgian Gardens* (1979)
G. and S. Jellicoe, P. Goode and M. Lancaster, *The Oxford Companion to Gardens* (1986)
David Ottewill, *The Edwardian Garden* (1989)
John Parkinson, *Paradisi in sole paradisus terrestris* (1629), facsimile ed., The English Experience, Walter Johnson Inc, Norwood N.J./Theatrum Orbis Terrarum, Amsterdam (1975)
Steen Eiler Rasmussen, *London: the Unique City* (1937)
Eleanour Sinclair Rohde, *The Story of*

the Garden* (1932; reprinted 1989)
John Stow, *A Survey of London* (1598; 2nd ed. 1603), edited by C. L. Klingsford (1908, reprinted 1968), Everyman ed. (reprinted 1987)
Dorothy Stroud, *Capability Brown* (1950)
—— *Humphry Repton* (1962)
David Stuart, *Georgian Gardens* (1979)
Gladys Taylor, *Old London Gardens* (1977)
David Jacques and Arend van der Horst, *The Gardens of William and Mary*
Peter Willis, *Charles Bridgeman and the English Landscape Garden* (1977)

THE MEDIEVAL GARDEN
A. M. T. Amhurst, *A History of Gardening in England* (1910)
P. Armitage and B. West, 'Formal Evidence from a late Medieval Garden Well of the Greyfriars, London', *Trans. London and Middx. Arch. Soc.*, vol. 36, pp. 107–136 (1985)
B. M. U. Boardman, 'The Gardens of the London Livery Companies', *Journal of Garden History*, vol. 2, no. 2, pp. 85–116
H. M. Chew and W. Kellaway (eds.), *London Assize of Nuisance 1301–1431*, London Record Society (1973)
H. M. Colvin (ed.), *The History of the King's Works, Vols. I and II*, 'The Middle Ages' (1963)
J. H. Harvey, *Mediaeval Gardens* (1981)
P. Hunting, *The Garden House* (1987)
T. McLean, *Medieval English Gardens* (1981)
A. R. Myers (ed.), *English Historical*

Documents, vol. IV (1969)
H. T. Riley (ed.), *Memorial of London and London Life in the XIIIth, XIVth and XVth Centuries* (1868)

GARDENS AND OPEN SPACE IN TUDOR AND EARLY STUART LONDON
Records of the Worshipful Company of Carpenters, vol. 4, Wardens' Accounts 1546–1571, ed. B. Marsh (1916), vol. 5, Wardens' Accounts 1571–91, ed. B. Marsh and J. Ainsworth (1937), vol. 7, Wardens' Accounts 1592–1614, ed. A. M. Millard (1968)
B. M. U. Boardman, 'The gardens of the London Livery Companies', *Journal of Garden History* vol. 2 no. 2 (1982)
N. G. Brett-James, *The Growth of Stuart London* (1935)
J. H. Harvey, *Early Nurserymen* (1974)
A. Procktor and R. Taylor (eds.), *The A to Z of Elizabethan London* (1979)
K. Thomas, *Man and the Natural World* (1983)
John Schofield (ed.), *The London Surveys of Ralph Treswell* (1987)

MEDICINAL AND KITCHEN GARDENING
J. de la Quintinie, *The Compleat Gard'ner: or, Directions for cultivating the right Ordering of Fruit-Gardens and Kitchen-Gardens; with divers Reflections on several parts of*

Husbandry – in six books. Made in English by John Evelyn, London (1693)

John Evelyn, *Kalendarium Hortense: or the Gardener's Almanac, directing what he is to do monthly throughout the year,* 2nd ed. London (1666)

—— *Fumifugium: or the Inconvenience of the Aer and Smoke of London Dissipated,* London (1661)

—— *Kalendarium,* Six Volumes – annotated ed. by E. S. de Beer 1620–1706, Clarendon Press (1955)

Thomas Hill, *The Gardener's Labyrinth: containing a discourse of the Gardener's life . . .,* completed by Henry Dethick, London (1577)

Sir Hugh Platt, *Delightes for Ladies, to adorne their Persons, Tables, Closets and distillatories: with Beauties, banquets, perfumes and Waters.* (1602)

D. C. Stuart, *The Kitchen Garden: A historical guide to traditional crops* (1984)

Stephen Switzer, *The Practical Kitchen Gardiner, or a New and Entire System of Directions, For his employment in the Melonry, Kitchen-garden and Potagery . . . being chiefly observations of a Person train'd up in the Neat-Houses or Kitchen Gardens about London* (1727)

FLOWERS AND PLANTS IN THE SEVENTEENTH CENTURY

A. K. Coats, *The Plant Hunters* (1969)

E. R. Duthie, *English Florist Societies and Feasts in the 17th and First Half of the 18th centuries,* Garden History Society (Spring 1982)

T. Hanmer, *The Garden Book of Sir Thomas Hanmer,* edited by Ivy Estob (1933)

J. Harvey, *Early Garden Catalogues* (1972)

P. Leith-Ross, *The John Tradescants* (1984)

K. Lemmon, *The Covered Garden* (1962)

O. Moreton, *Old Carnations and Pinks* (1955)

—— *The Auricula* (1964)

LONDON'S MARKET GARDENS IN THE EARLY MODERN PERIOD

Hugh Alley's Caveat. The Markets of London in 1598, ed. Archer, Barron and Harding, London Topographical Society (1988)

A. B. Appleby, *Famine in Tudor and Stuart England* (1978)

C. W. Chalklin, *Seventeenth Century Kent* (1965)

Thomas Cojan, *Haven of Health* (1596)

M. St. Clare Byrne (ed.), *The Elizabethan Home* (1949)

F. J. Fisher, 'The Development of the Lords Food Market, 1540–1640', *Economic History Review,* vol. V (1935)

T. Fuller, *The Worthies of England* (1662)

Richard Gardiner, 'Profitable Instructions for the Manuring, Sowing and Planting of Kitchen Gardens' (1599)

Wm. Harrison (ed. Georges Edden), *The Description of England* (1968)

P. V. McGrath, 'The Marketing of Food, Fodder and Livestock in the London Area in the Seventeenth Century', London M.A. Thesis (1948)

John Norden, *The Surveyor's Dialogue* (1607)

Sir Hugh Platt, *Sundrie Reward Artificial Remedies against Famine,* written by HP upon the occasion of this present dearth (1596)

The Public Markets of the City of London surveyed by William Leybourne in 1697, (ed) Betty R. Masters, London Topographical Society (1974)

Malcolm Thick, 'Market Gardening in England and Wales', ch. 18 *The Agrarian History of England and Wales,* vol. VII 1640–1750 (1985)

Ronald Webber, *The Early Horticulturists* (1968)

J. C. Drummond and Anne Wilbraham, *The English Man's Food* (1939)

C. Anne Wilson, *Food and Drink in Britain* (1973)

A TOUR OF LONDON'S GARDENS WITH JOHN ROCQUE

The Ambulator; Or a Pocket Companion for the Tour of London and the Environs (11th ed., 1806)

Buildings of England London 2: South (1983)

J. Cary, *Actual Survey of the Country Fifteen Miles Round London* (1786)

Geographia Greater London Street Atlas, Geographia Ltd and the Automobile Association

John Roque, *Twenty Miles Round London* (1746)

James Thorne, *Handbook to the Environs of London* (1876)

GARDENING AND THE MIDDLE CLASSES 1700–1830

T. Longstaffe-Gowan, 'James Cochran: Florist and Plant Contractor to Regency London', *Garden History,* vol. 15, no. 1 (Spring 1987)

—— 'Proposal for a Georgian Town Garden in Gower Street: The Francis Douce Garden', *Garden History,* vol. 15, no. 2 (Autumn 1987)

—— 'Plant Effluvia. Changing notions of the effects of plant exhalations on human health in the eighteenth and nineteenth centuries', *Journal of Garden History,* vol. 7, no. 2 (1987)

—— *The London Town Garden 1700–1830; the experience of nature in the eighteenth-century city* (1990)

Neil McKendrick, John Brewer and J. H. Plumb, *The birth of consumer society; the commercialization of eighteenth-century England* (1982)

LONDON GARDENS AND THE DECORATIVE ARTS 1680–1800

Elizabeth Adams, *Chelsea Porcelain* (1987)

Elizabeth Adams and David Redstone, *Bow Porcelain* (1981)

Wilfrid Blunt, *In for A Penny: A Prospect of Kew Gardens* (1978)

Frank Britton, *London Delftware* (1987)

Handasyde Buchanan, *Nature into Art* (1979)

G. Calman, *Ehret, Flower Painter Extraordinary* (1977)

Ray Desmond, *A Celebration of Flowers: Two Hundred years of Curtis's Botanical Magazine* (1987)

Ralph Edwards and Margaret Jourdain, *Georgian Cabinet Makers, c. 1700–1800* (1955)

The Glory of the Garden, Sotheby's and the Royal Horticultural Society (1987)

Christopher Gilbert, James Lomax and Anthony Wells-Cole, *Country House Floors, 1660–1850,* Temple Newsam Country House Studies no. 3, Leeds City Art Galleries (1987)

John Hardy and Maurice Tomlin, *Osterley Park House,* Victoria and Albert Museum (1985)

Ruth Hayden, *Mrs Delany her life and her flowers,* British Museum (1980)

Morrison Heckscher, 'Eighteenth-Century Rustic Furniture Designs', *Furniture History,* vol. XI, pp. 48–52 (1975)

Wendy Hefford, 'Thomas Moore of Moorfields', *The Burlington Magazine,* vol. CXIX, no. 897, pp. 840–847 (December 1977)

—— 'Huguenot Tapestry Weavers in and around London 1680–1780', *Proceedings of the Huguenot Society of London,* vol. XXIV, no. 2, pp. 103–112 (1984)

Paul Hulton and Lawrence Smith, *Flowers in Art from East and West,* British Museum (1979)

John Irwin and Katharine B. Brett, *Origins of Chintz with a catalogue of Indo-European cotton-paintings in the Victoria and Albert, London, and the Royal Ontario Museum, Toronto* (1970)

D. King (ed.), *British Textile Design in the Victoria and Albert Museum* (1980)

H. C. Marillier, *English Tapestries of the Eighteenth Century* (1930)

Florence Montgomery, *Printed Textiles: English and American Cottons and Linens 1700–1850* (1970)

Michael Snodin (ed.), *Rococo: Art and Design in Hogarth's England,* Victoria and Albert Museum (1984)

Lanto Synge, *Antique Needlework* (1982)

Patrick Synge-Hutchinson, 'G. D. Ehret's Botanical Designs on Chelsea Porcelain', *The Connoisseur,* vol. CXLII, pp. 88–94 (October 1958)

Maurice Tomlin, *Catalogue of Adam period Furniture,* Victoria and Albert Museum (1972)

Ward Jackson, *English Furniture Designs of the Eighteenth Century,* London, Victoria and Albert Museum (1984)

VICTORIAN PARKS

George Chadwick, *The Park and the Town* (1966)

Brent Elliott, *Victorian Gardens* (1986)

Charles Poulsen, *Victoria Park* (1976)

J. J. Sexby, *The municipal parks, gardens, and open spaces of London* (1898)

COMMERCIAL HORTICULTURE IN VICTORIAN LONDON
Mea Allan, *Tom's weeds: the story of Rochford's and their house plants* (1970)
J. G. L. Burnby and A. E. Robinson, 'Now turned into fair garden plots' (1983)
R. Webber, *Covent Garden: mud salad market* (1969)
—— *Market gardening* (1972)
E. J. Willson, *West London nursery gardens*, Fulham & Hammersmith Historical Society (1982)

GARDEN SUBURB, GREEN BELT AND WINDOWBOX
Susan Beattie, *A Revolution in London Housing, LCC Architects and their Work 1893–1914* (1980)
John Brookes, *Room Outside* (1969)
—— *The Small Garden* (1977)
Jane Brown, *Gardens of a Golden Afternoon* (1982)
—— *The English Garden in our Time from Gertrude Jekyll to Geoffrey Jellico* (1986)
—— *Lanning Roper and His Gardens* (1987)

Walter L. Creese, *The Search for Environment. The Garden City: Before and After* (1966)
David Crouch and Colin Ward, *The Allotment. Its Landscape and Culture* (1988)
Arthur M. Edwards, *The Design of Suburbia* (1981)
Nan Fairbrother, *New Lives New Landscapes* (1970)
R. S. R. Fitter, *London's Natural History* (1945)
Mark Girouard, *Cities & People* (1985)
Roy Hawkins, *Green London* (1987)
Susan Jellicoe and Margery Allen, *Town Gardens to Live In* (1977)
Dawn MacLeod, *The Gardener's London* (1972)
Paul Oliver, Ian Davis, Ian Bentley, *Dunroamin . The Surburban Semi and Its Enemies* (1981)
Alan Powers, *Oliver Hill. Architect and Lover of Life* (1989)
Lanning Roper, *Successful Town Gardens* (1954)
Anne Scott James and Osbert Lancaster, *The Pleasure Garden* (1977)
Peter Shepheard, *Modern Gardens* (1953)
David Thomas, *London's Green Belt* (1970)

Christopher Tunnard, *Gardens in the Modern Landscape* (1948)
Faith and Geoff Whiten, *Chelsea Flower Show* (1988)

LONDON'S PARKS AND GARDENS: A PICTURE GALLERY
'The Smythson collection of the Royal Institute of British architects', *Architectural History* (1962)
'Evelyn's own description of the layout of Sayes Court', *Illustrated London News* (30 August 1952)
The painters of Camden Town, Christie's catalogue (1988)
'A town garden' (previously Tissot's), *Country Life* (23 November 1912)
Felix Barker and Peter Jackson, *London: 2000 years of a city and its people* (1974)
John Harris, *The Artist and the Country House*
John Hayes, *Catalogue of oil paintings in the London Museum* (1970)
Roy Strong, *The Renaissance Garden in England* (1979)
Rosemary Weinstein, 'Southampton House and the Civil War', *Collectanea Londiniensia*, London & Middlesex Archaeological Society, Special Paper no. 2 (1978)

INDEX

INDEX

EDITOR'S ACKNOWLEDGMENTS

A book of this kind inevitably depends on the work of a great number of people. The key individuals are obviously those who have contributed essays, and, happily, many of them are Museum of London colleagues: Brent Elliott, Hazel Forsyth, Brian Halliwell, Vanessa Harding, John Harris, Nicola Johnson, Todd Longstaffe-Gowan, Tessa Murdoch, Peter Stott and Rosemary Weinstein. In particular, I should mention Celina Fox for her unfailing guidance and crucial fund-raising success. It was the generous sponsorship of Guardian Royal Exchange Properties Ltd that made the exhibition which inspired these essays possible.

I must then pay tribute to Yvonne McFarlane, Carey Smith and Nick Wells of Anaya Publishers. They have brought this publication to fruition against all odds and to quite unbelievable deadlines.

I am also endebted to the following people for their enthusiasm, work and support in the production of this book: Rex Banks, Mavis Batey, Brigid Boardman, Jane Brown, The Duke of Buccleuch, John Carlton-Smith, Harold Carter, David Challis, Carol Colson, Victor Corney, Jennifer Cox, Brian Curle, Penny David, Ray Desmond, John Dixon Hunt, Gina Douglas, June Drever, David Dueck, Ruth Duthie, Torla Evans, Karen Eyre, John Fisher, Barry Gray, Rosemary Harris, John Harvey, Ruth Hayden, Eve Hostetner, Ralph Hyde, Peter Jackson, Ann Jones, Martin Kauffmann, Krystyna Matyjaszkiewicz, Jennifer Montagu, Jonathan Riddell, Eva Rupprecht, John Sargeant, Nancy Segal, Mr and Mrs Michael Simpson, Jeremy Smith, Richard Stone, Sir Roy Strong, Roy Vickery, Shirley Waller, Michael Walpole, Roger Warner, Alex Werner, Caroline Williamson, Richard Woollard.

Finally, these acknowledgments would not be complete without my extending enormous thanks to my husband, Graham Baugh, for his efforts in unravelling my early drafts and providing an invaluable baby-sitting service.